Novum Organum

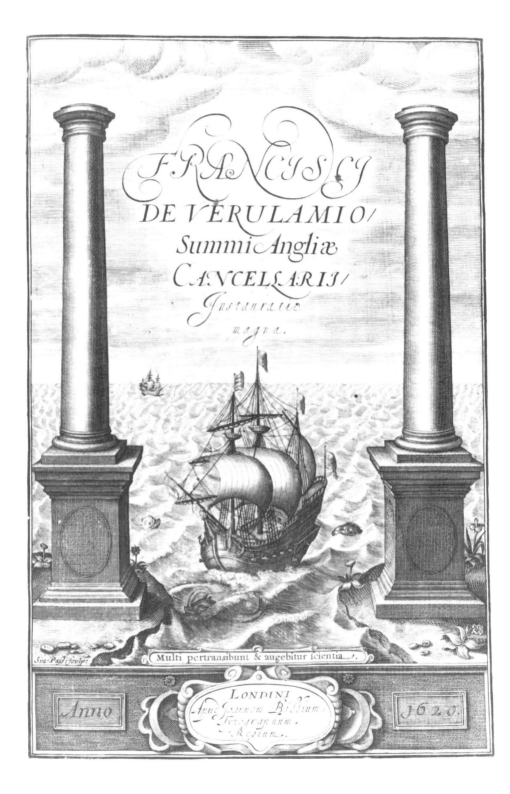

FRANCISCI
DE VERULAMIO,
Summi Angliæ
CANCELLARII,
Instauratio
magna.

Multi pertransibunt & augebitur scientia.

Sim: Pass: sculp:

LONDINI
Apud Joannem Billium
Typographum
Regium.

Anno

1620.

FRANCIS BACON

Novum Organum

With Other Parts of
The Great Instauration

TRANSLATED AND EDITED BY
PETER URBACH
AND
JOHN GIBSON

Open ✸ Court

Chicago and La Salle, Illinois

Volume 3 in the series: Paul Carus Student Editions

OPEN COURT and the above logo are registered in the U.S. Patent and Trademark Office.

© 1994 by Open Court Publishing Company

First printing 1994

Printed and bound in the United States of America.

Library of Congress Cataloging-in-Publication Data

Bacon, Francis, 1561–1626.
    [Novum organum. English]
    The novum organum ; with, The great instauration / Francis Bacon ; translated and edited by Peter Urbach and John Gibson.
       p.   cm. — (Paul Carus student editions ; v. 3)
    Includes bibliographical references and index.
    ISBN 0-8126-9245-4 (paper)
    1. Induction (Logic)—Early works to 1800.   2. Science—Methodology—Early works to 1800. I. Urbach, Peter. II. Gibson, John. III. Bacon, Francis, 1561–1626.   Instauratio magna. English. 1993. IV. Title: Novum organum. V. Title: Great instauration. VI. Series.
B1168.E5U7313   1993   93-39277
   192—dc20   CIP

CONTENTS

David Leonard Urbach
16th February 1953–31st March 1994
My dear brother

P. U.

ACKNOWLEDGEMENTS

We are pleased to have this opportunity to thank a number of friends and colleagues who gave us valuable help and advice in this project. First and foremost, Pat Gardner, who typed the first draft of the work and whose secretarial assistance throughout made the whole task much easier and more enjoyable; Timothy Childers, who assisted with a great deal of background research, and May Cameron, Steve Gould, Colin Howson, and Tom Hewlett, who helped clarify some points in the text; and Alasdair Cameron, who read a good portion of the translation, with a skilled eye to style. We are also grateful to Simon Blundell, Librarian of the Reform Club; to Elizabeth Earle and Dan Lewis of The Francis Bacon Library, Claremont, California; and especially to Elizabeth Wrigley, President of that Library, for permission to use its incomparable resources and for making the stay of one of us (P.U.) in Claremont so pleasant and rewarding. Finally, we thank Edward Roberts of the editorial staff of Open Court for the patience and care given to the preparation of this volume.

EDITOR'S INTRODUCTION

Francis Bacon (1561–1626) was born into a distinguished political family. His father, Sir Nicholas Bacon, was one of Queen Elizabeth's chief counsellors, and his mother was sister-in-law to Lord Burleigh, the Queen's Secretary of State. Although so favourably placed and also highly ambitious, Bacon commanded little patronage and was obliged to make his own way in the world, for his father died when he was only 18 years old, leaving him poorly provided for; and his uncle, Burleigh, was disinclined to assist, fearing—it is sometimes said—that Bacon would outstrip his own son in the race for political advancement.

Bacon was educated at the University of Cambridge for three years, from the age of 12; he then studied law at Gray's Inn, in London; and in 1584 was elected a Member of Parliament. He had to wait until James I succeeded Queen Elizabeth in 1603 for any substantial advancement in his career, though when it came it was meteoric: rapid and brilliant in its progress, catastrophic in its end. For in 1604 he became one of the King's Learned Counsel; in 1607 Solicitor General; in 1613 Attorney-General; in 1616 a Member of the Privy Council; a year later Lord Keeper of the Great Seal; and finally in 1618 he was appointed to one of the chief positions of state, head of the Judiciary, Lord Chancellor. Bacon's dignities kept pace and he steadily progressed in rank to Sir Francis Bacon, then Baron Verulam of Verulam and lastly Viscount St Alban.

But in 1621 Bacon was impeached by Parliament on a charge of accepting bribes. Bacon acknowledged the justice of the censure but claimed that the gifts he received never influenced his legal judgements; it has since been argued that Bacon was acting in accordance with the practical standards of the time and that his impeachment was motivated largely by political opposition to the King, rather than by moral outrage. The effect on Bacon was to propel him ignominiously from public life. *schimpflich*

His forced retirement gave Bacon more time to devote to the philosophy which had occupied him from an early age. His main philosophical concern was with the sciences and how they might be rescued from the lamentable state into which, in his view, they had fallen. He complained that the sciences of his day were sterile, in that although they issued in elaborate and polished formulations and endless commentaries, they seemed incapable of producing effects, especially ones of utility to mankind; and it was the achievement of just such effects, or 'works', that Bacon regarded as both a desirable goal in itself and the principal sign that the theories, or 'axioms', of a science were true. "All the philosophy of Nature which is now received," he said in one of his earliest writings, "is either that of the Grecians, or that other of the alchemists. . . . The one never faileth to multiply words, and the other ever faileth to multiply gold". Bacon saw his task as inaugurating the restoration, or 'Instauration', of the sciences.

Bacon's diagnosis of the trouble was that science had up to his day taken too little account of observation and given too much credit to tradition and authority; and even when observations were cited in a scientific work, their role, in Bacon's opinion, was not to test but merely to illustrate the scientific doctrines being advanced, giving a misleading impression of strongly confirming them. For when any observation was in accord with a favoured theory, it was paraded as favourable evidence; but when an observation conflicted with the theory, the practice was to ignore it, or cast doubt on it, or exclude it as an exception, or explain it away by some "frivolous distinction"; but not to regard the theory itself as mistaken.

Bacon set out his views in his *Great Instauration* (1620); however, he was unable to complete that work, not just through adverse circumstances, but much more because of the immensity, some say impossibility, of the task he had set himself. Its scale is indicated by the titles of its projected sections, which are listed in *The Plan of the Work,* below. The first section, called *The Divisions of the Sciences,* was intended as a survey of contemporary science. Bacon had in 1605 published a book entitled *The Proficience* [i.e., Improvement] *and Advancement of Learning, Divine and Human,* containing such a survey; this he translated and considerably expanded into the *De Dignitate et Augmentis Scientiarum (On the*

Dignity and Advancement of Learning) and designated the first part of the *Great Instauration.*

The second part of the *Great Instauration* was the *Novum Organum,* or *New Organon. Organon* is a Greek word meaning "instrument", in particular, an "instrument of reasoning." Bacon's use of the word alludes to Aristotle's famous work of that name, whose principles of demonstration and investigation he hoped to supersede. The *Novum Organum* was published in 1620 in two books (though Bacon indicates that others were planned), together with a Preface to the *Great Instauration,* a Dedication to King James, and an outline of the projected contents of the *Great Instauration,* entitled *The Plan of the Work.* Also included as part of, or a supplement to, the *Novum Organum* was a short piece setting out Bacon's principles for collecting a suitable store of observations upon which any scientific investigation could be based, entitled *A Description of a Natural and Experimental History.* The present edition reproduces, in a new translation, the contents of the 1620 edition.

The third part of the *Great Instauration* was entitled *The Phenomena of the Universe,* or *A Natural and Experimental History for the Foundation of Philosophy;* Bacon wrote several 'histories', or collections of observations, on a number of different subjects, which were probably intended as contributions to this part of the larger work. For example, there was the *History of Dense and Rare,* which reported, inter alia, Bacon's own measurements of the densities of various substances; the *History of Life and Death;* and *History of the Winds.* The most substantial such writing was the *Sylva Sylvarum (Collection of Collections),* which contains a remarkable catalogue of facts and supposed facts, as well as suggestions for new experiments on many different topics; this work was published posthumously, and turned out to be the work of Bacon's that enjoyed the most popularity in the seventeenth century.

No other part of the *Great Instauration* seems to remain, and our idea of what the rest was intended to contain must depend more or less entirely on the outlines given in *The Plan of the Work.*

The *Novum Organum* is one of Bacon's most polished writings, for he had worked on the main ideas contained in it over many years; thus we find adumbrations and what are in effect preliminary drafts of parts of the *Novum Organum* in a number of earlier writings. The *Novum Organum* is composed in aphorisms. These are not aphorisms in the sense of pithy maxims—indeed, many of the aphorisms in this volume amount to substantial essays; they are, in fact, intended to contrast with an expository technique advocated in contemporary theories of rhetoric and employed, according to Bacon, by many natural philosophers up to his time, whereby a whole subject would be partitioned under a variety of heads and carefully packaged so as to present the appearance of completeness and comprehensiveness. But Bacon held that the natural sciences of his day were far from satisfactory or complete, and that by making them appear so, philosophers were promoting an altogether too rosy picture of the sciences while at the same time stifling further investigations which might improve matters. "Knowledge", Bacon said, "while in aphorisms and observations . . . is in growth." Bacon regarded the theory of scientific method as similarly incomplete and in need of further improvement; hence his own aphoristic style.

Bacon died shortly after he was taken ill on a journey out of London in the course of which, he says, he was "desirous to try an experiment or two, touching the conservation and induration [i.e., hardening] of bodies". John Aubrey, in his *Brief Lives,* tells us that the experiment involved killing a hen and stuffing it with snow, though Bacon can hardly have been inquiring as to whether the flesh would be conserved by the cold, as Aubrey reports, since he already knew this and mentioned it in the *Novum Organum.* In his will Bacon directed that two lectureships in natural sciences be endowed at the Universities of Oxford and Cambridge, but the charges on his estate turned out to exceed its assets, so, unfortunately, Bacon's instructions could not be carried out.

For a long time after his death, Bacon was admired and venerated as a philosopher of science, and his writings clearly inspired some of the revival of experimental investigation in the seventeenth century. And when the Royal Society of London was founded in 1667, many regarded it as realising the kind of scientific brotherhood that Bacon had idealised in his *New Atlantis,* a utopian island state dedicated to pure scientific study. Indeed, Thomas Sprat treated Bacon as a sort of patron saint of that Society, prefacing his famous *History* (1667) of it with an ode "To the Royal Society" composed by *holprig*

Abraham Cowley. This doggerel verse commenced by deploring the rudimentary state of the natural knowledge of the day, and acknowledging Bacon as the inaugurator of a new scientific age: "*Bacon* at last, a mighty Man, arose/Whom a wise King and Nature chose/Lord Chancellor of both their Laws". There follow these mortal lines:

> From these and all long Errors of the way,
> In which our wandring Prædecessors went,
> And like th'old Hebrews many years did stray
> In Desarts but of small extent,
> *Bacon*, like *Moses*, led us forth at last,
> The barren Wilderness he past,
> Did on the very Border stand
> Of the blest promis'd Land,
> And from the Mountains Top of his Exalted Wit,
> Saw it himself, and shewed us it.

Bacon published the *Great Instauration* in Latin, in the hope of thereby gaining a wider European audience. But the standing of Latin as the universal language of learning was not to last much longer, with Descartes in 1637 setting a pattern of writing philosophy in the vernacular. There is an *Landes-* advantage to having the work in Latin, however, which is that *sprache* it invites a new translation from time to time, so that new scholarship may be incorporated and the work presented in the language of the day. The translation of the *Novum Organum* that for nearly 150 years has stood as the most authoritative is by Robert Leslie Ellis, published after his death, under the supervision of James Spedding. The present translation is an entirely new one, though we have often taken guidance from Ellis and Spedding and also from other authorities; it seeks to be as literal a translation as possible and tries at the same time to make Bacon's ideas as clear as possible. Our aim has been to present Bacon's rich and fascinating work in a more accurate, readable and accessible form for modern readers.

THE MODERNITY OF BACON'S PHILOSOPHY

Bacon's reputation as a man and as a philosopher has fluctuated dramatically. After his near deification in the seventeenth century as creator of the new experimental approach to science, he was largely eclipsed in the eighteenth, scarcely mentioned by the great philosophers of that era; and then the nineteenth century saw an enthusiastic revival of scholarly interest in Bacon. Moreover, scholars have to an unusual degree been inclined to range themselves passionately either on Bacon's side or against him. A particularly fierce opponent was Thomas Babington Macaulay, who in the *Edinburgh Review* of 1837 launched a famous attack, in magnificent purple prose, denouncing Bacon's moral character and philosophical skill. It was largely due to this provocation that James Spedding devoted the best part of his life to defending Bacon, producing meticulous, biographical analyses and a fine new edition and translation of Bacon's works and letters.   *akribisch*

Bacon is often admired chiefly as a man of letters and for the striking quality of his English style. Many too are intrigued by what they perceive as the mystic in Bacon. For example, some have seen Bacon as a crypto-Rosicrucian or as the true Shakespeare, seeking evidence for these propositions in supposedly coded messages hidden in his writings. There is a less eccentric version of the idea of Bacon as a mystic, supported by the distinguished scholars Frances Yates and Paolo Rossi, who regard Bacon's writings as steeped in alchemy and magic and betraying (in Yates's words) an "underlying cosmic mysticism".

The reader will not, I think, find much in the present volume of a mystical character. It has indeed a modern ring to it. Unlike his philosophical successors, such as Descartes, Leibniz, and even Newton, Bacon treats a question of current concern—how should scientists proceed in order to increase knowledge of the world?—in down-to-earth fashion, with virtually no admixture of theology, and none of the faulty "proofs" for God's existence upon which Cartesian epistemology so embarrassingly rests. But despite the familiar issues that Bacon raises and the accessibility of his treatment, he is not so clear and unambiguous as to escape conflicting interpretations by different students of his work.

According to one influential school of thought, Bacon believed it possible to generate infallible scientific axioms by universally applicable, mechanical procedure, and believed moreover that he himself had discovered such a mechanism. Now if Bacon did believe this, he was surely wrong; for it is a truism of scientific method that a finite set of observations can always be explained by *infinitely* many alternative hypotheses; but we can only ever accumulate finitely many observations, and so will always have infinitely many alternative theories to choose from, with no guarantee that any one that we might for some reason favour is in fact true. Thus the goal of an infallible science, let alone one reached with machine efficiency, is utterly unrealistic.

An alternative to the 'mechanical-infallible' interpretation of Bacon that has been gaining ground in recent years is what I have called the 'hypothetico-inductive' interpretation (Urbach 1987). This takes Bacon to be saying what many modern-day philosophers of science maintain, that scientific explanations are fallible and hypothetical, but that some have a better claim to truth than others. It is this more realistic idea that seems to reflect Bacon's philosophical position more accurately.

Interpretation and Anticipation of Nature
Bacon distinguished two inductive methods: "anticipation of Nature", which he held responsible for the inertia and poverty of much contemporary science, and "interpretation of Nature", which he regarded as the "true induction" that would, if applied, lead to better results in the future.

Anticipation is often equated with hypothetical reasoning, and interpretation with the infallibilist process I outlined earlier, for example by Karl Popper (1959, p. 279), who asserted that "Bacon's term 'anticipation' . . . means almost the same as 'hypothesis' (in my way of using the term)". But Bacon's own descriptions of the anticipation and interpretation of Nature do not bear out this reading. Let us examine what he said.

Bacon believed that the science of his day was both unsatisfactory and the product of anticipation:

> *The axioms now in use have been derived from a meagre and narrow experience and from a few particulars of most common occurrence; and these axioms have been framed, for the most part, so as just to fit them, hence it is no wonder they do not lead to fresh particulars; and if they chance to come up against an instance not previously noticed or known, the axiom is rescued by some frivolous distinction, when the more correct course would be for the axiom itself to be corrected. (NO, I, 25)*

These remarks do not take issue with accepted axioms of science for being fallible and hypothetical. Quite the reverse. Bacon is objecting that theories that anticipate Nature are, at any rate "for the most part", not hypothetical, since they have been carefully tailored to fit the relevant facts or observations. As Bacon put it elsewhere: "the sciences we now have are nothing more than nice arrangements of things already discovered, not methods of discovery or pointers to new works" (*NO, I, 8*).

Sometimes, Bacon says, anticipations of Nature do extend beyond the given particulars and lead to new ones. But the way of anticipation when such predictions are refuted is not for "the axiom itself to be corrected", which Bacon described as the "truer course", but rather for the axiom to be rescued by introducing "some frivolous distinction".

Another characteristic and grounds for complaint that Bacon saw in anticipations was their superficiality: "The discoveries that have been made up to now in the sciences have as a rule been such as closely underlie common notions" (*NO, I, 18*) and are "nearer the senses" (Preface to *The Great Instauration*; see p. 13). "Astronomy, optics, music, many of the mechanical arts, medicine itself . . . all lack depth, and merely glide over the surface and variety of things "(*NO, I, 80*).

The defects of anticipation were matched by corresponding merits in the interpretation of Nature. For example, there is the requirement that theories should not relate to surface phenomena only but should "penetrate further into the inner and more remote parts of Nature": scientific investigation should refer to the physical causes of phenomena, causes that are to be found only in the "smallest particles, or at least those too small to be perceived by the sense" (*NO, II, 6:* see also I, 80 and 107). The two examples of an interpretation of Nature, concerning heat and colour, which Bacon himself worked out in some detail, both fulfil this requirement, locating those phenomena in the smaller, and evidently invisible, particles of matter (*NO, II, 20 and 23*).

Secondly, interpretations of Nature are different from anticipations in that they encompass more particulars than they were originally made to explain and, moreover, some of those new particulars will have been checked and verified. This is how Bacon put it:

*in establishing axioms by means of this induction [i.e.,
interpretation], we must also examine and check whether
the axiom so established is only fitted to and made to the
measure of those particulars from which it is derived, or
whether it is larger and wider. (NO, I, 106)*

As we have seen, the first of these possibilities describes a
defect of theories that anticipate Nature, namely, that they do
not go beyond existing observations. It is the second possibility
that relates to interpretation; its theories are larger and wider
than the facts from which they are drawn. However, an axiom
that interprets Nature should do more. Bacon continued:

*And if it is larger or wider, we must look to see whether it
confirms its largeness and wideness by indicating new
particulars, as a kind of collateral security . . . (NO, I, 106)*

In other words an axiom that interprets Nature will not
only assert more than the known particulars, but it will also be
confirmed by correctly predicting new phenomena; this confirmation then acts "as a kind of collateral security", that is, I
suggest, as an indication of its truth.

Bacon's distinction between theories that anticipate Nature and those that interpret her is remarkably similar to one
that is often drawn, especially by philosophers such as Popper
and Imre Lakatos, between 'ad hoc' and 'non-ad hoc' theories.
Ad hoc theories, as they define the notion, are either ones that
make no new predictions (Lakatos calls these 'ad hoc$_1$'), or ones
which do make such predictions, none of which however is
verified ('ad hoc$_2$' in Lakatos's terminology). Both Popper and
Lakatos regarded ad hoc theories as "unacceptable". Accepta-
ble theories, in their view, are the non-ad hoc ones that do
predict new effects, especially where those predictions have
been verified.

Bacon particularly objected to the way that pet ideas were
often perpetually defended by the systematic use of anticipation. In such cases, a theory is advanced, one of its predictions
examined, and found to be false: the scientist then introduces
some minor variant of the theory which no longer yields that
prediction; if the new variant makes a fresh prediction which
is also refuted, the scientist will once more spring to the
defence with another modification, or "frivolous distinction",
ensuring that the main claim of the theory is left intact. The

same defence mechanism is then invoked every time any new counter-instance appears. Alchemy is a case in point:

> *the alchemist nurses eternal hope, and when the thing does not succeed, he blames some error of his own, and in self-condemnation thinks he has not properly understood the words of his art or of its authors, whereupon he turns to traditions and auricular whispers; or else thinks that in his performance he has made some slip of a scruple in weight or a moment in time, whereupon he repeats his experiments endlessly. (NO, I, 85)*

The role of hypotheses

Bacon's preference for interpretations over anticipations seems necessarily to involve a preference for interesting speculations over trivial certainties. What then accounts for the entrenched opinion that Bacon regarded hypotheses as unacceptable in science? One reason is that he seems often to have spoken sharply against hypotheses. Thus he objected that the method of anticipation "flies from the senses and particulars to axioms of the most general kind" (*NO*, I, 19); and said that "the understanding must not be allowed to leap and fly from particulars to remote and nearly the most general axioms" (*NO*, I,104). Such remarks appear incompatible with Bacon's requirements for the interpretation of Nature which call for new axioms to be larger and wider than the particulars from which they are drawn. The apparent conflict is, however, resolved by the contexts of the above quotations, which show Bacon's chief target to have been not speculation itself but, as always, the dogmatic defence of speculations, and the tendency to regard them as infallible or unalterable. Thus, the quotations restored to their contexts read as follows:

> *[Anticipation of nature] flies from the senses and particulars to axioms of the most general kind, and from these principles and their [supposed] immutable truth, proceeds to judgement and to the discovery of intermediate axioms . . . (emphasis added)*

> *The understanding must not be allowed to leap and fly from particulars to remote and nearly the most general axioms . . . and from their [supposed] unshakable truth, to prove and explain intermediate axioms. (emphasis added)*

Bacon made the same point in practically every one of the many places where he warned against the mind's taking flight to very general axioms, namedly, that the danger resides in such axioms being mistaken for unshakable truths. Here is another example:

> For the ancients . . . out of a few examples and particulars
> . . . flew to the most general conclusions or principles of
> the sciences, with respect to whose fixed and immoveable
> truth, through intermediate propositions, they extracted
> and proved inferior conclusions, and from these, they
> constructed their art. (NO, I, 125)

These remarks continue in a way that reveals the link in Bacon's mind between his rule against flying to generalities and his criticism of the conservative and dogmatic method of anticipation:

> And then, if any new particulars and examples were
> brought forward which would conflict with their opinions,
> they subtly fitted them into their system by distinctions or
> explanations of their rules, or else crudely removed them
> by provisos [i.e., by adding certain limiting clauses to their
> laws]; while for any particulars that were not conflicting,
> they laboured long and hard to find causes that agreed
> with their principles.

Bacon was, then, deploring not the use of hypotheses, but the tendency to treat them as if they were incorrigible. Such an attitude produces a reluctance to examine the hypotheses further ("the mind . . . scorns experience") and leads to the sterile science that Bacon saw around him.

Idols of the Mind

Bacon criticises and further elaborates the dogmatic approach that the anticipation of Nature represents in his famous Doctrine of the Idols (*NO*, I, 46–68). The idols were attitudes of mind that Bacon saw as supporting anticipations and as constituting obstacles to the true inductive method. The idols were not however tendencies to rest content with hypotheses, as is sometimes said by defenders of the infallible-mechanical view of Bacon's philosophy; they were, principally, tendencies to adhere to theories uncritically or defend them dogmatically, either avoiding counter-evidence, or ignoring it when it

presents itself, or finding ways round it when it cannot be ig-
nored.

Bacon described four groups of idols. The *Idols of the Tribe*
were so named because they were, in his opinion, characteristic of the entire human race. The first of these idols was the
tendency of the human understanding to suppose "a greater
order and uniformity in things than it finds" (*NO,* I, 45). Then,
having adopted those opinions, it "draws everything else to
support and agree with them. And though it may meet a
greater number and weight of contrary instances, it will, with
great and harmful prejudice, ignore or condemn or exclude
them by introducing some distinction, in order that the authority of those earlier assumptions may remain intact and unharmed" (*NO,* I, 46).

The human understanding is not only inclined to underrate negative evidence in this way; it will also exaggerate the
significance of the positive evidence, being "more moved and
excited by affirmatives than by negatives . . . rightly and properly it ought to give equal weight to both; rather, in fact, in
every truly constituted axiom, a negative instance has the
greater weight" (*NO,* I, 46).

This idol of the mind has often been noted by psychologists
and condemned by philosophers. People truly are inclined "to
take note of events where they are fulfilled" but "disregard
them and pass them by" where they are not, and they thereby
receive and impart a distorted picture of the real support that
their theories have (*NO,* I, 46). Such an approach indicated
"the dogmatic attitude" for Popper (1963, p. 50); it is, he said,
"related to the tendency to *verify* our laws and schemata by
seeking to apply them and to confirm them, even to the point of
neglecting refutations".

Another Idol of the Tribe was the mind's proclivity to be
most influenced by a few, familiar phenomena which "inflate
the imagination", leading it to believe that "everything else
behaves in the same way as those few things with which it has
become engaged". People are then unwilling to test their
theories by seeking "remote and heterogeneous instances, by
which axioms are tested as if in the fire . . .", because such a
course risks the unwelcome possibility that they will meet a
refutation (*NO,* I, 47).

Yet another tribal idol was the tendency to leave out of

scientific consideration the underlying causes of things, causes that are not immediately visible and possibly not visible at all: "contemplation", Bacon complains, "usually ceases with seeing, so much so that little or no attention is paid to things invisible. Therefore every action of the spirits enclosed in material bodies lies hidden and escapes us. In the same way also, we fail to see the more subtle change of schematism in the parts of denser substances (which is generally called alteration, though it is in fact movement in the smallest particles)". And as we noted in discussing the method of anticipation, Bacon believed that "unless those two things . . . are searched for and brought to light, nothing can be achieved in Nature, at least as far as works are concerned" (*NO,* I, 50).

The *Idols of the Cave* were prejudices arising from individual quirks rather than from universal tendencies; for instance, the pride some people have in their own inventions. It was this pride, said Bacon, which led Aristotle to impose his preconceived ideas on Nature, subjugating his natural philosophy to his logic (*NO,* I, 54). Similarly, some minds are "steady and acute", other "more lofty and discursive"; both are inclined to excess, leading in the first case to a concentration on the minute differences between things, in the second to consideration only of the most abstract resemblances (*NO,* I, 55). What is called for in science are "balanced judgements" taken from "the light of Nature and experience" (*NO,* I, 56). Bacon sums up discussion of this set of idols with the judicious advice that "anyone studying Nature should be suspicious of whatever allures and captivates his understanding" (*NO,* I, 58).

The *Idols of the Market-place* were tendencies to accept unwittingly and without question certain ideas that are, as it were, built into the very language. Bacon perceptively observed that language and our vocabulary were largely developed by unsophisticated people for ordinary discourse and so "divide things along lines most suited to common understanding". And when "someone of sharper understanding or more diligence in observation wishes to shift those lines, so as to move them closer to Nature, words shout him down" (*NO,* I, 59).

The *Idols of the Theatre* were related to erroneous theories and mistaken laws of demonstration, which impose themselves on uncritical minds. Bacon compared such theories and laws with elegant stage plays which represent reality as their authors would wish it to be, not as it is. There were three Idols of the theatre: *Sophistical or Rational, Empirical,* and *Superstitious.*

The *Rational* idols were doctrines that were apparently confirmed by observations, but in fact were preconceived ideas to which the experience was somehow forced to conform. Aristotle exemplified this idol for Bacon: "[he] corrupted natural philosophy with his dialectic, when he constructed the world out of categories . . . He dealt with the business of density and rarity . . . by the trivial distinction of Actuality and Potentiality, and asserted that particular bodies each have their own individual and natural motion, and if they partake of any other motion, that this must come from elsewhere, and he arbitrarily imposed numerous other things on Nature". To be sure, Aristotle's works report many experiments in defence of his theories, but these count for very little, in Bacon's view, for Aristotle had made up his mind beforehand and, "after laying down the law according to his own judgement, he then brings in experience, twisted to fit in with his own ideas, and leads it about like a captive" (*NO,* I, 63).

The *Empirical* idols were the inclinations to devise philosophies (for example, alchemy) on the basis of carefully performed experiments, but too few to support such large claims. Bacon observed that while most people would regard ideas of that kind as unbelievable and groundless, those who laboured over the experiments see them as probable and almost certain, and they are then inclined to "twist everything else in extraordinary ways to fit in with them".

Superstitious idols were the tendencies to import theological ideas into science, either by reading off their ideas concerning natural philosophy from the Bible, or by assuming purpose in the physical world and attributing reasons, or "final causes", to things. Not that the Bible is in any way false, however, but it is to be understood metaphorically. Nor again did Bacon deny that God brought everything about for a purpose; he merely thought that that aspect of phenomena was beyond our understanding and led to a sterile science. The healthy course, Bacon sententiously concluded, is to "give to faith only that which is faith's" (*NO,* I, 65).

Forms

Bacon characterised the aim of human knowledge as the discovery of what he termed the "forms" of given "natures", or qualities. And subordinate to this were the goals of discovering the largely hidden, causal process that occurs when a body is generated or changes, and the latent schematism, or hidden structure, of unchanging or static bodies.

Bacon acknowledged four kinds of cause: material, efficient, formal, and final (which we have already discussed). The first two were sufficient conditions of an effect, that is, conditions whose presence ensures that the effect is present, or that the property or nature will be generated. The formal cause, or form of a nature, included both the necessary and the sufficient conditions, so that if the form is present so must the nature be, and if it is absent, the nature must be absent too. Bacon also called the form of a nature "its true specific difference", and a "law of pure action" (see *NO*, I, 75), and said that the true form derives the given nature from some source of being that is inherent in more natures, and is more general than the form itself (*NO*, II, 4). These scattered remarks do not make the idea of a form very clear, but his examples of forms, of heat and of colour, do illustrate what he meant.

In the case of heat, the nature that is more general and inherent in more natures than heat itself is motion (motion is "like a genus of which heat is a species"). The "true differences that limit motion and constitute it as the form of heat" are (briefly) that the motion ocurs in the "smaller parts of bodies"; and is expansive, checked, upwards, and violent. The form of heat has also a practical aspect in that it tells us in general terms how heat may be generated, and it is in this sense that "the form of heat is the same thing as the law of heat" (see *NO*, II, 17).

The practical (or "operative") and speculative aspects of forms are thus very similar, making the "roads to human power and human knowledge . . . more or less the same", as Bacon famously observed. However, because speculative thinking is so inclined to lead people to rest in abstractions, Bacon recommended we start with practical questions such as how to create particular natures in a given body, e.g., yellowness in silver, or toughness in glass. And to this purpose, Bacon

Schmidbarkut

provided two "precepts or axioms". The first considers a body
as made up of simple natures, gold, for example, of yellowness
and, in particular degrees, weight, malleability, ductility, etc.
By discovering the forms of yellowness, weight, and the rest,
we would see how, if at all, particular materials could be
transformed into gold. The second kind of precept is concerned
with the discovery of latent processes, for example, the process
by which plants are generated "from the first coalescence of
juices in the earth, or from seeds, to the fully-formed plant"; it
was Bacon's view that this would be simpler and quicker than
enquiring into simple natures. Nevertheless, it is investigations of the latter sort that occupy the most prominent part of
the second book of _Novum Organum;_ Bacon's promise to
explain how latent processes should be investigated was,
however, never fulfilled.

Investigating forms
Bacon illustrates how he envisaged the investigation of the
forms of simple natures procceding using the example of heat.
Three tables of instances are compiled. The _Table of Existence
and Presence_ comprises instances where the nature under
investigation, heat in Bacon's example, is present. Of course,
there will normally be an immense number of such instances,
and Bacon did not intend them all to be mentioned; his idea
was that representative examples of diverse types of instance
should be listed. The _Table of Absence in Proximity_ was to
contain instances that lacked the nature in question. Again,
Bacon knew that it would be endless to list all such instances;
his solution was to select negative instances that were "most
akin to" corresponding positive instances in the Table of
Presence. Finally, the _Table of Degrees_ contained instances
where the nature increased or decreased in a given object, or
was present to different degrees in different objects.

The next stage in the inductive process was the rejection of
certain natures from the form of heat. Applying the idea to the
example of heat, Bacon says that the instances in the tables
allow him to "reject brightness" on account of boiling water.
And he "rejects brightness" again on account of the rays of the
moon. The two rejections are different, and what Bacon means
is this: the first rejection is of brightness as a necessary
condition for the presence of heat, since the existence of boiling

water shows that a body may be hot without being bright; the second rejection is of brightness as a sufficient condition for heat—the bright moon demonstrates that an object may be bright but not warm. Bacon uses his tables to demonstrate of a number of other qualities that they are either not necessary or not sufficient conditions for heat, and thus to show that they could not be part of the form of heat.

But this is not the end of the matter, since such a process of rejection "is not completed until it arrives at an affirmative". In other words, it is not enough for it to tell us that certain natures are not involved in the form of heat, without in the end revealing which are. But Bacon says that completion is not in prospect since "we do not yet have good and true notions of simple natures". And it is for this reason that Bacon allows the understanding at this stage to take a guess at the true form (he calls this the *Indulgence of the Understanding,* or the *Beginning of the Interpretation,* or the *First Vintage*), and his theory of the essential nature of heat—that it is a species of motion—is <u>adumbrated</u> above.   *Flüchtig skizziert*

There is a difficulty for anyone seeking a consistent interpretation of Bacon. Forms seem to be constituted by states of the hidden particles of matter, and if so, those observable qualities such as 'brightness', 'rarity', and the others that he rejects are not even candidates to be forms. Bacon may well have realized this because, when he reports his rejections, he never concludes by saying that such-and-such natures are not the form of heat; he always says that they "do not *belong to* the form of heat (*non sunt ex forma calidi*)". But if forms do involve the hidden particles of matter and are not identical to simple natures, Bacon was obliged to leave the tables of observations and make a guess as to the form. Why then does Bacon suggest that in an ideal world, where "good and true notions of simple natures" were available, the form could be arrived at without indulging the understanding and distilling a first vintage? I leave this problem to the reader!

The *Novum Organum* now turns to "other aids for the understanding in the interpretation of Nature", though of the nine such aids proposed, it only actually deals with one, the *Prerogatives of Instances.* These were particular kinds of instance with special roles in the inductive process. Bacon intended that many of the instances should be collected for inclusion in the tables, because instances endowed with these prerogatives "are like a soul among the common instances of presentation" and "a few count for many" (*NO,* II, 52). He listed twenty-seven prerogatives of instances, including, for example, "Crucial Instances", or as they are now often called, crucial experiments. In his discussion of the latter he antici- pates Newton by exploring the possibility of gravitational action on heavy bodies by the earth and describing an experi- ment to check it. Bacon's discussion of the prerogatives of instances is full of many other fascinating speculations and experiments, and information about contemporary scientific opinion, as well as insights into his own theoretical attach- ments and views on scientific method. It is clear, for example, from the discussion of the four Mathematical Instances (*NO,* II, 45–48), that Bacon rated precise, quantitative measure- ments highly and believed mathematics to have an important role in science, a point he made in other ways elsewhere (e.g., (*NO,* II, 8).

The prediction criterion

As we saw from the discussion of the Interpretation and Anticipation of Nature. Bacon held that a theory should lead to successful predictions and that if it merely explains facts already known, then it is less valuable as a contribution to knowledge. The idea that a theory is especially strongly confirmed by predictions is very plausible and has been defended by leading philosophers from Leibniz to Popper. But the prediction criterion has a very unsatisfactory consequence, for it implies that a given theory can receive conflicting evaluations from exactly the same evidence. Thus suppose a theory is suggested by a scientist in order to explain certain data but that it fails to lead to any new predictions. Since the theory is merely fitted to the known particulars, Bacon would criticise it as an anticipation of Nature. But imagine that another scientist knows only part of the data, and that he advances the very same theory to explain the facts of which he is aware. The theory is now larger and wider than the known facts and does lead to novel predictions; hence it interprets Nature. But this means that whether a theory is praised or dispraised hangs not only on its relation to the evidence but also on the historical accident of when the evidence was first cognized, and this of course may vary from scientist to scientist. In assessing a theory, we would have to ask who invented it and when, and in cases of simultaneous discoveries, our conclusions could be very different for one and the same theory, which I think would generally be considered absurd. (The prediction criterion is discussed, for example, by Hempel 1966, 38, and Howson and Urbach 1993.)

Bacon's gradualism

A more satisfactory aspect of Bacon's approach is his idea that one should not advance straight away to "the most general conclusions, or first principles of science", but should approach them gradually and in stages. Interpretation of Nature, Bacon said, "calls forth axioms from the senses and particulars by a gradual and continous ascent, to arrive at the most general axioms last of all" (*NO*, I, 19).

Bacon's circumspect, gradualist approach is sensible and seems to be original. The step-by-step approach also has a rationale within his philosophy. Bacon thought that theories could acquire, through experiment, a high degree of certainty. As a rule, if statement A implies statement B, then A cannot be more certain or plausible or probable than B, and will usually be less so. It is intuitively obvious, and can be rigorously shown, that the less certain a theory is at the outset, the more evidence it requires before it can reach some particular level of certainty. Hence, Bacon's aim of certainty, together with the supposition that theories are endowed with an initial or prior degree of certainty or probability, would justify his gradualism. Many modern philosophers of science would endorse Bacon's gradualism and this justification of it.

How good was Bacon's philosophy?

Many of Bacon's admirers, viewing his philosophy as a search for infallibility in science, have been forced to dismiss the bulk of his positivie precepts as ineffectual and thoroughly misguided and to see his merits in what Ellis called the "spirit" of his philosophy. By this Ellis meant Bacon's insistence that scientists should rely on experiment and observation, rather than on traditional belief and authority. But this is scarcely complimentary, for warnings such as these were by no means new in the seventeenth century. Other critics have dealt less kindly with Bacon, one, for example, seeing his supposed desire for a non-hypothetical science as a sign of "complacent ignorance" (Cohen 1949, 149).

But Bacon's ideas were not so uninteresting or wrong-headed. He expected his scientific method to produce not infallible knowledge, but well-confirmed hypotheses of steadily increasing generality. He was right to stress the importance of deep explanations that dealt with underlying physical causes over what he called the "simple enumeration" of surface properties. Bacon was the first to try to explore systematically the different kinds of experimental evidence and to lay down principles to guide the collection of "histories", or observational and experimental data. His anticipation of the modern kinetic theory of heat was inspired. He was also right to oppose the dogmatic method of anticipation, by which theories are defended, come what may, against adverse evidence. And he correctly, and with great originality, identified attitudes of mind that encourage it, and circumstances that encourage those attitutes of mind. All in all, a considerable achievement.

PETER URBACH

The Great
Instauration

Francis of Verulam

reasoning thus with himself came to this conclusion that the knowledge of his thoughts would be of advantage to present and future generations.

Believing that the human understanding creates difficulties for itself, and does not put to sober and sensible use the true means of help that are in man's power; from which manifold ignorance of things has come, and from that ignorance numberless ills; he thought that every effort should be made, by whatever means, to restore to its original condition, or at least to improve, that commerce between Mind *and* Things *(to which almost nothing on earth, or at least nothing that is of the earth, can compare). But there was never any hope at all that the errors that have flourished, and will for ever flourish, would (if the mind were left to go its own way) correct themselves one after the other, either by the natural force of the understanding or through the aids and instruments of dialectic. This is because the primary notions of things, which the mind readily and passively drinks in, lays up and accumulates (and from which all the rest flow) are defective and confused and carelessly abstracted from things; nor are the secondary and other notions any less arbitrary and unreliable. As a result, that entire human reasoning that we apply in the investigation of Nature is poorly put together and constructed, but is like some magnificent great pile without any foundation. For while men admire and extol the false powers of the mind, they pass by and abandon those that could be its true powers, were it given the proper assistance, and were the mind itself to wait on things instead of vainly trying to lord it over them. There was thus but one course left, namely to try the whole matter afresh with better means of support, and to bring about a complete* Instauration *of the arts and sciences* and all the learning of mankind, raised upon proper foundations. And while at the beginning this might appear infinite and beyond mortal capacity, once in train it will be found reasonable and sober, more so in fact than those things that have been done hitherto. For this matter has an end, whereas the affairs of science as they are now handled are a kind of giddy whirl, and perpetual motion in a circle. And while he well knew what a solitary undertaking this might be, and how hard it would be to bring it to credit and belief, nonetheless he did not think to desert either the task or himself, but resolved to enter on and explore that path that alone is open to the human mind. For it is better to make a beginning in a matter which can have an end, than to be involved in perpetual argument and striving in matters which have no end. And the paths of contemplation fairly resemble those celebrated paths of action, in that one, steep and difficult at first, ends in open country, while the other, at first sight easy and straightforward, leads to places trackless and precipitous.

Moreover, since he was unsure how soon these things would occur to anyone else, bearing in mind especially that he has so far found no one who has applied his mind to the same thoughts, he decided to publish at once as much as he has been able to complete. And this haste came not from ambition, but from anxiety for his work; that in the event of his death there should yet survive some indication or design of what he conceived; and that there should at the same time survive some sign of his sincere concern for the good of mankind. He certainly held any other ambition to be of less worth than that which he had in hand, seeing that the matter in question is either nothing, or is so great as to be content with its own merit, without seeking any further reward.

To Our Most Serene and Mighty Prince and Lord, James

by the Grace of God, King of Great Britain, France and Ireland, Defender of the Faith, Etc.

Most Serene and Mighty King,

Your Majesty could perhaps accuse me of theft for stealing so much time from your affairs as was needed for this work. I can offer no defence, for time can never be restored, unless the time taken from your business could perhaps be laid to the memory of your name and the honour of your age; if indeed these thoughts are of any value. They are certainly quite new, entirely new in kind, but taken from a very ancient model, namely, from the world itself, and from the nature of things and of the mind. To speak the truth, I myself like to consider this work a child of time rather than of intelligence, and the only surprising thing is that the first idea of the matter, and such great suspicions about established opinions, could have entered anyone's mind. The rest follows without difficulty. But no doubt there is an element of chance (as we say) and luck in what men think, no less than in what they do and say. And I wish this chance of which I speak to be so understood, that whatever good there is in what I offer may be ascribed to God's infinite mercy and goodness and to the felicity of your times; and that, as I have been a most honest and affectionate servant in my life, so after my death I may have the fortune to ensure, by lighting this new torch in the dark shades of philosophy, that this age will shine forth yet more gloriously to posterity. And surely it is to the times of the wisest and most learned of kings that the *Regeneration* and *Instauration* of the sciences rightly belongs. Lastly, I have a petition, one not unworthy of Your Majesty, and one that very greatly concerns this my work.

5

It is that you, who can compare with Solomon in so many things, in the gravity of your judgements, in the peace of your reign, in largeness of heart, in the noble variety of the books you have composed, would further follow his example and make it your care that a natural and experimental history be collected and completed, true and rigorous, free of anything philological,[1] such as philosophy may be built upon and such as I shall in its due place describe, so that at length, after these many ages of the world, philosophy and the sciences may no longer hang insubstantial in the air, but rest on the solid foundations of well-weighed experience of every kind. I have provided the *Organon,* but the materials must be sought from things them- selves. May God Almighty long preserve Your Majesty.

Your Most Serene Majesty's

most bounden and devoted

servant,

F R A N C I S   V E R U L A M ,
CHANCELLOR.

---

[1]A *philologus* was a man of letters and, in particular, an interpreter of the writings of others. As Bacon explains in Aphorism 3 of *Aphorisms on the Composition of the Primary History,* which is printed at the end of this volume, he was keen to exclude from such histories appeals to the authori- ty of ancient authors.

The Great Instauration
of Francis of Verulam

P R E F A C E

That the sciences are in an unhappy state, and have made no great progress; and that a path must be opened to man's understanding entirely different from that known to men before us, and other means of assistance provided, so that the mind can exercise its rightful authority over the nature of things.

Men seem to me to have a poor knowledge both of their resources and of their strengths, but in fact to overrate the one and underrate the other, with the result that they either put a senselessly high value on the arts they already possess, and do not seek to enlarge them, or else unfairly disparage themselves and spend their powers on trivial things, making no attempt at those things that bear on the heart of the matter. These [failings] are like pillars of fate[2] in the path of the sciences, since men have neither desire nor hope to encourage them to explore beyond. And since an assumption of wealth is among the greatest causes of poverty, and faith in things presently existing leads to neglect of true means of assistance for the future, it is useful, in fact absolutely necessary, that at the very threshold of my work I dispel the excessive fame and admiration accorded to those discoveries made hitherto (and that without any circumlocution and pretense), as a timely warning that men should not overestimate their number nor overpraise their value. For anyone looking carefully into all

[2]The pillars of fate, or of Hercules, are the pillars between which the ship of human reason in the frontispiece is attempting to steer a passage. Hercules' pillars were the two rocks on either side of the Straits of Gibraltar.

those different books that are the boast of the arts and sciences, will find throughout them numberless repetitions of the same things, all different in the ways they handle their subject but saying nothing new; so that while at first sight it all appears abundant, when looked at closely, it is found to be sparse. And as to their usefulness, it should be said frankly that that wisdom which we imbibed principally from the Greeks seems merely the boyhood of knowledge, with the characteristics of boys, that it is good at chattering, but immature and unable to generate. For it is fruitful of controversies, and barren of works. So much so, that the state of learning as it now is seems to agree to the life with the Scylla of fable, who had the head and features of a virgin, but was girt about the womb with a clinging pack of barking monsters. In the same way also, the sciences as we know them have charming and fair-seeming general features, but when it comes to details, down to the parts of generation as it were, where they should yield fruit and works, then arguments and barking disputations arise, and in these they terminate, and are all the issue they can yield.

Furthermore, if these sciences were not altogether defunct, what has been the case throughout the many ages now past could, it seems, hardly have come about, that they have stuck more or less motionless in their tracks and have made no advances worthy of mankind, often to the point where not only what was once asserted remains assertion still, but where also a question once raised remains a question still, not answered by discussion but fixed and fed thereby; while all the tradition and succession of schools represent only the characters of master and pupil, not of inventors or those who bring any distinction to things already invented. In the mechanical arts, on the other hand, we see the opposite happening, for they grow and become more perfect by the day, as if partaking of some breath of life; and in the hands of their first authors they often appear crude and somewhat clumsy and shapeless, yet in the course of time they take on new powers and usefulness, to such a degree that men's eager pursuit of them ceases and turns to other things before these arts shall have reached the summit of their perfection. By contrast, philosophy and the intellectual sciences stand like statues, worshipped and celebrated, but not moved forward. In fact they sometimes flourish most under their first authors, only to decline thereafter. For when men (like party politicians)[3] have once surrendered their minds and have given their allegiance to the opinion of one man, they bring no enlargement to the sciences themselves, but merely act as servile functionaries and attendants to glorify certain authors.

And let no one say that the sciences have been gradually growing and have finally reached a certain secure position, and now at last (as if they had run their full course) have a settled home in the works of a few writers; that nothing better can be found hereafter, the only thing left being to embellish and cultivate the discoveries already made.

Indeed, it is certainly much to be wished that matters were so, but the real truth is that these enslavings of the sciences arise from nothing more than the impudence of a few and the sloth and inertia of the rest. For after the sciences had perhaps to some extent been carefully studied and handled, some fellow has then popped up, of bold mind and popular and celebrated for his neat method of summarizing knowledge, who has to all appearance arranged them as an art but in reality has spoiled the efforts of his predecessors. This, however, is what later generations like, because it makes their work easy, and saves the tedium and impatience involved in any new investigation. But if anyone is persuaded by this long-established consensus, as if it were the judgement of time, he should know that the argument on which he relies is most fallacious and unsafe. For we by no means know everything that has been brought to light and published in science and art in every different age and place, and far less what has been explored and worked on in private by individuals. Neither the births, therefore, nor the miscarriages of time have survived in our records. Nor is the consensus itself and the long time it has lasted worth much at all. For however political systems differ, there is only one such system of the sciences; it always has been and will remain democratic. Now as far as the people are concerned, the doctrines that most flourish are either contentious and pugnacious, or bland and empty, such,

---

[3]Bacon uses the term *pedarii senatores*. Pedarians were said (though this is contested) to have been senators of an inferior grade, who had no vote of their own but could merely signify their assent to that of another.

that is, as either ensnare assent or win it by flattery.[4] And therefore the greatest minds in every age have doubtless felt their force; while being men of uncommon capacity and understanding they have nonetheless, with an eye to their popular reputation, submitted to the judgement of time and of the multitude; and as a result, any more exalted reflections that may have gleamed forth were straightway buffeted and extinguished by the winds of popular opinion. The result has been that Time, like a river, has brought down to us the light and inflated, while it has sunk the weighty and solid. In fact those same authors who set up a virtual dictatorship in the sciences and hold forth so confidently, when from time to time they come to themselves again, turn to complaints about the subtlety of Nature, the hidden recesses of truth, the obscurity of things, the tangled skein of causes and the weakness of the human intellect; not that that proves them any more modest, seeing that they would rather put the blame on the common condition of men and things than confess their own faults. In fact, quite often, when some art fails to attain its object, they declare on the strength of that same art that attainment is not possible. But an art cannot be condemned when it is itself judge and jury. That is therefore only said to save ignorance from ignominy.

Now the condition of the teachings handed down and accepted is, broadly speaking, that they are barren of works, but teeming with questions; late and slow in making any progress, giving an appearance of perfection in the whole, but half-hollow within; subject to the whim of popular opinion and doubted even by their authors, so that they are displayed to view hedged about with sundry artful devices. On the other hand, even those who have resolved to find things out for themselves and devote their efforts to extending the frontiers of knowledge have never ventured to tear themselves away entirely from received ideas and to seek the sources of things.

---

[4]The doctrines that ensnare assent and mislead it by flattery are those of the Idols of the Theatre; they are exemplified by Aristotle's philosophy and by those natural sciences which try to incorporate elements of theology. As Bacon explains more clearly in Aphorisms I, 65 and 67, it was the pugnacious dogmatism of these teachings which trapped their admirers.

Yet they think it a great achievement if they introduce and add anything of their own to the sum of knowledge, with the prudent thought that they gain a reputation for independence by the addition, and for modesty by their agreement with the rest. But so long as common opinion and custom have their say, these vaunted middle ways turn out to bring great harm to the sciences. For it is hardly possible at one and the same time to gaze with admiration upon authors and to excel them, knowledge being like water, which does not rise higher than the level from which it descended. Men of this sort therefore make a few changes but little progress; they bring some improvements, but not any great advance.

There have however been some bolder spirits who have taken the whole business upon themselves, and relying on the force of their intelligence, have beaten a path for themselves and their theories by overturning and destroying previous ones. But for all their commotion, there has been no great advance, since their aim has not been to enlarge the benefits and operations of philosophy and the arts but merely to exchange one doctrine for another and to assert their own rule over men's opinions. But little good has come of it, since although they are opposite errors, the causes of those errors are just the same.

And any who did not bind themselves either to other men's ideas or their own, but were inspired from a love of freedom to try to carry others with them in their search for truth, were well-meaning but ineffective in their attempt. For they seem to have followed only probable lines of thought and to have been carried around in a giddy whirl of arguments, and to have weakened the rigour of their investigation by the indiscriminate licence of their search. We find no one who has spent a proper time on things themselves and actual experience. And some again who have committed themselves to the waves of experience and almost become mechanics, nevertheless carry out a somewhat erratic investigation into that very experience and conduct their campaign in no systematic way. Moreover, most of them set themselves some trifling tasks, accounting it a great achievement if they were able to make just one discovery, a way of proceeding as slight as it is unskilful. For no one examines the nature of any matter correctly and successfully by looking at that matter alone; even after taking great pains in varying experiments, he does not find rest, but still finds something further to look for.

And there is another thing of first importance to be remembered, namely that all who have laboured in learning from experience have from the outset fixed upon certain definite works, which they pursued with immoderate and premature eagerness, and have sought, as I say, fruit-bearing, not light-bearing, experiments. They have not followed the example of the order in which God on the first day created light alone and devoted a whole day to that. Nor on that day did He bring forth any material work, but descended to those things in the days that followed.

And those who gave the first place to dialectic, and who believed that therein lay the most reliable aids to the sciences, have in very truth seen most clearly that human understanding left to itself is deservedly not to be trusted. But then the remedy is altogether too feeble for the disease; more than that, it is not free from disease itself. For the received dialectic, while quite correctly applied to civil affairs and those arts that are based on discourse and opinion, falls a long way short of the subtlety of Nature; and clutching at what it cannot hold does more to consolidate errors than to open the road to the truth.

To sum up, then, it does not seem that either trust in others or their own efforts in the sciences have succeeded in bringing light to men up to now, especially since neither the demonstrations nor the experiments known so far have been of much assistance. Rather, the great edifice of this world appears to the eye of human understanding to be labyrinthine in its structure, displaying on every hand such ambiguous paths, such deceitful likenesses and signs of things, such oblique and convoluted coils and knots of natures. And our journey has always to be made by the uncertain light of the sense, now shining forth, now hidden, through the forests of experience and particulars. And furthermore, as I have said, those who put themselves forward as guides for our journey are themselves also entangled and add to the number of errors and wanderers. In such a difficult pass there is no hope to be had from human judgement acting by its own power alone, nor from some lucky turn of chance. For no excellence of wit, however great, nor repeated throws of the dice of experiment can overcome these obstacles. Our steps must be guided by a thread, and the whole way from the very first perceptions of the senses must be laid down on a sure plan. Not that my remarks should be taken to imply that nothing at all has been achieved by the great labours of so many years; nor should we be ashamed of the discoveries made in the past. It is true that so far as intelligence and abstract thought are concerned, the ancients proved themselves remarkable men. But just as in earlier times, when sailors set their course by observations of the stars alone, they could, to be sure, skirt the coasts of the old continent or cross some lesser and inland seas; but before the ocean could be crossed and the regions of the new world discovered, the use of the mariner's compass had to become known as a more dependable and certain guide along the journey. In exactly the same way the discoveries made hitherto in the arts and sciences have been such as could be found by practice, reflection, observation and argument, being those that are nearer the senses and underlie common notions; but before we can reach the more remote and hidden parts of Nature, it is essential to introduce a better and more perfect method of using the human mind and understanding.

For my part at least, constrained as I always am by the desire for truth, I have committed myself to the uncertainties, difficulties and loneliness of the ways and, trusting in God's help, have held my mind steady against the violent forces and serried ranks of opinion, against also my own inward hesitations and scruples, no less than against the dark clouds of Nature and the phantoms flitting around me on every side; to the end that I may provide, at last, more trustworthy and safe guidelines for present and future generations. And any success I have had in this enterprise has been entirely because the way was made clear to me by a right and proper humility of the human spirit. For all who have applied themselves before me to the discovery of arts, after casting a brief glance at things and examples and experience, have immediately invoked their own spirits in some way to utter oracles, as if the art of discovery was simply a matter of thinking. I, on the other hand, dealing strictly and continually with things, have not taken my attention off them longer than was needed for their image and rays to meet (as happens in the sense of vision) with the result that very little is left for the power and superiority of intelligence.

And I have also followed the same humility in my teaching
which I applied to discovering. For I do not try either by
triumphant victories in argument, nor by calling antiquity to
my aid, nor by any usurpation of authority, nor by a veil of
obscurity either, to invest these my discoveries with any
majesty, which might easily be done by anyone trying to bring
lustre to his own name rather than light to the minds of others.
I have not, I say, brought nor am I preparing any force or guile
against men's judgement; I lead them rather to things themselves and the bonds of alliance between them,[5] so that they
may see for themselves what they have, what they can dispute,
what they can add and bring to the common store. And for
myself, if I have shown a misguided belief in some matter, or
failed to give full attention, as if I had nodded off, or if I have
turned aside from the way and broken off the investigation,
nevertheless I present the bare facts openly, in such a way that
my mistakes can be noticed and removed before they seriously
infect the main body of knowledge; and also so that it will be
easy for my labours to be carried on. And I think that I have in
this way established a true, lawful and lasting marriage
between the empirical and the rational faculties (whose sour
and ill-starred divorce and separation have brought confusion
to all the affairs of the human family).

For this reason, since these things are not for me to
determine, at the outset of my work I offer most humble and
fervent prayers to God the Father, God the Son and God the
Holy Spirit, that, mindful of the tribulations of mankind and
its journeys through this life, in which we toil through few and
evil days, They will vouchsafe through my hands to grant new
alms to the family of man. And this also I humbly ask, that
things human may not run counter to things divine, and that
from the unlocking of the paths of the sense and the more
intense kindling of the natural light there will arise no
unbelief or darkness in our minds towards the divine mysteries; but that rather, as from an understanding pure and
purged of empty phantoms, yet nonetheless obedient and
wholly submissive to the divine oracles, we may give to faith

---

[5]The Latin here is *rerum foedera,* which reflects the same idea as
Bacon's *Instantiae Foederis,* or Instances of Alliance, of Aphorism II, 35.

that which is faith's. And lastly that with knowledge rid of the poison instilled by the serpent, whereby the human mind becomes swollen and puffed up, we may not reach too high nor too far in our wisdom, but may seek the truth in Christian love.

Having thus said my prayers, I turn to men, with certain salutary admonitions and also moderate requests. My first admonition (which was also my prayer) is that, in things divine, men should confine the sense within its proper sphere. For the sense, like the sun, opens the face of the terrestrial globe, but shuts and seals up the face of heaven. On the other hand, in flying from that evil, they should not fall into the opposite fault, as they certainly will, if they think that any part of the investigation of Nature must be excluded, as if by an interdict. For it was not that pure and spotless natural knowledge, by which Adam gave names to all things according to their kind, that was the origin and occasion of the Fall, but that ambitious and headstrong greed for moral knowledge—of telling good from evil—so that man might desert God and make his own laws, that was the ground and manner of this temptation. On the contrary, of the sciences which concern themselves with Nature, the holy philosopher declares: "It is the glory of God to conceal a thing; but the glory of a king to discover a thing";[6] in much the same way as if the Divine Nature took pleasure in the innocent and good-natured children's game of hide-and-seek, and out of His indulgence and kindness to men chose the human soul to be His companion in play in this game. Lastly, I would like to give this general admonition to all men, namely, that they reflect on the true ends of knowledge, and that they seek it not from any intellectual satisfaction, nor for contention, nor to look down upon others, nor for reward, or fame, or power, or any of these baser things; but to direct and bring it to perfection in charity, for the benefit and use of life. For the angels fell through hunger for power; men through hunger for knowledge. But of love and charity there can be no excess, neither did angel or man ever run into danger thereby.

Now the requests I wish to make are these; for myself, I ask nothing, but for the matter in hand I urge men to think of

---

[6]Proverbs xxv, 2; the "holy philosopher" being Solomon.

it not as an opinion but as a task to be done; and to be well
assured that I am laying down foundations, not for any one
sect or teaching but for the advantage and enlargement of
mankind. Next I ask that they be fair to their own interests,
put off the zeal of opinions and prejudices, and take counsel
together for the common good; and freed and protected from
the errors and obstacles of the way by my safeguards and
assistance, that they may come forward and take part themselves in the labours that remain. I ask, moreover, that they be
of good hope and not imagine that my *Instauration* is something infinite and beyond the reach of man, when the truth is
that it is the proper end and termination of infinite error. And
it is not unmindful of the shortness of human life, since it does
not expect that it can bring its business to entire completion
within the course of one generation, but intends it to be taken
on by the next; and finally it seeks knowledge, not arrogantly
in little recesses of human ingenuity, but humbly in the wider
world. But it is the empty things that are of vast size: solid
things are the most compressed and occupy little room. And
last of all, I have just this to ask (lest anyone should perhaps
from unfairness to me endanger my whole enterprise), that
men should consider how far, from that which I must necessarily assert (if I wish to be true to myself), they have the right
to judge and pass sentence on these thoughts of mine; seeing
that for my part I reject all that premature human reasoning
that anticipates things and is rashly and far too quickly
derived from them, and is, as far as the investigation of
Nature is concerned, an inconstant thing, muddled
and badly built. Nor can I be expected
to abide by the judgement of a
method of reasoning that
is itself on
trial.

The Plan of the Work

It consists of Six Parts

First: *The Divisions of the Sciences.*

Second: *The New Organon, or Directions for the Interpretation of Nature.*

Third: *The Phenomena of the Universe, or A Natural and Experimental History for the Foundation of Philosophy.*

Fourth: *The Ladder of the Understanding.*

Fifth: *The Forerunners, or Anticipations of Second Philosophy.*

Sixth: *Second Philosophy, or Active Science.*[1]

---

[1]Ellis translates *philosophia secunda* as 'new philosophy', which is certainly supported by Bacon's description, towards the end of *The Plan of the Work,* of the sixth part of his *Instauration* as containing "the philosophy which, by the legitimate, chaste and rigorous enquiry, . . . is at length developed and established", and by a similar remark he makes in Aphorism I, 116. However, *secunda* standardly means "second", rather than "new". Bacon confuses the matter further by using the expression *philosophia prima,* or first philosophy, in the *De Augmentis* (III, i), to signify very general principles that apply to many different fields and sciences, for instance, "if equals be added to unequals, the whole will be unequal".

Bacon calls a science "active" when it has practical consequences and is not purely speculative.

BRIEF SUMMARIES OF EACH PART

It is a part of my intention to set out everything as openly and clearly as possible. For nakedness of mind is the companion of innocence and simplicity, as nakedness of body once was. In the first place, therefore, let me present the order and system of the work, which I divide into six parts.

1   The first part gives a summary or general description of the learning which mankind possesses today. For I thought it best to spend some time on what is already accepted, so that it might be easier both to bring the old to perfection and to lead on to the new. For I am just as eager to refine the old as to reach after things beyond. And this will also help my teaching to gain credence, since 'an uneducated man', as they say, 'will not take in the words of knowledge unless you tell him first what is in his own heart' [Proverbs xviii, 2]. I will therefore make a point of coasting along the shores of the arts and sciences that are now accepted, as well as conveying some useful things to them along the way.

However, the divisions of the sciences which I use include not only those [divisions] already discovered and known, but those that have hitherto been wrongly omitted. For in the intellectual world, just as in the terrestrial, we find both cultivated and desert regions. It should come as no surprise, therefore, if now and then I depart from the customary divisions. For an addition not only alters the whole but necessarily alters the parts and their sub-divisions too; and the accepted divisions are suited only to the accepted sum of the sciences, as it now stands.

As for those subjects that I shall note as omitted, I do not propose only to give brief titles and summaries of those that are required. For if ever I refer to something as having been omitted, the reason for which seems sufficiently obscure for me to suspect that men would not easily understand my meaning, or what work I had in mind, I shall always (so long as the subject is of any importance) take care either to devise precepts for the performance of such work, or else subjoin, as an example of the whole, some part of the work itself that I have already accomplished, thus providing assistance in every case with either works or advice. For I considered that it would serve my own reputation, and be useful to others, that it should not be thought that I have allowed only some hazy notion of those things to cross my mind, and that what I earnestly desire and aim for are no more than pious hopes; whereas they are in fact things entirely within men's power (if they are but true to themselves), and of which I have in my own mind a sure and well thought-out conception. For I am not just going to survey these regions in my mind, like augurs at their auguries, but will enter them like a general zealous to prove his worth. *Now this is the first part of the work.*

2 Having then sailed by the ancient arts, I shall next prepare the human understanding to advance further. The second part of my work is therefore devoted to instruction in the better and more perfect use of reason in the investigation of Nature, and in the true aids to the understanding: so that by its means (so far as the human condition and mortality allow) the understanding may be exalted, and its ability to overcome the difficulties and obscurities of Nature enlarged. And this art which I present (which I usually call the *Interpretation of Nature*) is a kind of logic, though the difference between it and ordinary logic is great, indeed immense. For the ordinary logic professes to devise and prepare means to help and assist the understanding; and in this one respect they agree. But my logic is completely different from the common sort, in particular at three points: viz., in its end, in its method of demonstration, and in the starting point of the inquiry.

For the end I propose for my science is the discovery not of arguments but of arts, not of things that are consistent with first principles, but of the principles themselves, not of probable reasons but of indicators and directions for works. As my intention is different, so therefore is the result. The result of the one is to overcome an opponent by disputation, of the other to overcome Nature by action.

And the nature and order of the demonstrations themselves are suited to such an end. For in the ordinary logic, almost all the work is performed around the syllogism, and logicians seem to give scarcely any serious thought to induction, passing it by with a casual mention, and hastening on to the formulas of disputation. I, on the other hand, reject demonstration by syllogism for acting too confusedly and allowing Nature to slip from its grasp. For although no one can doubt that propositions that agree on a middle term agree also with each other (this being a kind of mathematical certainty),[2] nevertheless there is this underlying deception, that the syllogism consists of propositions, propositions of words, and words are tokens and symbols of notions. If therefore the very notions of the mind (which are, as it were, the soul of words, and the basis of the whole system and structure) are badly and carelessly derived from things, and vague, inadequately defined and circumscribed, in short, if they are defective in many ways, then everything collapses. I therefore reject the syllogism; not only as regards first principles (for even the logicians do not apply it to those) but also as regards the intermediate propositions, which while they are indeed derived from the syllogism and owe their existence to it, are barren of works, far removed from practical results, and entirely inadequate for the active part of the sciences. Although, therefore, I concede to the syllogism and famed and vaunted demonstrations of that kind their jurisdiction over arts that are popular and based on opinion (which I leave undisturbed), yet in regard to the nature of things, I use induction throughout, both for minor and for major propositions. For I consider *Induction* to be that form of demonstration which upholds the sense, presses down upon Nature and is intent on and closely bound up with works.

It follows from this that the order of demonstration is also entirely inverted. For hitherto the proceeding has been at the beginning to fly from the sense and particulars to the greatest generalities, as if to fixed poles around which the disputations revolve; and from these to derive the rest by middle terms: a route that is certainly short, but precipitate, and affording no passage to Nature, but well inclined and suited to disputations. On the other hand, going by my method is to derive axioms gradually, in a connected succession, so as only at the end to arrive at the most general; however, when they do come forth they are not purely speculative but are well-defined, and such

---

[2]The syllogism is a form of logical argument with two premises and containing, in all, three different terms. The term common to the premises is what Aristotelians referred to as the 'middle term'. An example of a syllogism is 'All As are Bs; All Bs are Cs; therefore, All As are Cs', with B as the middle term.

as Nature would really recognize as better known to herself,[3] and which lie at the very marrow of things.

But far the greatest change I make is in the very form of induction, and the judgement made from it. For the induction of which the logicians talk, which proceeds by simple enumeration, is a childish affair, unsafe in its conclusions, in danger from a contradictory instance, taking account only of what is familiar, and leading to no result.[4]

Now what the sciences need is a form of induction that will analyse experience and take it apart, and through due exclusions and rejections necessarily come to a conclusion. And if that common art of judgement[5] of the logicians involved so much labour and exercised such great intellects, how much more work is involved in this other method, which is drawn not only from the inner recesses of the mind, but also from the very bowels of Nature?

Nor is this all, for I also lay down and strengthen the foundations of the sciences more firmly, and sink the beginnings deeper than men have ever done, submitting to examination those things that the ordinary logic takes on trust from others. For the logicians take the first principles of the sciences from each of the sciences themselves; they also venerate the first notions of the mind; and finally they acquiesce in the immediate informations of the sense when it is well-placed. I, on the other hand, maintain that true logic ought to enter each province of the sciences with a greater authority than belongs to the principles of those sciences themselves, and should compel those putative principles to submit to examination, until they are entirely established. And as for the first notions of the understanding, there is not one of these that is conceived by the understanding when left to itself that I would not regard as suspect, and in no way

---

[3]Footnote 12 to Aphorism I, 22, discusses the concept of being "better known" to Nature.

[4]Simple enumeration, that is, generalisation from observed instances, is described in footnote 62, *below*.

[5]*Judgement* was a scholastic logical term signifying the part of logic that included the syllogism and reasoning by induction—see footnote 75 to Aphorism I, 82.

established, until it has submitted to a new art of judgement and a pronouncement had been made on it in accordance with that art. And the information given by the sense itself I also examine in many ways. For the senses are certainly fallible, but they also indicate their errors; yet while the errors are right before us, the indications of how to cure them are remote and have to be looked for.

Now the sense is doubly culpable: for it either forsakes us, or it deceives us. Thus in the first place, there are many things that escape the sense, even when the latter is unhindered and rightly placed to receive them; either from the subtlety of the whole body [under observation], or the minute size of the parts, or from the distance of the position, or either the slowness or speed of motion, or the familiarity of the object, or for other reasons.[6] Nor again, when the senses do take hold of a thing, is their grasp of it very firm. For the evidence and information given us by the sense has reference always to man, not to the universe; and it is a great mistake to say that the sense is the measure of things.

To remedy these things, I have sought most carefully everywhere to find helps for the sense, and supply substitutes where it forsakes us, and correctives where it is at variance [from the truth].[7] And I try to bring this about not so much with instruments as by experiments. For the subtlety of experiments is far greater than that of the sense itself, even though assisted by the most delicate instruments. (I am speaking of those experiments that are skilfully and expertly thought out and framed for the purpose of the inquiry.) I do not therefore attach much importance to the immediate and natural perception of the sense; but I arrange it so that the sense judges only the experiment, the experiment the point in Nature. And for this reason I think that, as regards the sense (from which all knowledge of Nature must be sought, unless we wish to act like madmen), we stand before it as a priest of religion and skilful interpreter of its oracles; and while others

---

[6]These limitations on the powers of the senses are described in Aphorism II, 40, together with methods for overcoming them.

[7]Aids for the senses and substitutes to make up for their limitations are discussed in Aphorisms II, 39 and 42, respectively.

only profess to support and cultivate the sense, I do so in actual fact. These then are the preparations that I make for kindling and bringing to bear the light of Nature. And they would be sufficient by themselves, if the human understanding were even and like a clean sheet of paper. But since men's minds are obsessed to such an extraordinary extent that they entirely lack any unblemished and smooth surface on which to receive the true rays of things, I think it incumbent on me to seek a cure for this also.

Now the *idols* that dwell in the mind are either adventitious [i.e., coming from without], or innate. The adventitious migrate into men's minds either from the doctrines and sects of philosophers, or from faulty laws of demonstration. But the innate are inherent in the very nature of the understanding, which is found to be far more prone to error than the sense. For however much men delight in admiring, almost worshipping, their own cleverness, one thing is very certain, that just as an uneven mirror, by reason of its particular shape and cross-section, distorts the rays of things, so the mind also, when it is acted upon by things through the sense, treacherously implants and mixes its own nature into the nature of things, in the process of forming its erroneous notions.

And while those first two kinds of *idols* are only with difficulty eradicated, these last kinds cannot be eradicated at all. All that can be done is to point them out, and to mark and convict that insidious power of the mind, lest from the destruction of the old errors, shoots of new ones may perhaps spring up at once like blemishes out of that same ill complexion of the mind, and the end result will be that errors will not be extinguished, but only interchanged; and rather to lay it down, once and for all, as a settled maxim, that the mind can only pass judgement by means of induction, and that moreover, in its legitimate form. This doctrine, then, of the purging of the understanding so as to adapt it to the truth, is accomplished by three refutations: the refutations respectively of philosophies, of demonstrations, and of native human reason. Once these have been explained, and it has been made clear what is due to the nature of things and what to the nature of the mind, I think I shall, with God's good help, have prepared and adorned the bridal chamber of the mind and the universe. And the prayer of the nuptial hymn should be that from this marriage may come help for mankind, and a long line of inventions which will in some part alleviate man's wretched and needy condition. *This is the second part of the work.*

3 But I intend not only to show and prepare the ways, but also to enter them, and therefore the third part of the work embraces the *Phenomena of the Universe;* that is, every kind of experience, and a natural history such as can serve as the foundation on which to build philosophy. For while a superior method of demonstration or form of interpreting Nature may protect the mind from falling into error, it cannot thereby furnish it with the material for knowledge. But for those who intend to discover and to understand, not to indulge in conjectures and soothsaying, and rather than contrive imitation and fabulous worlds plan to look deep into the nature of the real world and to dissect it—for them everything must be sought in things themselves. And even if all the world's brains came together, no amount of ingenuity or meditation or argument could ever replace or make up for this hard work and investigation and world-wide survey. Either this, then, must be done, or the business abandoned for good. But such have been men's actions up to now that it is little wonder that Nature does not give herself up to them.

For in the first place, the way that the sense itself is informed, both deserting and deceiving us; observation, careless, irregular and fortuitous; tradition, empty and based on rumours; practice, slavishly bent on its work; the conduct of experiment, blind, stupid, vague and broken off too soon; and finally, natural history, slight and scanty—all these have contributed the worst possible materials to the understanding for fostering philosophy and the sciences.

Then an attempt is made to put things right by preposterously subtle argument and the airing at too late a stage of quite hopeless matters, which entirely fails either to set the business right or to separate the errors. No hope therefore can be entertained of any major increase or advance, except through a restoration of the sciences.

Now the first beginnings of this restoration must only be made by a natural history, and that of a new kind and compiled on a new system. For it would be useless to polish the mirror if there were no images to be reflected, and obviously there must be suitable material prepared for the understanding, as well as safeguards for dealing with it. But just as my logic differs from that now in use, so also does my history differ in many respects: in its end or purpose, its size and compilation, and in its subtlety, and also in the way it is selected and arranged in due order for what follows.

For first, I propose a natural history that does not so much charm with its variety or gratify by the immediate fruit of experiments, as provide light for the discovery of causes and supply the first mother's milk to the infant philosophy. For though I am principally in pursuit of works and the active part of the sciences, I am nevertheless content to wait for harvest-time, and do not attempt to reap moss or the green corn; knowing well as I do that axioms rightly discovered bring with them hosts of works, not in ones and twos but thick and fast. And that premature and childish desire to snatch up hastily some kind of pledges of new works I utterly condemn and reject, as being like Atalanta's apple,[8] which delayed her in the race. This then is the purpose of my natural history.

Now as to how it should be compiled, I arrange it as a history, not only of Nature free and untrammelled (that is when she flows along of her own accord and on her own business)—as is a history of the heavenly bodies, of meteors, of the earth and sea, minerals, plants and animals—but much more of Nature constrained and vexed; by which I mean when, by the art and intervention of man, she is forced out of her natural state and is pressed and moulded. I would therefore

---

[8]In Greek mythology, Atalanta was born in Arcadia. She was determined to live in perpetual celibacy, yet her great beauty attracted many admirers. To free herself from these importunities, she proposed to run races with her suitors, and being very swift-footed, she was always confident of victory. Her suitors were to run without arms, and she was to carry a dart in her hand. Atalanta's lovers were to start first, and whoever arrived at the goal before her was to be rewarded with her hand as the prize, but all those whom she overtook were to be killed with her dart. Many of her suitors died in the contest until Hippomenes proposed himself. Venus had presented Hippomenes with three golden apples and as soon as he had started the course, he artfully threw down the apples. While Atalanta stopped to pick up the tempting fruit, Hippomenes outstripped her and thereby won the race and her hand in marriage.

describe at length all experiments in the mechanical arts, and in the operative part of the liberal arts,[9] and in those practical crafts that have not developed into an art of their own, as far as it may be possible to inquire, and as conduces to my purpose. In fact, to tell the truth, I care nothing for men's pride and regard for appearances, and I take many more pains and precautions over this part of the work than over the former, seeing that the nature of things betrays itself more readily under the vexations of art, than in its natural freedom.

And I shall not confine my history to material bodies, but have made it my care also to prepare a separate history of those powers that can be considered cardinal in Nature, and which plainly constitute the primary forces of Nature, as the foremost passions and desires of matter, viz., *dense, rare, hot, cold, consistent, fluid, heavy, light* and many others.

Moreover, to speak of subtlety, what I am looking for is a kind of experiment far more subtle and simple than those that present themselves. For I root out and drag from the darkness many things that no one would think of investigating unless he were proceeding with fixed determination towards the discovery of causes; since in themselves they are of no great use, and are quite clearly not sought for their own sake, but have exactly the same relation to things and works as have the letters of the alphabet to speech and words, which, though useless in themselves, are the elements of all discourse.

Now in the selection of factual accounts[10] and experiments, I think I have been more cautious than those who have been

---

[9]The term *liberal* was traditionally applied to arts or sciences that were considered worthy of a free man, as opposed to servile or mechanical arts. The former consisted of the *trivium*—grammar, rhetoric and logic— and the *quadrivium*—music, arithmetic, astronomy, geometry. Medicine and architecture were later added to these seven. These arts were the basis of all education in the Middle Ages, and indeed, long after in some countries; the mechanical arts consisted of manual crafts and manufacture.

The operative part of science relates to the production of effects and is distinguished from the speculative part, which concerns the inquisition of causes. (*De Augmentis,* III, iii, *Works,* IV, p. 343)

[10]We have translated *narratio* as "factual account"; in the terminology of sixteenth century rhetoric, the narration was that part of an oration in which the facts are stated.

engaged in natural history hitherto. For I accept everything that was actually seen, or at least examined with some degree of rigour, so that nothing is exaggerated to appear miraculous, but so that my factual accounts may be pure and unblemished by fables and vanity. And I expressly denounce and condemn all false tales that are accepted and go around (which by extraordinary negligence have persisted for many generations and become inveterate), and will have the sciences no longer troubled with them. For someone has wisely remarked that the fairy tales and superstitions and trifles that nursemaids instil into children cause grave damage to their minds; and the same thought makes me concerned and even anxious, lest from the start, when with my natural history I have the care and charge of philosophy's infancy, I accustom it to empty stories. And in every experiment that is new and slightly more subtle, even if to my mind it is certain and proved, I nevertheless add a clear statement of the method I used in conducting it, so that men, having a clear picture of all the details, may see whether there could be any underlying faults and devise more reliable and, if possible, more delicate tests; and lastly I sprinkle warnings and scruples and cautions like water over the whole exercise, to drive away and ward off all phantasms, as if by some religious rite of exorcism.

Lastly, knowing as I do how much men's mental vision is distracted by experience and history, and how difficult it is at first (especially for pliant or preoccupied minds) to familiarize themselves with Nature, I quite often add observations of my own, these being, as it were, the first dealings and leanings and glances of history towards philosophy; both as an assurance to men that they will not be kept tossing forever in the billows of history, and so that when the time comes for the understanding to start work, everything may be in a better state of readiness. And I believe that by means of a natural history such as I describe, a sure and convenient approach may be made to Nature, and a sound and well-prepared store of material provided for the understanding.

4 Now after we have surrounded the understanding with the most trusty helps and guards and brought together, after most rigorous selection, a whole army of divine works, it may seem that nothing more needs doing before we make a start on philosophy itself. But in such an arduous and uncertain

enterprise a few things seem to be called for, partly to assist my teaching and partly for immediate advantage.

The first[11] of these is to set out examples of investigation and discovery according to my method, which should be displayed in certain subjects, chosen preferably from those subjects which of those investigated are the most noble and most widely different from each other, so as to have an example in each kind. I do not mean those examples that are introduced to illustrate particular precepts and rules (for I provide a great number of them in the second part of the work), but entire types and models which make visible, as it were, in certain diverse and notable subjects, the general mental process and its structure and sequence involved in discovery from beginning to end. For it occurs to me that in mathematics it is clear and easy to follow a demonstration with the help of a machine;[12] but without that advantage, everything seems complicated and more intricate than is really the case. To examples of this kind, therefore I devote the fourth part of my work, which is really just a particular and explicit application of the second part.

5   The fifth part is only for use during the time before the rest of the work is completed, payable like interest until the principal can be obtained. For I do not so blindly pursue my goal as to neglect any useful things met along the way; and for this reason, I include in the fifth part those things that I have myself either discovered or proved or added; not, however, by means of my methods and precepts for interpreting [Nature], but by the ordinary use of the understanding that others usually employ in inquiry and discovery. For while I hope that my continuous close contact with Nature will produce greater things from my reflections than could be expected from my mental ability, I hope too that these will serve like wayside

---

[11]Bacon seems to be commencing a list of points but only gets as far as this first one.

[12]Bacon sometimes refers to astronomy as mathematics, in accordance with contemporary terminology, and the machine he is here referring to may be some kind of mechanical representation of planetary motion. In Aphorism II, 36 (*4*), Bacon tells us that he once had such a model "built with iron wires, as in a machine".

inns, where the mind on its journey to more certain discoveries may rest a little time. At the same time, however, I put it on record that I have no wish to be bound by these aforementioned discoveries, which were neither discovered nor proved by the true principles of interpretation. But no one should disapprove of such a suspension of judgement in a teaching that asserts, not that nothing can be known at all, but that knowledge is only possible by following a certain method and path; and yet halts for the time being at certain degrees of certainty for help and support until the mind may arrive at an explanation of causes on which it can stand. For even those schools of philosophers which held to an unconditional doctrine of acatalepsy [i.e., that knowledge of the world is impossible] were no worse than those who usurped a licence to pronounce [upon Nature]. They, however, provided no aids either to the sense or the understanding, as I have done, but simply proffered faith and authority, which is a very different thing, and more or less the opposite.

6 And finally the sixth part of my work (to which all the others are as servants and attendants) contains and sets out the philosophy which by the legitimate, chaste and rigorous inquiry (which I have earlier prepared and explained) is at length developed and established. But to bring this final part to perfection, and lead it to its conclusion, is a thing both above my strength and beyond my hopes. I have made a beginning that, I hope, is not to be despised; the fortune of mankind will give the outcome, such as men in the present state of things and of minds may perhaps be unable to grasp or measure. For the matter in hand is not just a pleasant speculation, but in truth concerns the affairs and fortunes of mankind and all the power of its works. For man is only the servant and interpreter of Nature and he only does and understands so much as he shall have observed, in fact or in thought, of the course of Nature; more than this he neither knows, nor can do. No force whatever can unfasten or break the chain of causes, and Nature is only overcome by obeying her. So it is that those two objects of mankind, *Knowledge* and *Power,* come in fact to the same thing; and the failure of works derives mostly from ignorance of causes.

And all depends on keeping the mind's eye fixed on things themselves, so that their images are received exactly as they are. For God forbid that we should give out a dream of our imagination for a pattern of the world; but may He rather grant of His grace that we may write a revelation or true vision of the footsteps and imprint of the Creator upon created things.

Therefore, Oh Father, who gavest us the light to see things as Thy first work of creation, and didst breathe into the face of man the light of the understanding as the highest of Thy works, guard and govern this work, that, begun by Thy goodness, returneth to Thy glory. When Thou didst turn to look at the works which Thy hands had made, Thou didst see that all was very good, and Thou didst rest. But man hath turned to the works that his hands have made and hath seen that all was vanity and vexation of spirit; and he hath had no rest. Wherefore, if we toil and sweat in Thy tasks, Thou wilt make us partakers of Thy vision and Thy sabbath. We humbly pray that this mind may stay firm in us; and that
Thou wilt wish to have the family of man endowed
with new mercies through my hands, and
the hands of others to whom
Thou wilt give the same
purpose.

THE
FIRST PART OF THE
INSTAURATION
WHICH COMPRISES THE
DIVISIONS OF THE SCIENCES,
IS WANTING.
But some account of them will be found in the
Second Book of the "Advancement of
Learning, Divine and Human."

———————

Next comes
THE SECOND PART OF THE
INSTAURATION,
WHICH EXHIBITS
THE ART ITSELF OF
INTERPRETING NATURE,
AND OF THE TRUER EXERCISE OF THE
UNDERSTANDING;
Not however in the form of a regular Treatise,
but only a summary arranged into aphorisms.

Novum
Organum

THE SECOND PART OF THE WORK
WHICH IS CALLED
THE NEW ORGANON;
OR,
TRUE DIRECTIONS
CONCERNING THE INTERPRETATION
OF NATURE

PREFACE

Those who have ventured to pronounce on Nature as if it were a thing already explored, whether they have done so out of self-confidence, ambition or professional habit, have inflicted the greatest harm on philosophy and the sciences. For, persuasive as they were, they have been just as effective in smothering and stopping inquiry, and they have done more harm by spoiling and putting an end to other men's efforts than good by their own. Those on the other hand who have taken the opposite road, and have declared that absolutely nothing can be known—whether they have sunk to this opinion from dislike of the ancient sophists,[1] from vacillation of mind, or even from a certain weight of erudition—have adduced reasons for it that are not to be despised; however, they did not derive this opinion from the right beginnings, and in their zeal and eagerness they have carried their argument too far. But the earlier Greeks,[2] whose writings have been lost, were more careful to steer a course between a boasting certainty and despairing Acatalepsy;[3] and though more often indignantly complaining of the difficulty of inquiry and the obscurity of things, and fairly champing at the bit, they still pressed on with their object and engaged with Nature, thinking, it seems, that it is best not to argue that nothing can be known, but rather to try and find out. Even they, however, trusted in the power of their intellect and applied no rule, but based everything on keen meditation and perpetual turning and twisting of mind.

---

[1]The ancient sophists were teachers and intellectual showmen in fifth century BC Greece, who travelled the country offering for a fee instruction in various subjects. Bacon is referring to Plato as having introduced and advocated Acatalepsy (as he makes clear in Aphorism I, 67, *below*). In Plato's dialogues *Protagoras* and *Gorgias,* Socrates is represented as undermining with sceptical questioning the supposed knowledge of the sophists. However, popular contemporary opinion (reflected, for example, in Aristophanes's play *The Clouds*) regarded the sophists as no less sceptical than Socrates—a reputation they gained through their practice and teaching of rhetoric, the art of arguing equally convincingly for either side of any dispute.

[2]A list of some of the earlier Greek philosophers whom Bacon had in mind is given in Aphorism I, 71, *below.*

[3]Acatalepsy is the doctrine that the world is incomprehensible.

Now my method, though hard to practise, is easy to explain. It is that, in order to establish degrees of certainty, we should reduce the sense to its proper rank; but I reject for the most part that mental process that follows the sense. Instead, I open up and lay down a new and certain road for the mind to take, starting from those perceptions of the senses. And this was certainly recognized even by those who attributed so much importance to dialectic, obviously looking for intellectual props, not being entirely confident in the natural unassisted working of the mind. But this remedy comes too late, to matters already lost, after the mind, through the daily inter-course of life, has become occupied with received and false doctrines, and is beset with the vainest *idols*. So, therefore, that art of dialectic, coming, as I said, too late to the rescue, and never getting the matter straight again, has done more to fix errors than to reveal truth.

There remains but one cure, one healthy course: the whole operation of the mind must be completely re-started, so that from the very beginning it is not left to itself, but is always subject to rule; and the thing accomplished as if by machinery. Certainly, if men had attempted mechanical tasks, using their bare hands alone, without the powerful assistance of instru-ments, in the way that they have not hesitated to handle intellectual tasks with bare force of mind, their achievements would have been small indeed, however strenuously they all laboured together.

Now (to pause for a while upon this example and look at it as under a [magnifying] glass) let us suppose some enormous obelisk for the decoration of a triumph or similar splendid occasion had to be moved from its place, and men tried to do this with their bare hands, would not any sober-minded spectator think this the height of folly? And madder still if they simply brought in more workers, or took out the weaker, and chose only strong and sturdy ones, hoping to achieve their end in this way at least? And if, not content with that, they decided to bring in all the resources of athletic skill, summon-ing men whose every muscle, nerve and limb was expertly anointed with embrocation, would not that spectator cry out that they were only taking pains to show a kind of method and discretion in their madness?

Yet it is with the same senseless effort and useless

combination of forces that men proceed in intellectual matters. They hope for great things, either from the number and consensus of clever minds, or from their excellence and sharpness, or even fortify their mental sinews with dialectic (which can be considered an athletic art), yet all the time, however great their eagerness and effort, on a true judgement, they are always applying their bare understanding to the matter. Whereas, in any great work to which men put their hands, it is clearly not possible for either the full strength of each to be exerted or that of many to be combined, unless with the aid of instruments and machines.

Following on from these initial remarks, I must mention that there are two things that men should be clearly warned not to overlook. The first is that it so happens, fortunately as I believe for the quenching and dispelling of controversy and swollen-headedness, that the honour and respect due to the ancients can be preserved intact and undiminished, and that at the same time I may carry out my designs and yet gather the fruits of my modesty. For if I were to declare that, while following the same road as the ancients, I had produced better results than they, that would be certain to lead to comparison and argument over our respective talents and mental abilities, such as no smooth words could avoid. Not that there would be anything wrong or novel in my doing so, for why should I not have the right common to all to point out and criticize anything in their work that was ill-founded? Yet such a rivalry, however just and permissible, would perhaps be an unequal one, as a measure of my powers. As it is, though, since my contention is that an entirely new way, untried and indeed unknown to them, lies open to the understanding, the case is altered. No more partisan strife; I merely appear as a guide, a position of quite modest authority, owing more to luck than to superior ability. This warning concerns persons only; the other concerns the matter itself.

I am not trying in the least to disturb the philosophy that now flourishes, nor any other more correct and complete philosophy that may exist now or in the future. For I do not wish to hinder this received philosophy, or others like it, from nourishing disputes, ornamenting learned discourse, or providing employment for professors, and benefits for civic affairs. I go further, in fact, and declare openly that the philosophy I am advancing will be of little use for those purposes. It does not present itself in a hostile manner, cannot be picked up in passing, does not flatter the understanding with preconceived ideas, nor descend to popular acceptance, except through its usefulness and results.

Let there be, therefore, as a boon and blessing for each side, two sources of knowledge and two ways of organizing it; and likewise two tribes of thinkers and philosophers, two clans as it were, not in any way hostile or alien to each other, but linked in mutual support: in short, let there be one method for the cultivation of knowledge, and one for its discovery.

And as for those who prefer the former, either because they are in a hurry, or from civic considerations, or because they lack the mental capacity to absorb and embrace the latter (which must apply to most men), I hope that they succeed in their purposes, and obtain what they are pursuing. But if there are any men who have the wish and the will not only to cling to and make use of knowledge already discovered, but to penetrate further; to conquer, not an opponent in argument, but Nature herself in action: to seek, in short, not elegant and probable conjectures, but certain and demonstrable knowledge: such men, true sons of learning, I invite to join me, if they will, so that we can pass by the outer halls of Nature, which any number of men have already trodden, to where at length the way into her inner chambers shall be revealed. And to make my meaning clearer and familiarize what I have in mind by giving them names, I have chosen to call one method *Anticipation of the Mind* and the other *Interpretation of Nature.*

One thing more I ask. I have devoted much thought and care to ensuring that my propositions should not only be true but also accepted easily and without strain into men's minds (however strangely they are already occupied and obstructed). On the other hand, in such a great restoration of learning and knowledge, it is only fair to ask that any man who seeks to form an opinion on these my ideas, whether from the evidence of his own senses or from the host of authorities, or from the forms of demonstrations which nowadays have almost the force of judicial laws, should not think he can do so in passing or in the midst of other business; but should get to know the subject thoroughly, and try for a while himself the way that I describe, so that he becomes aware of the subtlety of things that experience will show him; and let him take due time to correct those misleading, deep-seated habits of thought. Only then, when he has begun to be his own master, let him (if he will) use his own judgement.

*A Summary of the Second Part,
arranged into
Aphorisms*

Aphorisms Concerning the Interpretation of Nature and the Kingdom of Man[4]

APHORISM

1

Man, the servant and interpreter of Nature, only does and understands so much as he shall have observed, in fact or in thought, of the course of Nature; more than this he neither knows nor can do.

2

Neither the bare hand nor the understanding left to itself are of much use. It is by instruments and other aids that the work gets done, and these are needed as much by the understanding as by the hand. And just as instruments improve or regulate the movement of our hands, so instruments of the mind provide suggestions or cautions to the understanding.

3

Human knowledge and human power come to the same thing, for where the cause is not known the effect cannot be produced. We can only command Nature by obeying her, and what in contemplation represents the cause, in operation stands as the rule.

---

[4]This comparison of the interpretation of nature—Bacon's proposed method of discovery—and "the kingdom of man" is made a little clearer in Aphorism I, 68, *below.*

4

With respect to works,[5] man can only bring natural objects together or separate them; Nature does the rest by her internal operations.

5

The mechanic, mathematician, physician, alchemist and magician[6] all immerse themselves in Nature, with a view to works, but all so far with feeble effort and slight success.

6

It would be irrational, and self-contradictory,[7] to suppose that things that have never yet been done could be done, except by means not yet tried.

7

The products of mind and hand seem very numerous in books and handiworks, but all that variety consists in minute subtlety, and derivations from the few facts already known, not in the number of axioms.

---

[5]Works were practical effects, particularly those of utility to mankind, which Bacon expected a properly constituted science would bring in abundance.

[6]A mechanic is a practical scientist or craftsman. By mathematician Bacon almost certainly means astronomer here. He sometimes identifies the two and indeed this was not unusual. Thus in the *Advancement of Learning,* Bacon refers to "the mathematicians [who] cannot satisfy themselves, except they reduce the motions of the celestial bodies to perfect circles". Magic was the art of producing striking effects by exploiting the hidden qualities of bodies. John Baptista Porta (ca. 1535–1615) published an immensely popular book called *Natural Magic* in 1558.

[7]The phrase *in se contrarium,* which we translate as "self-contradictory", does not however signify a logical contradiction.

8

Even the works already invented owe their existence to casual experience more than to the sciences; for the sciences we now have are nothing more than nice arrangements of things already discovered, not methods of discovery or pointers to new works.

9

There is a single root cause of nearly all the evils in the sciences, namely, that while we wrongly admire and extol the powers of the human mind, we fail to look for true ways of helping it.

10

The subtlety of Nature is far greater than that of the sense and the understanding, so that all our beautiful speculations and guesses and controversies are absurd, only there is no one at hand to observe this fact.

11

Just as the sciences we now have are of no use in discovering works, so the logic we now have is of no use in discovering sciences.[8]

---

[8]*Logic* in Bacon's day was often used synonymously with *dialectic,* though the two terms were also often distinguished, as Aristotle had done; in fact, it was a subject of discussion in the sixteenth century whether or not they should be distinguished. Bacon seems to make no sharp distinction. Logic and dialectic were both aspects of the art of reasoning; they included methods of analysing propositions and determining what can be said for and against them as well as the theory of formal inference, including the syllogism, and induction. Bacon calls the latter "ordinary" induction, which he opposes to his own "true induction" (Aphorism I, 17); he also includes the latter under the head of logic (*The Plan of the Work, 2, above*).

12

The logic now in use serves to reinforce and fix those errors that are founded on commonly held notions rather than to help the search for truth, and so does more harm than good.

13

The syllogism does not apply to the principles of the sciences, and is applied in vain to the intermediate axioms, being quite unequal to the subtlety of Nature. Therefore, while it commands assent, it fails to take hold of things.

14

The syllogism consists of propositions, propositions of words, and words are tokens of notions. Therefore—and this is the heart of the matter—if the notions themselves are muddled and carelessly derived from things, the whole superstructure is shaky. The one hope, therefore, lies in true *induction*.

15

There is no soundness in our notions, whether the logical or the physical: *substance, quality, action, passion* [i.e., *being acted upon*], even *existence* itself, are poor notions; much worse are *heavy, light, dense, rare, moist, dry, generation, corruption, attraction, repulsion, element, matter, form* and the like; all these are ill-defined and fantastical.[9]

16

Our notions of individual species, such as *man, dog, dove,* and of immediate perceptions of the sense, *hot, cold, white,*

---

[9]The logical notions are the first of the two sets listed here, *substance, quality, action* and *passion,* which are four of Aristotle's so-called categories—see footnote 38 to Aphorism I, 63, *below.*

black, are not very misleading. Yet even they are sometimes confused, as a result of the flux of matter and the mingling of things with each other. All the other notions which men have adopted up to now are aberrations, improperly abstracted and derived from things.

17

There is as much capriciousness and aberration in the construction of axioms as in the abstracting of notions; and the same is true of those principles themselves that depend on ordinary induction.[10] But this fault is much worse in the axioms and lower propositions yielded by the syllogism.

18

The discoveries that have been made up to now in the sciences have as a rule been such as closely underlie common notions. To penetrate further into the inner and more remote parts of Nature, it is necessary that both notions and axioms be drawn from things by a more certain and guarded way, and that an altogether better and surer intellectual operation be introduced.

19

There are and can be only two ways of inquiry into and discovery of truth. The one flies from the senses and particulars to axioms of the most general kind, and from these principles and their [supposed] immutable truth, proceeds to judgement and to the discovery of intermediate axioms. And

---

[10]By "ordinary induction" Bacon is referring to a kind of generalisation from particular instances which was a standard part of the logic of his day. Thomas Wilson, in his influential textbook of logic, *The rule of Reason, conteinyng the art of Logique, set forth in Englishe,* 1551, provides a typical example: "Rhenyshe wine heateth, Malmesey heateth, Frenchewine heateth, neither is there any wyne that doth the contrary: Ergo all wine heateth."

this is the method that is now in use. The other calls forth axioms from the senses and particulars by a gradual and continuous ascent, to arrive at the most general axioms last of all. This latter is the true but untried way.

20

The understanding left to itself takes the same (that is, the former) path which it takes when it proceeds in dialectical order. For the mind likes to leap to positions of greater generality, that it may rest there, and after a short while it scorns experience. But these evils are at length increased by dialectic, on account of the solemn rituals of disputations.[11]

21

The understanding left to itself, in a sober, patient and serious mind (especially if unhindered by received doctrines) tries sometimes to follow the second way, the right one, but does not get far. For the intellect alone, unregulated and unaided, is unequal to the task and quite unfitted to overcome the obscurity of things.

22

Each way starts from the sense and particulars and comes to rest in the greatest generalities, but there is an immense difference between them. While the former just cursorily skims experience and particulars, the other engages properly and methodically with them; the former, again, sets up certain abstract and useless generalities from the beginning, the other

---

[11]*Dialectic* was standardly described as the "art of disputing well", for example, by Peter Ramus (Pierre de la Ramée, 1515–1572), the most famous logician of the sixteenth century (he was murdered in Paris two days after the Massacre of St Bartholomew's Day).

rises up gradually to those things that are more general in Nature.[12]

23

There is a great difference between the idols of the human mind and the ideas of the divine mind; that is to say, between certain empty opinions and the genuine signatures and marks impressed on created things, as they are found to be.[13]

24

It cannot be that axioms established by argumentation should have any value for discovering new works; for the

---

[12]The Latin here translates literally as follows: "to those things which are more known to Nature (*notiora sunt naturae*)". Bacon uses the same phrase in Aphorism II, 4, when discussing his doctrine of forms. These are certain arrangements and states of the minute parts of matter, which constitute, as it were, the essence of some observable property (or 'nature'), such as heat, and whose discovery is a principal goal of Bacon's inductive science: ". . . the true form is such that it derives the given nature from some source of being that is inherent in more natures, and is (as they say) better known to Nature (*notior naturae*)". A few lines later he glosses this by saying that in the search for a form, "another nature [should] be discovered which is interchangeable with the given nature, and yet is a limitation of a more known nature (*notioris naturae*)". Then in Aphorism II, 15, Bacon, clearly recapitulating these earlier comments, says: "What we have to find . . . is a nature of such a kind that it is always present or absent with the given nature, and always increases and decreases with it, and is, as I have said above, a limitation of a *more general* (*magis communis*) nature [italics added]". It seems likely, therefore, that "more general" is how we should render *notiora,* rather than Ellis's "better known in the order of Nature", which is hard to interpret.

Bacon's use of the term derived from Aristotle, who employed it in the sense of, or at least as implying, "more general". For instance: "the things which are most knowable are first principles and causes" (*Metaphysics* 982a30–982b1); and "By 'prior' or 'more knowable' in the absolute sense I mean that which is further from it [i.e., our perception]. The most universal concepts are furthest from our perception, and particulars are nearest to it" (*Posterior Analytics* 72a2–6).

[13]The idols, certain attitudes and habits of mind antipathetic to the true inductive method, are explained in detail in Aphorisms I, 38–68.

subtlety of Nature is far greater than that of argument. But axioms properly and methodically derived from particulars can very well point to and indicate new particulars again, and so render the sciences active.

25

The axioms now in use have been derived from a meagre and narrow experience and from a few particulars of most common occurrence; and these axioms have been framed, for the most part, so as just to fit them, hence it is no wonder they do not lead to fresh particulars; and if they chance to come up against an instance not previously noticed or known, the axiom is rescued by some frivolous distinction, when the more correct course would be for the axiom itself to be corrected.

26

To help in my teaching, I generally call the reasoning which we apply to Nature *Anticipations of Nature,* because it is rash and premature; but that reasoning which is drawn from things by proper means, I call *Interpretation of Nature.*

27

Anticipations are strong enough to produce agreement; for even if men went mad in one and the same way, they could agree among themselves well enough.

28

Anticipations are certainly much better at producing agreement than interpretations, because, being gathered from a few particulars, and those mostly of familiar occurrence, they immediately touch the understanding and fill the imagination; whereas *interpretations,* being gathered here and there from a great variety of widely scattered things, cannot strike our mind so quickly; and of necessity, as far as general opinions go, they seem harsh and discordant, much as do the mysteries of faith.

29

In sciences that are based on supposition and opinion, there is a proper use for anticipations and dialectic, for in them the object is to command assent, not to master the thing itself.

30

There can never be any great progress in the sciences through anticipations, even if all the clever minds of all the ages were to meet and work together and transmit the combined fruits of their labours, because radical errors in the first digestion by the mind are not cured by the excellence of subsequent actions and remedies.

31

We can look in vain for advancement in scientific knowledge from the superinducing[14] and grafting of new things on old. A fresh start (*instauratio*) must be made, beginning from the very foundations, unless we want to go round for ever in a circle, making trifling, almost contemptible progress.

32

The honour of the ancient authors, in fact of all authors, remains undiminished, because the comparison that is being drawn does not concern their talents or abilities, but the path they were following; and I would not be a judge so much as a guide.

---

[14]*To superinduce* is "to bring in or induce something on top of something already present"; Bacon uses the term a good deal in Book II of this work, when treating the possibility of adding new 'natures' or properties to a given body.

33

It must be clearly said that no judgement on my method, or whatever may be found by it, can be reached by using *anticipations* (that is, the method of reasoning now employed). For it cannot be that my method should be judged by one that is itself on trial.

34

It is no easy matter even to teach and explain what I am proposing, for things new in themselves will still be understood by reference to things already known.

35

Borgia said of the expedition of the French into Italy that they came with chalk in their hands to mark out their billets, not with weapons to force their way in.[15] In the same way, I intend that my teaching should enter quietly into minds well suited and able to receive it. There is no use in challenging where we disagree on first principles and the notions themselves, and even on the forms of demonstrations.

36

In truth, there remains for me but one simple method of teaching, namely, to lead men to particulars, and their se-

[15]The Borgia referred to was Pope Alexander VI, and the expedition was undertaken by Charles VIII, who in September 1494 "was allowed to take Italy with scarcely an effort, and as it were with merely a piece of chalk", because, according to Machiavelli, the Italians depended on mercenaries, who he reckoned were by nature disloyal. (*The Prince,* ch. 12) The French army reached Naples early the following year, and remained there for nearly a month fraternizing with the largely welcoming populace; the events of this sojourn led, incidentally, to the first recorded outbreak of syphilis, which became known as the Neapolitan sickness in France, and the French sickness in Italy. See Claude Quétel, *History of Syphilis* (Polity Press: Cambridge, 1990).

quence and order; and they for their part must force themselves to give up for a time their notions and to begin to familiarize themselves with things.

37

My method and the reasoning of those who held the doctrine of Acatalepsy [that knowledge of anything is impossible] are somewhat similar in their initial stages, but in their outcome are very far apart, and indeed opposed. While they roundly assert that nothing can be known, I say that we cannot know much of Nature through the means which are now in use. While they proceed to destroy the authority of the sense and understanding, I devise and furnish ways of helping them.

38

The idols and false notions that have hitherto occupied the human understanding, and lie deep-seated there, have not only so beset men's minds that their approach to the truth becomes difficult; but even when access to it is given and conceded, they will present themselves and interfere in that very restoration (*instauratio*) of the sciences, unless men are forewarned and protect themselves against them as far as possible.

39

There are four kinds of idols besetting human minds. To help in my teaching, I have given them names. I call the first, *Idols of the Tribe;* the second, *Idols of the Cave;* the third, *Idols of the Market-place;* and the fourth, *Idols of the Theatre.*

40

The formation of notions and axioms by true *induction* is of course the proper remedy for warding off and clearing away these idols, but just to point them out is very useful. For the doctrine concerning idols is to the *Interpretation of Nature* as the doctrine of Sophistical Refutations[16] is to ordinary dialectic.

41

The *Idols of the Tribe* lie deep in human nature itself and in the very tribe or race of mankind. For it is wrongly asserted that the human sense is the measure of things.[17] It is rather the case that all our perceptions, both of our sense and of our minds, are reflections of man, not of the universe, and the human understanding is like an uneven mirror that cannot reflect truly the rays from objects, but distorts and corrupts the nature of things by mingling its own nature with it.

42

The *Idols of the Cave* are those specific to individual men.[18] For besides the errors common to human nature in general, each of us has his own private cave or den, which breaks up and falsifies the light of Nature; either because of his own distinct and individual nature, or because of what he has been taught

---

[16]This is a reference to Aristotle's work *De Sophisticis Elenchis* (*On Sophistical Refutations*), in which he expounds and attempts to solve various sophistical puzzles that arise from verbal ambiguities and equivocations. Sophistical refutations were "arguments which appear to be refutations but are really fallacious and not refutations" (164a20). And in this work, Aristotle characterised dialectical arguments as ones "which, starting from generally accepted opinions, reason to establish a contradiction" (165b3).

[17]This presumably alludes to Protagoras of Abdera (fifth century BC), the first and most notable of the Greek sophists, whose famous contention was "Man is the measure of all things, of things that are that they are, and of things that are not that they are not". This seems to have been intended as an expression of scepticism and relativism, though Bacon is evidently reading it in the opposite sense. We have noted before (footnote 1 to the Preface to the *Novum Organum*) that Bacon did not regard sophist teachings as sceptical.

[18]Bacon is alluding here to Plato's Myth of the Cave, from the seventh book of the *Republic,* which depicts mankind as trapped in a cave, mistaking the shadows passing across the walls of the cave for realities.

or gained in conversation with others, or from his reading, and the authority of those whom he respects and admires; or from the different impressions [he gains from things], according as they present themselves to a mind prejudiced and already committed, or to one impartial and moderate, or the like. So that the human spirit (according to how it is distributed in individual men) is variable and always in commotion, and as it were, subject to chance. Whence Heraclitus[19] has well said that men seek knowledge in lesser worlds, and not in the greater or common world.

43

There are also idols arising from the dealings and association of men with one another, which I call *Idols of the Market-place,* because of the commerce and meeting of men there. For speech is the means of association among men; but words are applied according to common understanding. And in consequence, a wrong and inappropriate application of words obstructs the mind to a remarkable extent. Nor do the definitions or explanations with which learned men have sometimes been accustomed to defend and vindicate themselves in any way remedy the situation. Indeed, words plainly do violence to the understanding and throw everything into confusion, and lead men into innumerable empty controversies and fictions.

44

Finally, there are idols which have crept into human minds from the various dogmas of philosophies, and also from faulty laws of demonstrations. These I call *Idols of the Theatre,*

---

[19]In the *Advancement of Learning,* I, (*Works,* III, p. 292) Bacon makes his meaning much clearer: "Heraclitus gave a just censure, saying, *Men sought truth in their own little worlds, and not in the great and common world;* for they disdain to spell and so by degrees to read in the volume of God's works; and contrariwise by continual meditation and agitation of wit do urge and as it were invoke their own spirits to divine and give oracles unto them, whereby they are deservedly deluded". (Heraclitus of Ephesus was a Greek philosopher who was born around 500 BC.)

because I regard all the philosophies that have been received or invented as so many stage plays creating fictitious and imaginary worlds. Nor am I only speaking of present philosophies, nor indeed only of the ancient philosophies and their sects, for numerous other plays of the same kind may yet be composed and contrived, since the most diverse errors spring sometimes from similar causes. Nor again do I mean this only in regard to universal philosophies, but also to many principles and axioms of the sciences, which have become established through tradition, credulity and neglect.

But I now must speak at greater length and more precisely about these separate kinds of idols, to warn the human understanding about them.

45

The human understanding on account of its own nature readily supposes a greater order and uniformity in things than it finds. And though there are many things in Nature which are unique and quite unlike anything else, it devises parallels and correspondences and relations which are not there. Hence the fiction that 'in the heavens all things move in perfect circles,' spirals and dragons[20] being completely rejected (except in name). Hence, too, the element of fire with its own orb is introduced to make up the square with the other three which fall under the sense.[21] Hence, too, the ratio of density of the so-called elements is arbitrarily fixed at ten to one; and other

---

[20]Dragons are presumably some kind of serpentine coil, in the sense also employed by Virgil (*Aeneid,* II, 199–249), when he describes in blood-curdling detail how the serpents (*dracones*) squeezed Laocoön and his sons to death. It is evident from what Bacon says in his *De Augmentis,* III, iv, that he regarded dragons and spirals as different kinds of curve, with the latter "winding and unwinding towards the tropics".

[21]In Aristotelian philosophy, all matter apart from celestial matter was supposed to be formed out of combinations of four elements, which were called earth, water, air and fire, and physical changes were understood in terms of those elements. Each had its 'natural place' in the sublunary world: earth's natural place was the centre of the terrestrial globe; that of water was in the outer shell of a sphere, or orb, whose centre was the earth; and the natural places of air and fire were the outer shells of successive concentric spheres centred on the earth.

dreams of that kind.[22] And that sort of vanity is rife not only in dogmas but also in simple notions.

46

The human understanding, once it has adopted opinions, either because they were already accepted and believed, or because it likes them, draws everything else to support and agree with them. And though it may meet a greater number and weight of contrary instances, it will, with great and harmful prejudice, ignore or condemn or exclude them by introducing some distinction, in order that the authority of those earlier assumptions may remain intact and unharmed. So it was a good answer made by that man who, on being shown a picture hanging in a temple of those who, having taken their vows, had escaped shipwreck, was asked whether he did not now recognize the power of the gods. He asked in turn: "But where are the pictures of those who perished after taking their vows?"[23] The same reasoning can be seen in every superstition, whether in astrology, dreams, omens, nemesis and the like,[24] in which men find such vanities pleasing, and

---

[22]The elements Bacon had in mind here were almost certainly the traditional ones of air, fire, water and earth, just referred to. Thus in his study of density he comments: "The conceit of the Peripatetics, that the variety of the elements compared one with the other is in a proportion of ten to one, is a thing fictitious and arbitrary. For it is certain that air is at least a hundred times rarer than water, and flame than oil; but that flame is not ten times rarer than air itself." (*History of Dense and Rare, Works,* V, p. 354)

[23]This story is told by the Roman statesman and writer Marcus Tullius Cicero (106–43 BC) in his *De Natura Deorum (On the Nature of the Gods),* III, xxxvii: "Diagoras, named the Atheist, once came to Samothrace, and a certain friend said to him, 'You think that the gods disregard men's affairs, do you not remark all the votive pictures that prove how many persons have escaped the violence of the storm, and come safe to port, by dint of vows to the gods?' That is so, replied Diagoras; 'it is because there are nowhere any pictures of those who have been shipwrecked and drowned at sea'".

[24]These were various forms of divination. Paracelsus characterised divination through dreams thus: "If anything is presented to a person by means of a dream, be it present, future, or past, be it knowledge, a treasure, or any other secret, it bears reference to this art" (*The Hermeti-*

take note of events where they are fulfilled, but where they are
not (even if this happens much more often), they disregard
them and pass them by. But this evil lurks far more insidiously
in philosophies and sciences, in which an opinion once adopted
infects and brings under control all the rest, though the latter
may be much firmer and better. Moreover, even without this
pleasure and vanity I have spoken of, the human understanding still has this peculiar and perpetual fault of being more
moved and excited by affirmatives than by negatives, whereas
rightly and properly it ought to give equal weight to both;
rather, in fact, in every truly constituted axiom, a negative
instance has the greater weight.

<h3 align="center">47</h3>

The human understanding is most moved by things that
strike and enter the mind together and suddenly, and so fill
and inflate the imagination; and it then imagines and supposes, without knowing how, that everything else behaves in
the same way as those few things with which it has become
engaged. The understanding is slow and awkward at ranging
over the whole field of remote and heterogeneous instances, by
which axioms are tested as if in the fire, unless it is constrained to such action by strict rules and a powerful authority.

<h3 align="center">48</h3>

The human understanding is restless; it cannot stop or
rest, but presses on, though in vain. Thus it is unthinkable
that there should be any end or limit to the world, but always,
as if of necessity, the thought arises that there is something
beyond. Nor can the understanding conceive how an eternity
has passed before the present day, since that distinction which
is commonly accepted between 'an infinite time in the past and
in the future' simply cannot stand; because from that it would

---

cal and Alchemical Writings of Paracelsus, II, p. 296). Nemesis, presumably, is the art of reading divine retribution into human misfortunes.

follow that one infinity is greater than another, and that eternity is running out and coming near to being finite. A similar subtlety, arising from an immoderation of thought, concerns the perpetual divisibility of lines.[25] But this immoderation of our mind is much more harmful in the discovery of causes. For while the most general things in Nature must be positive [i.e., not dependent on other things], just as we find them, and cannot themselves be caused, nevertheless the human understanding, unable to rest, still seeks greater generality (*notiora*).[26] Thus it is that in reaching out for things further away, it falls back upon nearer ones, namely final causes,[27] which have relation entirely to human nature rather than to the universe, and have thus corrupted philosophy to an extraordinary degree. It is no less the mark of an unskilful and superficial philosopher to require a cause in the most general things, than not to do so in things that are dependent and particular.

49

The human understanding is not a dry light,[28] but is infused by desire and emotion, which give rise to 'wishful science'. For man prefers to believe what he wants to be true. He therefore rejects difficulties, being impatient of inquiry; sober things, because they restrict his hope; deeper parts of

---

[25]Bacon is here referring to one of the paradoxes of Zeno of Elia (a Greek philosopher of the fifth century BC), that if a line were infinitely divisible, the infinite parts must either each be of finite length, in which case the line itself is infinitely long, or else each has no length, in which case, so has the line.

[26]For the meaning of *notiora*, 'better known', in this context, see the note, *above,* to Aphorism I, 22.

[27]The final cause of a thing or change is the purpose for which it was made or occurred. The different Aristotelian "causes" are described below in a note to Aphorism II, 2.

[28]A dry light is an unprejudiced light, untinged by personal predilection. In his *Apophthegms* (268), Bacon writes: "Heraclitus the obscure said: *The dry light was the best soul.* Meaning, when the Faculties Intellectual are in vigour, not wet, nor, as it were, blooded by the Affections". (The fragments of Heraclitus's writings preserved in the form of quotations by later authors are often very cryptic, so earning him the title *Obscure*.)

Nature, because of his superstition; the light of experience, because of his arrogance and pride, lest his mind should seem to concern itself with things mean and transitory; things that are strange and contrary to all expectation, because of common opinion. In short, emotion in numerous, often imperceptible ways pervades and infects the understanding.

50

But by far the greatest impediment and aberration of the human understanding arises from the dulness and inadequacy and deceptions of the senses, in that those things which strike the sense outweigh things which, although they may be more important, do not strike it directly. Hence, contemplation usually ceases with seeing, so much so that little or no attention is paid to things invisible. Therefore every action of the spirits enclosed in material bodies lies hidden and escapes us. In the same way also, we fail to see the more subtle change of schematism[29] in the parts of denser substances (which is generally called alteration, though it is in fact movement in the smallest particles). Yet unless those two things I have mentioned are searched for and brought to light, nothing much can be achieved in Nature, at least as far as works are concerned. Again, the nature of common air and of all the many bodies thinner than air is almost unknown. For the sense in itself is a weak thing and prone to aberration, nor are instruments for magnifying or sharpening the senses of much use. But all truer interpretation of Nature is built up from instances, and adequate and suitable experiments, where the sense judges only of the experiment, the experiment of Nature and the thing itself.

51

The human understanding is of its own nature given to abstractions, and assumes to be constant those things that are

---

[29]*Schematism* means "structure" or "constitution". A note on Bacon's use of the term is appended to Aphorism II, 1.

in flux. But rather than turn Nature into abstractions, it is better to dissect her, as did the school of Democritus, which delved further into Nature than others. Matter rather should be our study and its schematisms and changes of schematism, and pure action and the law of action or motion; for forms are fictions of the human mind, unless we choose to call those laws of action forms.

52

Thus idols of this kind I call *Idols of the Tribe;* they arise either from the uniformity of substance of the human spirit, or from its attachment to preconceived ideas, or from its narrowness, or its restlessness, or from an infusion of emotions, or from the inadequacy of the senses, or from the mode of impression.[30]

53

The *Idols of the Cave* arise from the individual's particular nature, both of mind and body, and come also from education, habits and by chance. Though there are many different kinds, I shall cite those which call for the greatest caution, and which do most to pollute clear understanding.

54

Men become attached to particular sciences and contemplations either because they think themselves their authors and inventors, or because they have done much work on them and become most habituated to them. But men of this kind who apply themselves to philosophy and to contemplations of

---

[30]The first six causes of Idols of the Tribe enumerated in this aphorism recapitulate Aphorisms I, 45 to 50, respectively. This suggests, rather implausibly, that the last-mentioned cause—the mode of impression (*impressionis modo*)—relates to Aphorism 51; on the other hand, it appears to refer to a remark in Aphorism 42 on the different ways that things impress themselves on the mind.

things in general, distort and corrupt them as a result of their preconceived fancies. The most striking example of this is seen in Aristotle, who utterly enslaved his natural philosophy to his logic, rendering it more or less useless and contentious. And the race of alchemists have built up from a few experiments with a furnace a fantastic philosophy having regard to few things. Gilbert, likewise, after the most painstaking studies of the loadstone, immediately erected a philosophy that suited his own favourite subject.[31]

55

There is a very great, one might say radical, distinction between human minds as they are applied to philosophy and the sciences: some minds are more suited to and capable of marking the differences between things, others their similarities. Minds that are steady and acute can study and dwell upon every subtlety of differences, while those that are more lofty and discursive both recognize and bring together the slightest and most general similarities. Either sort of mind easily falls into excess, grasping either at minute differences of things or at shadows.

56

We find that some minds are given to an extreme admiration of antiquity, others to a fondness for and attachment to things new; not many have the temperament to hold the mean,

---

[31]Bacon's oblique criticism of his contemporary, William Gilbert (1540 or 1544–1603), appears to be directed not at his brilliant investigations of magnetism, which Bacon clearly admired, but at the hypothesis of the diurnal motion of the earth, which Gilbert defended with uncharacteristic dogmatism and poor argumentation in the last chapter of his book *On the Magnet*. See Peter Urbach, *Francis Bacon's Philosophy of Science* (La Salle, IL: Open Court Publishing Company, 1987), pp. 109–21.

Loadstone is the naturally-occurring magnetic mineral iron oxide, or magnetite, which William Gilbert employed in his investigations.

neither tearing down the sound ideas of the ancients nor spurning what has been rightly added by the moderns. This however is much to the detriment of the sciences and philosophy, since these preferences are rivalries between antiquity and modernity, rather than balanced judgements; whereas truth should be sought, not in the felicity of any particular age, which is a variable thing, but in the light of Nature and experience, which is eternal. Such rivalries should, therefore, be abjured, and care taken that the understanding is not hurried away by them into assent.

57

Contemplations of Nature and of bodies in their simplicity break up the understanding and fragment it, while contemplations of Nature and of bodies in their composition and configuration confuse and dissolve it. This is best seen in the school of Leucippus and Democritus,[32] compared with other philosophies. For it is so taken up with the minute parts of things that it almost overlooks the structure, whereas the others so marvel at the sight of the structure of things that they fail to penetrate to the simplicity of Nature. We ought therefore to consider and adopt each kind of contemplation in turn, so that the understanding can become at once penetrating and comprehensive, and the aforesaid inconveniences avoided, along with the idols that come from them.

58

This then should be our thought and care in warding off and removing the *Idols of the Cave,* which arise chiefly from preconceived ideas, or from the over-emphasis either of composition and division, or from a partiality for particular ages, or

---

[32]Leucippus and Democritus were fifth century BC Greek philosophers credited with having originated the atomic theory.

from the magnitude or minuteness of the objects.[33] In general, therefore, anyone studying Nature should be suspicious of whatever allures and captivates his understanding, and should be all the more cautious over theories of this kind, so that the understanding can be kept impartial and pure.

59

The *Idols of the Market-place* are the most troublesome of all; these are idols that have crept into the understanding through the alliance of words and names. For while men believe their reason governs words, in fact, words turn back and reflect their power upon the understanding, and so render philosophy and science sophistical and inactive. For words are usually applied according to common comprehension, and divide things along lines most suited to common understanding. When then someone of sharper understanding or more diligence in observation wishes to shift those lines, so as to move them closer to Nature, words shout him down. Hence it is that great and solemn debates between learned men often end in arguments over words and names, when it would be more prudent, as the careful mathematicians do, to begin with them and, through definitions, bring the debates to order. Yet even definitions cannot cure this evil, so far as they concern natural and material things. For definitions themselves consist of words, and words beget words, so that we have to go back to particular instances and to their due order, as I shall say in a moment when I come to the method and plan for the construction of notions and axioms.

60

The idols that are imposed by words on the understanding are of two kinds. Either they are names of things that do not exist (for just as there are things without names because they have never been seen, so also there are names without [corre-

---

[33]This sentence summarises the contents of Aphorisms I, 54 to 57, *above,* respectively.

sponding] things, as a result of fanciful suppositions); or they are names of objects which do exist but are muddled and vague, and hastily and unjustly derived from things. Words of the first kind are 'fortune', 'prime mover', 'planetary orbs', 'the element of fire', and other fictions of this kind, the product of groundless and false theories. And this class of idols is easier to get rid of, because they can be destroyed by steadfast denial and rejection of the theories.

But the other kind is obscure and deep-seated, and is derived from an incorrect and unskilled abstraction. For example, let us take any word, *moist,* say, and see how far the things which are signified by this word agree with each other; we shall find this word *moist* is nothing but a confused mark of different actions, which do not allow reduction to any consistent meaning. For it signifies not only something that readily surrounds another body, but also something with no definite boundaries and unable to become solid; something which yields easily in every direction; something which easily subdivides and scatters itself; or easily coalesces and becomes one; easily flows and is set in motion; easily adheres to another body and makes it wet; and which easily liquefies, or melts, when it was previously solid. So when we predicate the word in one sense, a flame is moist, in another, air is not moist, in another, fine dust is moist, in another, glass is moist.[34] Thus it is easy to see that this notion [of moistness] is carelessly abstracted only from water and common and ordinary liquids, without any proper verification.

In words there are, however, certain degrees of wrongness and error. A less faulty class is that of the names of substances, especially of well-derived species of the lowest [type] (for the notion of chalk or mud is good, that of earth is bad). A more defective kind is that of actions like *to generate, to corrupt, to alter;* the most defective of all is that of qualities (other than those that are the immediate objects of the sense), such as *heavy, light, rare, dense,* etc.[35] And yet among all of these there

---

[34]These different senses of the term 'moist', and much of the discussion, derive from Aristotle's *On Coming-To-Be and Passing-Away,* II, 2.

[35]The three classes of qualities mentioned here coincide with three Aristotelian categories (see footnote to Aphorism I, 15, *above*).

are inevitably some notions that are slightly better than others, depending on how many things strike the human sense.

61

The *Idols of the Theatre,* on the other hand, are not innate, nor are they secretly insinuated into the understanding, but are imposed and received entirely from the fictitious tales in theories, and from wrong-headed laws of demonstration. To attempt to refute them would be quite inconsistent with all I have said. For since I disagree with both their principles and their demonstrations, there is no place for argument. And this is fortunate, in that it leaves the good name of the ancients unimpaired. For they are not disparaged, since the question concerns only the path. For, as the saying goes, a lame man on the right road will beat a runner on the wrong one. In fact, as is clear, the more active and faster a man is, the further astray will he go when he is running on the wrong road.

However, my method of scientific discovery leaves only a small role to sharpness and power of wits, but puts all wits and understandings more or less on a level. For just as drawing a straight line or a perfect circle simply by hand calls for a very steady and practised hand, but little or no skill if a ruler or pair of compasses is used, so it is with my method.

Now although there is no point in contesting particular opinions, there is something I must say about the sects and the general divisions of these kinds of theories [Aphorisms I, 63–65]; something also, a little later, about the outer signs indicating that they are faulty [Aphorisms I, 70–77]; and lastly about the causes of such an unsatisfactory state of affairs and such enduring and general agreement in error [Aphorisms I, 78–92], so that the approach to the truth may be less difficult and the human understanding may more willingly be purged and rid of its idols.

62

The *Idols of the Theatre,* or of Theories, are many, and many more are possible and will perhaps arise. For if the minds of men through the ages had not been occupied with religion and philosophy; and if civil governments also, especially monarchies, had not been hostile to such novelties, even if they were just speculations; so that men who engaged in them did so at the risk of their lives and fortune, being not only unrewarded, but even exposed to contempt and envy; [had it not been, I say, for these things] many more sects and schools of philosophy would no doubt have sprung up, similar to those which once flourished in great variety among the Greeks. For just as there can be many hypotheses framed on the phenomena of the heavens, in the same way and indeed to a much greater extent, various doctrines can be based and built upon the phenomena of philosophy.[36] And fictitious tales of this kind also have this in common with those of poetic drama, that narratives written for the stage are neater and more elegant and more as one would wish them to be than true accounts drawn from history.

In general, however, philosophy takes for its material either a great deal from a few things, or only a little from many, so that either way, philosophy is founded on too narrow a basis of experience and natural history and pronounces on the authority of too few cases. For the Rational school of philosophers seizes from experience a variety of common [instances] without properly checking them, or thoroughly examining and weighing them, and leaves the rest to cogitation and agitation of wit.

There is another class of philosophers who, after toiling with great care and precision over a few experiments, have presumed to devise and produce philosophies from them, twisting everything else in extraordinary ways to fit in with them.

---

[36]The main theories of the heavens which Bacon considered were based on the idea that the heavenly bodies revolved around the earth (the Ptolemaic system) or around the sun (the Copernican system). According to these systems, either a planet itself moved in a circle round the principal centre, or it revolved in an epicycle about a subsidiary centre, which in turn circled the principal centre. Higher order epicycles were also admitted. Bacon is alluding to the fact that such systems, whether geocentric or heliocentric, could, in the traditional phrase, 'save the phenomena' equally well.

There is also a third kind who out of faith and piety mix
theology and tradition with their philosophy; among these, the
vanity of some has led them astray to look for and derive
science from spirits and supernatural beings. Thus the root
cause of error and *false philosophy* is threefold, *Sophistical,*[37]
Empirical and *Superstitious.*

63

The most striking example of the first kind is in Aristotle,
who corrupted natural philosophy with his dialectic, when he
constructed the world out of categories, and classified the
human soul, the noblest substance of all, as a thing of second
intention.[38] He dealt with the business of density and rarity,
by which bodies occupy greater or smaller dimensions or
spaces, by the trivial distinction of Actuality and Potentiality,[39] and asserted that particular bodies each have their own
individual and natural motion, and if they partake of any other

[37]The Sophistical idols are the same as those Bacon called "Rational"
in the preceding paragraph, and which he calls "Sophistical or rational" in
Aphorism I, 64, *below.*

[38]Aristotle's categories are, roughly speaking, classifications of predi-
cates. The main categories were those of substance, quantity, relation and
quality; there were also the categories of action, and passion, which Bacon
refers to in Aphorism I, 15, *above.* The category of substance referred to
existent things—Aristotle and Socrates are in this class, as are earth, fire
and water (*Metaphysics,* V, 8). Aristotle called the class of substances
'primary'; they were the primary conceptions of things, or first intentions,
formed by the first application of the mind to the things themselves.
Second intentions were secondary concepts, formed by the application of
thought to first intentions in their relations to each other, for instance,
the concepts of identity and difference. The distinction between terms of
first and second intention derives from the fourteenth century logic of
William of Ockham.
Aristotle regarded the soul as a modification of the substance of a
body, just as a body's shape or colour are modifications of the matter
composing the body. Thus the soul is not a substance since it is not
separable or independent of other things (*On the Soul* II, 1).

[39]Actuality and potentiality were important notions for Aristotle, who
held that a body's potential to act or be acted upon has a real existence in
the body. He employed the notions in explanatory contexts. Thus, in his
Physics (IV, 9), Aristotle denies that a body's density reflects the amount

motion, that this must come from elsewhere, and he arbitrarily imposed numerous other things on Nature. He was much more anxious about how anyone delivering an opinion should explain himself, and that any point should be made positive in words, than about the inner truth of things. This is best shown in a comparison of his philosophy with others well known among the Greeks. For the Homoiomera of Anaxagoras, the atoms of Leucippus and Democritus, the heaven and earth of Parmenides, the strife and friendship of Empedocles, the resolution of bodies into the undifferentiated nature of fire and their re-fashioning into solids, as held by Heraclitus, all have in them something of the natural philosopher and a taste of things of Nature and experience and natural bodies.[40] Whereas in Aristotle's *Physics,* you hear little but the words of dialectic; and in his *Metaphysics* too, under a more imposing name, and

---

of void it contains, and denies too that the movement of bodies in the universe requires a void. He held that just as the matter of a body is unchanged when it is heated or cooled, so too when it is expanded or contracted. "This is manifestly the case", Aristotle claimed, "for when water is transformed into air [vapour], the same matter, without taking on anything additional, is transformed from what it was, by passing into the actuality of that which before was only a potentiality to it" (*Physics,* 217a27–30). Aristotle explained change with the notoriously obscure formula: "Change is actuality of the potential *qua* such" (*Physics,* 20a11–12).

[40]Anaxagoras, a Greek philosopher born ca. 500 BC, believed matter to be composed of minute particles, but he thought different bodies consisted of different kinds of identical primary particles (or 'Homoiomera'), gold, for example, being composed of similar gold particles, bone of identical bony particles.

Parmenides of Elea, born around 519 BC, held that the principles of things are heat and cold, the prevalence of cold in the lower regions producing terrestrial matter, and of heat in the superior producing the heavens.

Empedocles, a philosopher, physician and statesman, who flourished in Sicily around 450 BC, held the two primal forces in the universe to be love and strife, which tend to keep like bodies together and unlike ones apart and by these means to form the multiplicity of things. Bacon appealed to forces of 'friendship' and 'strife' in his own natural philosophy (Aphorisms II, 48[8] and 50 [6]).

Heraclitus of Ephesus (born ca. 500 BC) held everything to be in a state of flux, and change to be the only actuality. The underlying principle of change was 'fire', a warm, dry, soul-like vapour, out of which all things are condensed and into which all things are again resolved.

more evidently as a realist than a nominalist, he has gone over the same ground again. Nor should it count for much that in his books *On Animals,* and in his *Problems* and other treatises, he often cites experiments. For he had come to his decision beforehand, without taking proper account of experience in setting up his decisions and axioms; but after laying down the law according to his own judgement, he then brings in experience, twisted to fit in with his own ideas, and leads it about like a captive. So in this respect also he is more culpable than his modern followers, the schoolmen philosophers, who have abandoned experience altogether.[41]

64

But the *Empirical* school of philosophy yields more deformed and monstrous ideas than the *Sophistical* or rational, because it is based, not on the light of common notions (which although faint and showing the surface only is yet to some degree universal and applicable to many things) but on the narrow and obscure foundation of only a few experiments. So that to those who are daily involved in such experiments and have infected their imagination with them, a philosophy of this kind seems probable, and almost certain; but to everyone else, unbelievable and groundless. A notable example of this is [to be found] in the alchemists and their teachings. It is not found much elsewhere these days, except perhaps in the philosophy of Gilbert. Even so, we must still be cautious in considering these philosophies, because I foresee that if men, alerted by my warnings, bid farewell to sophistical doctrines and devote themselves seriously to experience, then because of the premature and excessive hurry of their understanding and their leap or flight to generalities and the principles of things, philosophies of this kind will threaten great danger, against which evil we must even now proceed.

---

[41]The schoolmen, or scholastics, were philosophers who combined Christian theology with a science of nature that was much influenced by the ideas of Aristotle and other ancient thinkers. They flourished from the eleventh to the fifteenth century, and included Anselm, Albertus Magnus, Thomas Aquinas and William of Ockham.

65

But the corruption of philosophy by a combination of superstition and theology is much more widespread, and does the greatest harm both to whole philosophies and to their parts. For the human understanding is subject to impressions of the imagination just as much as to those of common notions. And while the contentious and sophistical kind of philosophy ensnares the understanding, that other, fanciful and inflated and almost poetic, misleads it more completely by flattery. For there is in man, especially in lofty and high-minded spirits, an ambition of the understanding no less than of the will.

There is a very clear example of this kind among the Greeks, chiefly in Pythagoras, though here mixed with more outright and oppressive superstition; and also a more dangerous and subtle one in Plato and his school. This fault is found also in parts of other philosophies, where they introduce abstract forms and final causes and first causes,[42] very often omitting intermediate causes, and the like. We must be exceedingly cautious on this point. For the very worst thing is the apotheosis of errors, and the veneration of empty ideas is a veritable plague of the understanding. Yet some of the moderns have, with the greatest frivolity, indulged so far in this foolishness, as to try to found a natural philosophy on the first chapter of Genesis and the book of Job and other sacred writings—"seeking the dead among the living".[43] It is all the more important to guard against and check this foolishness, for an unhealthy mixture of the divine and the human leads not only to fanciful philosophy but also to heretical religion.

---

[42]The abstract forms referred to here are the ideal types, or forms of a thing or quality, which Plato postulated. In his philosophy, there is, for instance, the form of beauty, in which all beautiful things 'participate' to a greater or lesser degree. The final cause is the 'purpose' or 'goal' of any change; these played a prominent role in Aristotelian natural philosophy (see footnote 115).

[43]Bacon is here ironically twisting the words of Luke xxiv, 5: "Why seek ye the living among the dead?" The allusion is to "the school of Paracelsus, and some others" (*Advancement of Learning,* book II, *Works,* III, p. 486), and also perhaps to Dr Robert Fludd (1574–1637), whose quasi-scientific writings drew very largely on the Bible, including the Book of Job.

The healthy course therefore is to keep a sober mind and give to faith only that which is faith's.[44]

66

So much then for the pernicious sway of philosophies based on common notions [Aphorism 63], or on few experiments [Aphorism 64], or on superstition [Aphorism 65]. I want now to discuss the defective subject matter of studies, especially those in natural philosophy.

Now the human understanding is infected by what it sees in the mechanical arts, where objects are most often altered by compounding or separating them, so that it believes that something similar happens in the universal nature of things. From this came the fiction of the elements and of their coming together to form natural bodies. Again, when man looks at Nature in its free state, he comes upon species of things, of animals, of vegetables and of minerals, and so slips easily into the thought that there are in Nature certain primary forms of things which Nature is striving to bring forth, and that the remaining variety results from the hindrances and aberrations met by Nature in her work, or from the conflict between different species and the transplanting of one into another. The first thought has given us primary elementary qualities, the second, occult properties and specific virtues, both of them belonging to those empty collections of ideas in which the mind finds rest and is turned away from things of more substance.[45]

---

[44]This famous advice of Bacon's is no doubt modelled on the biblical injunction: "Render therefore unto Caesar the things which are Caesar's; and unto God the things that are God's" (Matthew xxii, 21).

[45]The elements alluded to are air, water, fire and earth; the primary qualities, moist, dry, hot and cold; in Aristotle's philosophy, they were supposed to be combined in pairs in the elements, fire being hot and dry, air hot and moist, water cold and moist, and earth cold and dry (Aristotle, *On Coming-To-Be and Passing-Away,* II, 3).

Specific virtues were powers of certain potions that were alleged to act on particular parts of the body. Paracelsus in his *Archidoxies (Hermetical and Alchemical Writings of Paracelsus,* II) lists several specifics. Thus the "Attractive Specific", he says, "draws to itself everything that is superfluous in the body, and leads out whatever evil may adhere to it." He then reports some fantastic cases of such specifics, for example, one that "has

Physicians, on the other hand, work to better purpose on the secondary qualities of things and the processes of attraction and repulsion, of attenuation and inspissation, of dilation and astriction, of discussion, maturation, and the like.[46] But they would have made better progress still if they had not spoilt these other effects, which they correctly observed, with those two collections just mentioned, namely of elementary qualities and specific virtues, reducing them to primary qualities and their subtle and incommensurable mixtures, or failing to extend them by greater and more thorough study to tertiary and quaternary qualities, breaking off their studies too soon.[47] And virtues of this kind (I do not say they themselves, but similar ones) are to be looked for not only in the medicines of the human body, but also in changes in other natural bodies.

Yet it is a much greater evil that they give so much attention and inquiry to static principles—*from which*[48]—rather than to moving principles—*how* things happen. For the former lead to talk, the latter to works. And those specific differences of motion, which are observed in the received

---

drawn a man's lungs into his mouth and so suffocated him", and another which drew the pupil of the eye from its position right down to the nose, from which it could not be removed! Other specifics mentioned by Paracelsus include the Purgative, the Styptic and the Corrosive.

[46]These are all now-obsolete medical terms familiar in Bacon's day: *Attraction* was the action of drawing out humours, for example by a poultice; *repulsion* was the action of forcing back humours or eruptions; *attenuation* was the thinning of humours or solid masses in the body, and *inspissation* the opposite of this; *astriction* was the binding together of soft bodily tissues and could also signify constipation; *discussion* was the dispersal of morbid matter or humours; *maturation* was the development or 'ripening' of morbid bodily conditions, such as the formation of pustules.

[47]Porta, in his *Natural Magic,* book 2, ch. 4, describes "certain secondary qualities, which attend as it were upon the first; and these are said to work in a second sort; as to soften, to ripen, to resolve, to make less or thinner", which are secondary qualities of heat. Moisture "brings forth milk, urine, monthly flowers [menstrual blood], and sweat; which the physicians call third qualities". Sometimes these qualities "have their operations in some certain parts, as to strengthen the head, to succour the reins [loins or kidneys]; and these, some call fourth qualities".

[48]Principles "from which" (*principia, "ex quibus"*) presumably refers to the material causes of things, as Fowler has suggested, while *principia moventia, "per quae"* signify the efficient.

natural philosophy, *generation, destruction, increase, diminution, alteration* and *local motion,* are not much use either.[49] What they mean no doubt is this: local motion is when a body, otherwise unchanged, moves from its place; if it remains in one place and of one kind but changes in quality, that is alteration; if, as a result of that change, the bulk and size of the body does not remain the same, that is the motion of increase or diminution; if they change to such an extent that they alter their whole essence and substance and become something else, that is generation and destruction. But all these things are merely popular, and do not go deeply into Nature at all; they are only measures and limits, not actual kinds of motion; they indicate *how far,* not *how* or *from what source.* They tell us nothing about the appetites [i.e., the natural tendencies] of things, or the process going on in their parts. Only when this motion shows a thing to the sense in a palpable way as different from what it was before do they begin to examine its division. Even when they wish to say something about the causes of motions and to establish a division out of them,[50] they foolishly introduce a distinction between natural and violent motion;[51] one which comes entirely from a common notion,

---

[49]For Aristotle the term *motion* had a wider connotation than it does for us, signifying change in general. He acknowledged four kinds of motion, relating respectively to substance, quantity, quality and place. The first takes the form of coming into being and passing out of existence and is sometimes referred to as generation and destruction (or corruption)—for example, a lump of clay becoming a statue of Apollo, or ink and paper becoming a copy of *Novum Organum.* Motion with respect to quantity was also known as *increase* and *decrease,* or *growth* and *diminution;* with respect to quality it was called *alteration,* e.g., a change from black to white or soft to hard; and motion with respect to place was *local motion* (or *locomotion*).

The rationale for regarding all these changes as forms of motion may be explained in the following remark of Aristotle's: "Instead of saying what was air is now water, we can say where air formerly was, there is now water".

[50]"To establish a division out of them": that is, to partition motions into distinct types, as Bacon himself does in Aphorism II, 48.

[51]Bacon is referring to the medieval theory according to which the continuation of a projectile's motion was caused, not, as Aristotle said, by the continued pushing of the air, but by a force remaining within the projectile which was regarded as 'violent' and so subject to attenuation by friction and the natural tendencies of the body.

since every violent motion is, in fact, also natural; the external efficient cause[52] merely making Nature behave in a different way from before.

Leaving these matters aside, if one notices, for example, that there is in bodies an appetite for mutual contact, so that they will not allow the unity of Nature to be torn apart and thus yield a vacuum; or if one should say that there is in bodies a tendency to regain their natural dimensions or tension, so that if compressed within or extended beyond them, they at once strive to recover and resume their old volume and extent; or again, if one should say that bodies have a natural tendency to congregate into masses of bodies all similar to themselves— of dense bodies, say, towards the globe of the earth, of thin and rare ones towards the circumference of the sky—then these and their kind are truly physical types of motion. The other sort are plainly logical and scholastic, as this comparison of the two kinds makes clear.[53]

And it is no less an evil that, in their philosophies and studies, their work is devoted to the investigation and consideration of the first principles of things and the ultimate parts of Nature, whereas everything of practical utility depends on things intermediate. Hence it is that men never stop abstracting Nature until it becomes potential matter, without form;[54] and, on the other hand, never cease from dissecting Nature until they arrive at the atom, things which, even if true, can be of little help to the welfare of mankind.[55]

67

The understanding must also be on its guard against the intemperance shown by philosophies in giving or withholding assent, because intemperance of this kind appears to fix, and in some way perpetuate, idols, so that it becomes impossible to reach and remove them.

---

[52]The efficient cause of a thing is a cause in the modern sense; it is the antecedent physical change which brought the thing about.

[53]In this paragraph, Bacon is summarizing the detailed categorization of motions he gives in Aphorism II, 48.

[54]"Matter without form": that is, inert matter, lacking specific qualities.

[55]Bacon enlarges somewhat on this claim in Aphorism I, 104, *below*.

This excess is twofold: one kind is shown by those who are always ready to hold forth, and render the sciences arbitrary and magisterial; the other by those who have introduced the doctrine of Acatalepsy, and a search without aim or end. The first subdues the understanding, the other unnerves it. Thus Aristotle's philosophy, having by pugnacious confutations slain all others (as the Ottomans do their brothers),[56] has laid down the law on every point; and proceeds to raise questions he has himself determined, and then demolishes them, so that everything is left certain and decided; a practice which is still prevalent among his successors.

The School of Plato, on the other hand, introduced the doctrine of Acatalepsy, at first in jest and irony, and in dislike of the ancient sophists, Protagoras, Hippias and the rest, who feared nothing so much as to seem to be in doubt about anything.[57] But the New Academy[58] taught Acatalepsy as a

---

[56]Until the early seventeenth century, succession to the Turkish throne was not regulated by primogeniture, but by survival of the strongest of the deceased sultan's male offspring; the successful son needed then to secure his position by removing all other claimants. One of the most spectacular instances of such fratricide occurred in 1595, when Mahommed III, on his accession, put to death 19 of his brothers and 10 or 12 women who were said to be carrying his father's children. The need for such extreme measures was explained by Ogier Ghiselin de Busbecq, Spanish ambassador to Turkey from 1552–1562, in his *Letters:*

> *The position of the sons of the Turkish Sultans is a most unhappy one; for as soon as one of them succeeds his father, the rest are inevitably doomed to die. The Turks tolerate no rival to the throne; indeed, the attitude of the soldiers of the bodyguard makes it impossible for them to do so. For if a brother of the reigning monarch chances to remain alive, they never stop demanding largesses; and if their requests are refused, cries of 'Long live the brother!', 'God save the brother!' are heard, whereby they make it pretty clear they intend to put him on the throne. Sultans of Turkey are thus compelled to stain their hands with their brothers' blood and so inaugurate their reign by murder (The Turkish Letters of Ogier Ghiselin de Busbecq, Oxford: Clarendon Press, 1927, translated by E. S. Forster, p. 30).*

[57]Cicero accuses the Epicureans in these words (*On the Nature of the Gods,* I, viii, 18).

[58]The original Academy was the philosophical school founded by Plato around 387 BC in a locality in the northwest outskirts of Athens called Akademeia. Three periods in the history of the Academy are often distin-

dogma, a declared tenet of belief. And although this is a more honest procedure than recklessly laying down the law, since they say they would not do away with inquiry altogether, like Pyrrho and the Ephectics,[59] but would have some things to be followed as being probable, but nothing maintained as true; yet once the human mind has lost hope of finding the truth, its interest in everything becomes fainter, and this is the reason why men turn aside to pleasant disputations and discussions, roaming around things as it were, rather than steadily pursuing rigorous inquiry. But I have said from the start, and I stress it again and again, that the human senses and understanding, for all their weakness, must not have their authority disparaged, but should rather be supported.

68

So much then for the several kinds of idols and their trappings, which must be steadily and sternly disowned and renounced, and the understanding entirely rid and purged of them, so that the entry into the kingdom of man, which is founded on the sciences, may be like the entry into the kingdom of heaven, 'which is only to be entered as a little child.'[60]

69

Faulty demonstrations are, as it were, the forts and defence-works of idols, and the ones we see in dialectic have the effect of giving over and enslaving the world entirely to human thought, and thought to words. Demonstrations are in effect philosophies and sciences themselves. For whatever they

---

guished: the Old, the Middle and the New. The Old is that of Plato and his earlier successors; the Middle Academy was created around 270 BC by Arcesilaus of Pitane, who adopted a thorough-going scepticism; and the New Academy began with Carneades of Cyrene ca. 219–179 BC and continued with the sceptical tradition.

[59]Ephectics were those ancient sceptics who claimed one should suspend judgement in all things.

[60]Luke xviii, 17.

are like, and according as they are soundly based or not, so too will be the philosophies and views that follow from them. But the demonstrations which we use in the whole process leading from objects and the sense to axioms and conclusions are deceptive and inadequate. That process is fourfold and its faults likewise. In the first place, the impressions of the sense itself are faulty, for the sense both deserts and deceives.[61] Its desertions require substitutes, its deceptions rectifications. Secondly, notions are badly abstracted from sense impressions and are vague and confused, whereas they ought to be definite and clear cut. Thirdly, it is a bad induction to infer principles of science through simple enumeration,[62] not making use, as it should, of exclusions and resolutions, or separations of Nature.[63] Finally, that method of discovery and proof, whereby the most general principles are first laid down, and then intermediate axioms applied and proved by reference to them, is the mother of errors, and a disaster for all science. I will speak at greater length about those things which I have now merely touched upon, when, having completed these expiations and purgings of the mind, I shall propose a true method of interpreting Nature.

70

But the best demonstration by far is experience, so long as it holds fast to the experiment itself. For if it is transferred to other cases which are thought to be similar, unless this transfer is made by a correct and regular procedure, the result is false. But the method of learning from experience in current use is blind and silly, so that while men roam and wander

---

[61]Bacon enlarges on these failings and explains the means by which he proposes to rectify them in Aphorisms II, 40 and 42.

[62]Simple enumeration, we may assume, is the same as "ordinary induction" or generalization from observed instances described above in the footnote to Aphorism I, 17.

[63]The important role Bacon reserved for exclusions, that is, rejections or refutations, is described in Aphorism II, 16, and succeeding aphorisms. Separations or resolutions of Nature are cases of phenomena which do not always appear together, such as "Instances of Divorce" (Aphorism II, 37) and "Instances of Hostility" (Aphorism II, 33).

along without any definite course, merely taking counsel of such things as happen to come before them, they range widely, yet move little further forward; sometimes enthusiastic, sometimes distracted, and always finding there is something further to be sought. Indeed it generally happens that men conduct experiments frivolously and as if they were playing a game, altering slightly those already known, and if the thing does not succeed, they grow scornful and abandon the attempt. And even if they devote themselves more seriously and pertinaciously and painstakingly to experiments, they nevertheless apply their efforts to working out some single experiment, as Gilbert with the loadstone, and the alchemists with gold. This course that men take is as foolish as it is unprofitable, for no one investigates the nature of a thing successfully by scrutinizing only the thing itself; the inquiry must be widened so as to become more general.

And even when they manage to build some science and dogmas from their experiments, in their premature and hasty eagerness, they almost always turn aside to practical application of it; not only for the sake of the use and fruits of such application, but so that in some new work they can as it were snatch an assurance that their labour in other matters will not be profitless; and also to show themselves off to others, in order to improve the reputation of the work in which they are engaged. Thus, like Atalanta, they turn out of their path to pick up the golden apple,[64] interrupting their run and letting the victory slip from their hands. Whereas in the true course of experience, one that will bring new works, divine wisdom and order should be the pattern before us. For God on the first day of creation created light only, devoting to that task an entire day, in which He created no material substance. In the same way and from experience of every kind, we should first of all discover causes and elicit true axioms; and seek experiments that bring light, not fruit. Indeed, axioms that are correctly devised and established assist in practical application to no small degree and bring hosts and troops of works in their train. But I shall have something to say later about the ways of learning from experience, which no less than the paths of

---

[64]The fable of Atalanta is related in a footnote to *The Plan of the Work* (*3*).

judgement are beset with hindrances. So far I have only discussed ordinary experience as a bad kind of demonstration. But now, to keep things in their right order, I must add a few words about those aforementioned signs that current philosophical inquiry is in an ill condition, and the causes for this fact, which at first sight is so strange and incredible. For a knowledge of the signs prepares for assent; an explanation of the causes removes the strangeness; and these two will greatly assist in making it easier and less painful to root out the idols from the understanding.

71

The sciences which we have came down to us mostly from the Greeks; for the additions made by Roman or Arab writers, or those of more recent times, are few and of little importance; and such as there are have been built on the foundation of Greek discoveries. Now the wisdom of the Greeks was professorial and much given to disputations, which is a kind of wisdom most hostile to the search for truth. For this reason, that name of Sophists, which was contemptuously turned back and transferred by those who wanted to be thought true philosophers, to the rhetoricians of old, Gorgias, Protagoras, Hippias and Polus, also applies to the whole tribe, to Plato, Aristotle, Zeno, Epicurus, Theophrastus and their successors, Chrysippus, Carneades and the rest. There was this difference only, that the former were mercenary wanderers, going about from town to town, advertising their wisdom and taking fees for it. The others were more dignified and high-minded men, with fixed abodes, who opened schools and taught philosophy without payment. But both kinds, though different in other ways, were professorial, reducing the matter to disputations, founding and contending for sects and philosophical heresies, so much so, that their teachings, as in Dionysius's shrewd criticism of Plato, were "only the words of idle old men to ignorant youths".[65]

---

[65]In Diogenes Laertius, *Lives of Eminent Philosophers,* III, 18, Dionysius, Tyrant of Sicily, is reported as having angrily exclaimed to Plato "you talk like an old dotard", when Plato held forth against tyrannical rule. Bacon is alluding to this story.

The earlier Greek philosophers on the other hand, Empedocles, Anaxagoras, Leucippus, Democritus, Parmenides, Heraclitus, Xenophanes, Philolaus and the others (I omit Pythagoras, as one full of superstition) did not open schools, so far as we know, but applied themselves to the search for truth more quietly, austerely and without fuss, making no great show or parade about their work. They did their work better, in my opinion, only their teachings have been obscured over the passage of time by those shallower men who pay more attention and regard to the grasp and wishes of common people. Time, like a river, brings down to us what is lighter and more puffed up, and lets the heavier, solid matter sink. Yet even they were not entirely free from that fault of their nation, and were too much inclined to the ambition and vanity of founding a sect and catching the wind of popular applause. But the search for truth must be despaired of when it turns aside to inanities of this kind. One cannot forget that verdict, or rather that prophecy, of an Egyptian priest about the Greeks "that they were always children, having neither antiquity of knowledge nor knowledge of antiquity".[66] And certainly they are like children: they chatter readily, but cannot procreate. Their wisdom appears full of words but is barren of works. Thus, the signs we get from the fount and birthplace of present-day philosophy are not good.

72

Nor are the signs that we can perceive from the nature of the time and age much better than those from the nature of the place and nation, for throughout that age, knowledge either of history or of the world was narrow and scanty, which is by far the worst thing, especially for those who set great

---

[66]"Whereupon one of the [Egyptian] priests, a prodigiously old man, said, 'O Solon, Solon, you Greeks are always children: there is not such a thing as an old Greek'. And on hearing this he asked, 'What mean you by this saying?' And the priest replied, 'You are young in soul, every one of you. For therein you possess not a single belief that is ancient and derived from old tradition, nor yet one science that is hoary with age'." Plato, *Timaeus*, 22b.

store by experience. For they had not even a thousand years of history worthy of the name; nothing but stories and hearsay of times past. They knew only a very small part of the regions and territories of the earth, indiscriminately calling all the peoples to the north Scythians, and those to the west Celts; knowing nothing of Africa beyond the nearest part of Ethiopia, nor of Asia beyond the Ganges; and much less did they know about the territories of the New World, not even by report or any well-founded rumour. They actually pronounced to be uninhabitable many climes and regions where vast populations live and have their being; while even the travels of Democritus, Plato and Pythagoras, not really expeditions to distant lands, but rather suburban excursions, were hailed as great achievements. In our own times, on the other hand, both many regions of the New World and the furthest parts of the Old in every direction are becoming known. Our wealth of experiments has become enormous; so if any signs are to be gathered from the time of their birth, or nativity (as the astrologers would say), it seems that nothing much is signified by those philosophies.

73

Of all the signs, none is more certain or worthy than that which comes from fruits; for fruits and practical discoveries are, as it were, guarantors and sureties for the truth of philosophies. Yet from those philosophies of the Greeks, and their ramifications in particular sciences, hardly one experiment can be adduced in all those years that has contributed to helping and raising man's estate, and can truthfully be said to come from the speculations and doctrines of philosophy. And Celsus frankly and wisely admits as much when he observes that without doubt, experiments in medicine were made first, and it was afterwards that men philosophized around them, looking for and assigning causes, instead of the other way about, using their philosophy and knowledge of causes to invent and devise experiments.[67] It was not surprising, there-

---

[67]Celsus, born around 25 BC, was the celebrated author of an encyclopaedia, of which only the medical part, *De Medicina,* has survived. In the

fore, that among the Egyptians, who accorded divine and sacred status to inventors, there were more images of beasts than of men, because beasts have, through their natural instincts, produced many discoveries, whereas men with all their talk and reasoned conclusions have produced few or none.

It is true that alchemists have some achievements from their labours, but these came by chance, incidentally, or by some variation of experiments, such as mechanics are accustomed to make, and not from any art or theory; for the theory they have formed brings more confusion than help to their experiments. Those too who have applied themselves to natural magic,[68] as they call it, have made few discoveries, and those trivial, and more like deceptive tricks. Just as in religion we are cautioned that faith is shown by works, the same well applies to philosophy, that it should be judged by its fruits, and be considered barren if it bears no fruit; and all the more so if it yields not the fruits of grape and olive but the thistles and thorns of disputes and contentions.

74

Signs can also be drawn from the increase and growth of philosophies and the sciences. For things that are based on

Preface to this work, empiricists are reported as objecting to rationalist medicine, that is, medicine that arrives at remedies from supposed hidden causes, on several grounds, including the following: "When the remedies had been discovered, only then did they begin to discuss the reasons for them: and the art of medicine was not a discovery following upon reasoning, but after the discovery of the remedy, the reason for it was sought out". The empiricists conclude from this, with Celsus's explicit support, that a prior knowledge of the cause is not required, because such a knowledge would have either led to the same remedy, in which case it was not needed, or to a different one, in which case it would have been wrong. So, as Spedding pointed out, Celsus's views were in fact directly opposed to Bacon's.

[68]By "natural magic" was meant the art of producing remarkable alterations in a body through an understanding of its hidden powers. Though Bacon regarded much of contemporary magic as superstitious in character, he did approve of *magic* in what, in Aphorism II, 9, he called a purified sense of the word; in Aphorism II, 51, Bacon lists a number of "magical" effects.

Nature grow and develop; but those based on opinion are
variable and fail to develop. If, therefore, those doctrines had
not been torn like plants from their roots, as plainly they have
been, but had stayed attached to the womb of Nature and
drawn nourishment from her, that would hardly have happened, which we see after two thousand years has now come to
pass; namely, that sciences have stuck fast in their tracks and
remained in virtually the same position, without any noticeable development; rather the reverse, flourishing most when
under their first authors, but going downhill ever since. In the
mechanical arts, on the other hand, based as they are on
Nature and the light of experience, we see the very opposite
happening. So long as they find favour, they are always
thriving and growing, as if endowed with a certain spirit; at
first, primitive, then useful, finally highly developed, and
always improving.

75

There is also another sign we should take note of (if sign is
the right word, since it is rather testimony and indeed the
strongest testimony of all). This is the admission of the very
authorities whom men now follow. For even those who utter
such confident pronouncements on things turn in their more
sober moments to complaints about the subtlety of Nature, the
obscurity of things and the weakness of the human mind. Now
if this were all they did, while some more timid spirits might
perhaps be deterred from further inquiry, others keener and
more optimistic might be spurred and encouraged to further
progress. But not content to speak merely for themselves, they
lay it down that anything unknown to or beyond the reach of
themselves or their masters must be beyond the bounds of
possibility, and they therefore declare, as though this derived
from their art, that it cannot possibly be known or done. In
their extreme pride and ill-will they turn the weakness of their
own discoveries into an accusation against Nature herself, and
to a denial of hope to all others. From this came the New
Academy school, which held Acatalepsy as a declared tenet of
belief and condemned men to everlasting darkness. From this
came the view that forms or the true differences of things

(which really are laws of pure action) are impossible to discover, and beyond the reach of man.[69] From this too came those opinions concerning the active and operative part, such as the heat of the sun and of fire being totally different from each other; lest, I suppose, men should think that by the use of fire they could produce and fashion anything like those things which occur in Nature. Hence, finally, the view that man can do no more than bring things together, and that only Nature can produce a compound; lest men should hope by their own art to create or transmute natural bodies.[70] By this sign, therefore, men will readily be persuaded not to involve their fortunes and their work in dogmas that are not only hopeless but dedicated to hopelessness.

76

There is another sign we must not omit, namely that there was in the past so much controversy between philosophers, and such wide differences between the schools themselves. This shows well enough that the road from the senses to the understanding was badly built, since the same raw material of philosophy, namely the nature of things, was torn and broken into such wandering and manifold errors. And although in these days disagreements and differences in dogma concerning first principles and entire philosophies are mostly dead, yet

---

[69]Bacon characterises forms, the principal goal of his science, in more detail in Aphorisms II, 1–10.

[70]In his *Masculine Birth of Time* (a work which he did not himself publish), Bacon excoriated the celebrated physician Galen (ca. AD 130–ca. 200) thus: "You would have us believe that only Nature can produce a true compound; you snatch at the notion that the heat of the sun and the heat of the fire are different and opposite things; you parade this opinion with the malicious intention of lessening human power whenever you can and bolstering up ignorance to all eternity through despair of any improvement".

Spedding was unable to trace the claim about the heterogeneity of the heat of the sun and of fire to Galen. The claim is however implicit in Aristotle, who held that the celestial region, in which the sun is situated, is not hot or fiery, and that the sun produces the heat we feel through its motion (*Meteorology*, I, 3).

there still remain around parts of philosophy numberless questions and controversies, so that there is clearly nothing certain or sound in the philosophies themselves, nor in the methods of demonstration.

77

As for the common belief that in the philosophy of Aristotle at any rate there was a great consensus, since after it appeared, the philosophies of earlier thinkers fell out of favour and were abandoned, and in succeeding ages nothing better was found, his philosophy being so well established as to draw after it both earlier and later periods; in the first place, this belief that the ancient philosophies languished after Aristotle's works were published is quite untrue, for the works of the ancient philosophers lived on long after that, right down to Cicero's day and for centuries afterwards. It was only in still later times, with the flooding of the barbarians into the Roman Empire and the virtual shipwreck of human learning, that the philosophies of Aristotle and Plato, like light and insubstantial flotsam, survived the waves of time. And as for general consensus, men are wrong there too, if they look more carefully at what has happened. For a true consensus is one that, through the exercise of a free judgement and after the matter has been investigated, brings people to agreement. But far the greatest number of those who agreed with Aristotle's philosophy enslaved themselves to it through prejudice and on the authority of others; so that it was more a case of following and joining in than of consensus. And even if it had been a true and widespread consensus, so far from implying a real and solid confirmation, it rather furnishes a strong presumption to the contrary. For in intellectual matters it is the worst omen of all that an idea commands general consent, except in sacred matters and in politics, where there is the right to vote. For, as I said earlier, nothing pleases the multitude, unless it strikes the imagination, or ties up the understanding in knots of common notions. We can therefore very well transfer from morals to intellectual matters that remark of Phocion, that "when all men agree with us and join in our praise, we should immediately look within to see what mistake or wrong we have been guilty of".[71] This sign then is one of the most unfavourable.

I conclude therefore that the signs of truth and soundness in the philosophies and sciences that are current are not at all good, whether taken from the origins of those ideas, or from their fruits or their growth, or the admissions of their founders, or the fact of their common acceptance.[72]

78

I come now to the causes of errors, and why they have persisted for so many centuries. These causes are extremely numerous and powerful, so it is not at all surprising that the ones I shall now mention have hitherto escaped men's notice; only surprising rather, that they could now at last occur to any man, and enter his thought. But this, I think, is more a matter of good fortune than of anyone's superior mental ability; and should be considered the child of time rather than of genius.

In the first place, when the matter is rightly considered, those many long ages shrink to only a narrow compass. For of the more or less twenty-five centuries over which the memory and learning of mankind extends, one can hardly pick out six that were fertile in sciences and favourable to their onward progress. For times no less than regions have their deserts and waste places, and only three revolutions and eras of learning can rightly be so called: those of the Greeks, of the Romans, and lastly of ourselves, that is the nations of Western Europe, to each of which barely two centuries can fairly be assigned. The intervening ages of the world were miserable, as far as any bounteous or happy harvest of scientific knowledge is concerned. Nor is there any reason to mention the Arabs or the

---

[71]This anecdote is taken from *The Life of Phocion,* viii, which was written by Plutarch, Greek biographer, around the first century AD: "And when, as he was once delivering an opinion to the people, he met with their approval, and saw that all alike accepted his argument, he turned to his friends and said: 'Can it possibly be that I am making a bad argument without knowing it?'"

[72]In this concluding comment, Bacon is summarizing the points from Aphorisms I, 72, 73, 74, 75, 76 and 77, respectively.

schoolmen, who in the intervening periods did more to crush science with their numerous treatises than increase the sum of knowledge. On a proper consideration of the facts, then, the chief reason for the feeble progress of the sciences has been the shortness of those periods favourable to them.

79

In the second place, we have a cause that is certainly of great and universal importance, namely that in the very ages when the genius and literature of mankind most flourished, or even when it was moderately flourishing, only a very small share of men's effort was allotted to natural philosophy,[73] even though it ought to be regarded as the great mother of the sciences. For all arts and sciences, once torn from this root, may perhaps be polished and shaped for man's use, but will hardly grow. Indeed, it is well known that, after Christianity became accepted and grew in strength, most outstanding minds devoted themselves to theology, which was accorded the largest rewards, and furnished in abundance with every kind of assistance. This zeal for theology chiefly occupied that third age among us Western Europeans, the more so, in that about this time both literature began to flourish and religious controversies to spring up, while in the previous age, during that second period of the Romans, the most influential and diligent thoughts and efforts of philosophers were wholly taken up with moral philosophy, the theology of the pagans. In those times, moreover, the best minds applied themselves to civic matters, because of the great size of the Roman Empire, which required many men's services. And that age when natural philosophy was seen to flourish most in Greece lasted only a very short time; since both in the earlier period of the so-called Seven Wise Men, all except Thales devoted themselves to moral and political philosophy,[74] while in later years, after Socrates had brought philosophy down from heaven to

---

[73]"Natural philosophy" is the study of the interior causes of things, as Bacon indicates towards the end of the next aphorism.

[74]Thales of Miletus (sixth century BC), reckoned to be the founder of Greek philosophy, was the first among seven to be accorded the title of *Wise*.

earth, moral philosophy grew stronger still, and turned men's minds away from natural philosophy.

But that very time when scientific inquiry was being vigorously pursued was bedevilled with controversies and the ambition for novel opinions, and rendered useless. Seeing therefore that during these three eras natural philosophy was for the most part neglected or hindered, and men's attention was entirely elsewhere, it is not surprising that men made little progress in it.

80

There is also the fact that even among those who have studied it, natural philosophy has hardly ever found a man able to give it his whole and undivided attention, particularly in these latter days, except perhaps some monk studying by candlelight in his cell, or some gentleman in his villa; but it has always been made, as it were, a passage-way or bridge to other things.

The great mother of the sciences has thus been demoted to the highly undignified role of a maidservant, who assists with the work of medicine or mathematics, and washes the unripe minds of adolescents and imbues them with some first tincture of learning, the better to fit them for another later. However, let no one expect much progress in the sciences—especially in their practical aspects—unless natural philosophy is extended to particular sciences, and particular sciences in turn lead back to natural philosophy. This is the reason why astronomy, optics, music, many of the mechanical arts, medicine itself and, more surprisingly, moral and political philosophy and the logical sciences all lack depth, and merely glide over the surface and variety of things. This is because, after those particular sciences have been scattered and set up, they are nourished no more by natural philosophy; if [picking up the several arts mentioned above] they had truly studied the sources of motions, light rays, sounds, the structure and schematism of bodies, affections [i.e., states of the body] and the mental faculties of understanding, they might have been able to impart to them new vigour and development. Small wonder, then, that the sciences fail to grow, cut off as they are from their roots.

81

There is another substantial reason why the sciences have made so little progress, namely, that it is not possible to keep a true and proper course if the goal itself has not been correctly placed and fixed there. Now the only true and proper goal of the sciences is to bring new discoveries and powers to human life. But the great majority, intent only on monetary gain and professional esteem, have no appreciation of this; unless some craftsman, cleverer than the rest and thirsting for fame, were perhaps to work on some new invention, very often at his own expense. But in general, men are so far from adopting as their goal an increase in the sum of human science and art, that out of the sum already at hand they take or seek only what they can turn to professional use or pecuniary advantage or enhanced reputation, or benefits of that kind. And if, out of all that multitude, there were one who practised science for its own sake with sincere feeling, even he would be found to pursue variety in speculations and doctrines, rather than an earnest and unbending search for truth. And again, if there should perhaps be a more earnest seeker after truth, even he will take as his goal only that aspect of the truth that gives him mental and intellectual satisfaction in assigning causes to things known already, not to that aspect that will bring the promise of new works and the new light of axioms. Since no one has yet rightly set out the end of the sciences, it is not surprising that error follows in those things which are subordinate to the end.

82

But not only have men misplaced the end and goal of the sciences; even if it had been correctly placed, they have still chosen an entirely wrong and impassable road towards it. To a mind rightly considering the matter, it must seem extraordinary that no mortal man has ever taken the trouble to open up and establish such a road for the human understanding to follow, leading from the sense itself and well-prepared and properly ordered experience. But as it is, all has been left either to the fog of traditions or the giddy whirl of arguments or the fluctuations and meanderings of chance and rambling and disorderly experience. Let anyone soberly and carefully consider the sort of method which men are accustomed to use in their inquiry or discovery of anything: he will no doubt see first of all the very simple and artless method which men usually follow, which is simply this. Anyone preparing and girding himself to make some discovery will first look up and study what others have said on the subject; then he adds his own thought and with much mental agitation exhorts his own spirit, invokes it almost, to utter oracles to him. The whole method is without any proper foundation, and turns upon nothing but opinions.

Another may call in dialectic to discover things for him; but this is relevant in name only to the matter in hand. For dialectical invention[75] is not of principles and special axioms, of which arts are composed, but only of those things that seem consistent with them [i.e., with those principles]. For to those more curious and persistent in their questioning, full of their own concerns, and interrupting dialectic over proofs and inventions of principles or of primary axioms, she gives her well-known reply; it is the appeal to faith, as if to an oath of allegiance owed to every art.

There remains simple experience which, if taken as it comes, is called accident; if it is deliberately sought, it is called experiment. But this kind of experience is nothing but an unbound besom, as they say, [in other words, an utter confusion] a mere groping, as one does in the dark, testing the ground in every direction in the hope of finding one's way, when it would be more sensible either to wait for daylight or to kindle a light, and only then go forward. On the other hand, the right order for experience is first to kindle a light, then with that light to show the way, beginning with experience ordered and arranged, not irregular or erratic, and from that

---

[75]Following Aristotle's example, scholastic philosophers distinguished two separate parts of logic: invention and judgement. The first purported to supply methods by which debatable propositions could be analysed to determine what could be said for and against them; the second, methods of arranging words into propositions, propositions into syllogisms or inductions, and the latter into whole discourses. See W.S. Howell, *Logic and Rhetoric in England, 1500–1700* (New York: Russell and Russell, Inc., 1961).

deriving axioms, and from the axioms thus established deriving again new experiments, just as the word of God operated in an orderly way on the unformed matter of creation.

So men should cease to wonder that the course of the sciences is not yet run, since they have entirely lost their way, either abandoning experience altogether, or else becoming entangled in it and wandering as if in a labyrinth; whereas a method rightly set up leads them through the forests of experience to the open country of axioms by an unbroken path.

83

One evil that has grown to an extraordinary degree comes from a certain opinion or belief, long-standing but self-important and harmful, namely, that it is beneath a man's dignity to spend much time and trouble on experiments and particulars that come under the senses and are materially bounded, especially since they are usually laborious to look into, too base for serious thought, awkward to explain, degrading to carry out, endless in number and minute in subtlety. So in the end it comes about that the true path is not only untrodden, but actually shut off and barred, experience being not so much abandoned or badly handled as rejected with disdain.

84

Another factor holding men back from progress in the sciences has been the veneration, the almost spell-bound reverence for antiquity, and the authority of those held to be the great figures in philosophy, and then by a general consensus. And I have already had something to say about that [in Aphorism I, 77].

On the subject of antiquity, the idea that men have of it is utterly careless and hardly agrees with the meaning of the word. For the world's old age is its true antiquity and should apply to our own times, not to the world's youth, when the ancients lived. For their age, which from our own point of view is ancient and older, from the world's point of view is new and younger. And, in fact, just as we expect a greater knowledge of human life and a more mature judgement from an old man than from a young one, because of his experience and the range and wealth of matters which he has seen and heard and thought about; so we can likewise fairly expect much greater things from our own times, if only they knew their strength and had the will to exert it, than from former times, seeing that the age of the world is now more advanced and enriched with a multitude of experiments and observations.

Nor should we ignore the fact that the distant voyages and overland travels which have become frequent in our day, have opened up and revealed to us many things in Nature which can throw new light on philosophy. And surely it would be disgraceful in a time when the regions of the material globe, that is, of the earth, the seas and stars, have been opened up far and wide for us to see, if the limits of our intellectual world were restricted to the narrow discoveries of the ancients.

As regards authors, it is utterly feeble to grant them so much but to deny his rights to Time, the author of authors and indeed of all authority. For Truth is rightly described as the daughter of Time, not of Authority. It is not surprising then that those spells cast by antiquity and by authority and general consent have so bound up men's strength that they have become, as if bewitched, powerless to make intimate contact with things themselves.

85

Nor is it only the admiration of antiquity, authority, and general consent that has forced the industry of man to rest satisfied with discoveries already made, but also admiration of those abundant works which for long have been the possession of the human race. Indeed, when one turns one eyes to the great variety and beauty of all the artefacts which the mechanical arts have brought together for man's use, one is more inclined to admire men's wealth than feel their poverty; hardly recognizing that the primitive observations of man and the operations of Nature (which are the life and first impulses of all that variety) are few and not deeply sought, and the rest only a matter of men's patience and the delicate and controlled movement of their hands or instruments. The making of clocks, for example, is certainly a delicate and precise work, and such as seems to imitate the heavenly bodies in its wheels and the pulse of animals in its regular and successive motion, and yet it depends on just one or two axioms of Nature.

But, on the other hand, consider that subtlety of the liberal arts,[76] and that subtlety too which relates to the preparation of natural substances by the mechanical arts, as for example, the discovery of the motions of the heavenly bodies in astronomy, of harmony in music, of the letters of the alphabet (which to this day are not in use in the Chinese Kingdom) in grammar; or again, in things mechanical, the discovery of the products of Bacchus and Ceres, that is, of the making of wine and beer, and bread, or again of the delicacies of the table, distilled liquors and the like. And reflect and bear in mind too what long ages it has taken to bring these things to their present state of perfection (for they are all ancient, except distillation);[77] and also (as I have just said about clocks) how little they owe to observations and axioms of Nature, and how easily and obviously and from chance ideas they were discovered. You will then, I maintain, quickly free yourself from all admiration, and rather pity man's condition, in that so many centuries have yielded so poor and barren a harvest of arts and discoveries. But these very discoveries I have just mentioned were older than philosophy and the intellectual arts, so that if truth be told, useful inventions ceased just when the rational and dogmatic sciences began.

And if one turns from workshops to libraries and marvels at the enormous variety of books one sees there, on examining and looking more carefully into the subject matter and contents of those books, one will surely marvel the other way; for seeing the endless repetitions, and how men keep doing and saying the same things, one will pass from admiration of the variety to wonder at the poverty and scarcity of those things that have up to now possessed and occupied the minds of men.

Again, if one descends to consider things thought more curious than rational, and looks more closely into the works of alchemists and magicians, one will perhaps doubt whether to laugh or weep at them. For the alchemist nurses eternal hope,

---

[76]The idea of a liberal art is described in footnote 9 in the *Plan of the Work, (3), above.*

[77]Distillation originated around the first century AD but was introduced into Europe, through translations of Arabic texts, only in the twelfth century.

and when the thing does not succeed, he blames some error of his own, and in self-condemnation thinks he has not properly understood the words of his art or of its authors, whereupon he turns to traditions and auricular whispers; or else thinks that in his performance he has made some slip of a scruple in weight or a moment in time, whereupon he repeats his experiments endlessly; and if, meanwhile, among the chances of his experiments he lights on some things that appear either novel or of commendable utility, he feeds his mind with good omens of this kind, magnifies and makes much of them, supporting the rest with hope. It is not to be denied, of course, that alchemists have discovered a good many things, and given useful inventions to mankind. But they are like the fable of the old man who bequeathed to his sons some gold buried in his vineyard, pretending he did not know the exact spot. They then fell to work with might and main to dig up the vineyard and found no gold, but the vintage was made more plentiful by that working of the ground.[78]

Those, on the other hand, who cultivate natural magic, who explain everything by the sympathies and antipathies of things, have by their useless and indolent conjectures ascribed virtues and amazing operations to things, and if ever they produce works, they are such as aim at surprise and novelty, not at useful and fruitful results.[79]

In superstitious magic,[80] on the other hand, if we must mention that too, the chief thing to notice is that they are only subjects of a certain and definite kind, in which the curious and superstitious arts, throughout all nations and ages and even religions, have held sway or played. I dismiss them therefore. All in all, then, it is not surprising if supposition of plenty shall have been the cause of poverty.

---

[78]This is one of Aesop's fables.

[79]Porta, in his *Natural Magic,* book 1, ch. 7, supports the Greek doctrine that as a result of the "hidden and secret properties of things", bodies are imbued with sympathies and antipathies, or consents and disagreements, which cause them to interact either favourably or destructively. Porta saw no prospect of discovering the reasons for these tendencies: "neither will any wise man seek after any other cause hereof but only this, that it is the pleasure of Nature to see it should be . . .".

[80]"Superstitious magic" is sorcery, or the production of results by the invocation of spirits.

86

Moreover, the admiration of men for doctrines and arts, of itself rather naive and almost childish, is increased by the cunning and artifice of those who have practised and handed down the sciences. For they propound them with such ambition and affectation, and present them to view so shaped and masked, as if they were in all parts complete and finished. And if you look at their method of exposition and their partitions, they will seem to embrace and include every single thing that can fall within that subject.[81] But although these divisions of the subject are badly filled out, and are like empty cases, yet to the common understanding they present the form and plan of a perfect science.

But the first and earliest seekers after truth, with greater frankness and better success, were in the habit of casting the knowledge which they gathered from their study of things and which they intended to keep for use, into *aphorisms,* short and scattered sentences, not linked to each other by a rhetorical method of presentation; nor did they pretend or profess to embrace the entire art. But the way things are done now, it is hardly surprising that men look no further into matters that are handed down to them, as if they were perfect and long since complete in every respect.

87

Moreover, the reputation and credit of the ancient systems has been much increased by the idleness and superficiality of those who have proposed new ones, especially in the active and

---

[81]*Method* was a technical term of rhetoric, much discussed by sixteenth century logicians, signifying ways of abridging and partitioning a subject, in order to assist in learning or teaching it. Bacon considered the partitions and divisions of rhetorical method artificial and decried the false impression they created of the subject as complete and perfect. Thus in the *De Augmentis,* VI, ii (*Works,* IV, p. 448), Bacon says that those rhetoricians who apply such a method "press matters by the laws of their method, and when a thing does not aptly fall into those dichotomies, either pass it by or force it out of its natural shape"; he opposes this rhetorical method to his own aphoristic method; the former, he says, being useful for transmitting knowledge, the latter for initiating investigation. See W.S. Howell, *Logic and Rhetoric in England, 1500–1700.*

operative branch of natural philosophy. For there has been no
lack of empty talkers and dreamers who, partly from credulity,
partly by imposture, have loaded the human race with promises, proffering and holding out the hope of the prolongation of
life, the delaying of old age, the relief of pain, the repair of
inborn defects, the deception of the senses, suppression and
stimulation of desires, illuminating and heightening of intellectual faculties, the transmutation of substances, strengthening and multiplying of motions at will, impressions and
alterations of air, the drawing down and procuring of celestial
influences, divinations of future events, representations of
remote ones, revelations of things concealed and many more.[82]
But of these lavish promisers it would be fair to say that there
is as great a difference in philosophical doctrine between their
baseless utterances and true arts as there is in historical
narrative between the exploits of Julius Caesar or Alexander
the Great and the deeds of Amadis of Gaul or Arthur of
Britain.[83] For those illustrious commanders are found in fact to
have done greater things than these shadowy heroes are even
feigned to have done, and indeed by ways and means that were
neither fabulous nor miraculous. Not that it is fair to slight the
credibility of authentic memory for now and then being im-
pugned and wronged by fables. But all in all, it is not
surprising if novel propositions (especially when works are
also mentioned) meet a good deal of prejudice, in view of those
impostors who have tried to do the same, since their over-
weening vanity and arrogance have to this day brought about

---

[82]Probably one of the empty talkers Bacon had in mind was Paracelsus, who explained the skill of the magus, or magician, as that of being
able to "draw down virtues from heaven and infuse them into a subject".
The science of 'nigromancy', Paracelsus says, is that of seeing "in crystals,
mirrors, polished surfaces, and the like, things that are hidden, secret,
present or future, which are present just as though they appeared in
bodily presence". (*The Hermetic and Alchemical Writings of Paracelsus*, II,
p. 301 and p. 296, respectively) He was also author of *A Book Concerning
Long Life,* and another *Concerning Renovation and Restoration,* which
offered various nostrums for preserving the human body and curing its
ailments.

[83]Amadis of Gaul was the mythical hero of a romance of that name,
popular in the sixteenth century; he is represented as poet, musician, king
and the very model of chivalrous knighthood.

the destruction of all greatness of mind in attempts of this kind.

88

Far worse harm, however, has been done to knowledge by the feebleness of spirit and the smallness and slightness of the tasks which human industry has set itself; and yet, which is worst of all, that same pusillanimity is often accompanied by pride and arrogance.

For, in the first place, we find in all the arts a now familiar precaution that is taken by their authors, who blame Nature for any deficiency in their art; and what their art cannot achieve they declare, on the authority of that same art, to be a natural impossibility. But surely an art cannot be condemned if it is itself the judge. Moreover, the philosophy that is now practised holds certain ideas or tenets close to its bosom, by which (if the matter be more carefully examined) it hopes to persuade men that nothing difficult, nothing that dominates and overcomes Nature, can be expected from art or human labour. I have already mentioned this in what I have written concerning the difference between the heat of a star and that of fire, and about compounding [in Aphorism I, 75]. These things, if noted more accurately, all amount to a malicious restriction of human power and to a far-fetched and artificial despair, which not only disturbs the auguries of hope but also cuts the stimulus and vigour of industry and throws away the chances that experience itself might yield. While their only care is that their art should be thought perfect, working for the empty and wretched glory of having it believed that whatever has not been discovered and understood up to now could in no way be discovered or understood in time to come.

And even if a man should try to apply himself entirely to things and make some new discovery, he will still only concentrate and settle on one discovery—no more—to draw out and study closely, such as the nature of the magnet, the flow and ebb of the sea, the system of the heavens, and things like that, which seem to have some secret in them, and have been handled with little success up to now. For it shows a great want of judgement to investigate the nature of anything in that one thing alone, since the same nature that in some things seems hidden and concealed is obvious and almost palpable in others; and in the former it excites wonder, in the latter it hardly attracts attention. This we find in the nature of consistency, which in wood or stone is not noticed, but passed over under the name of solidity, without further inquiry as to why separation or solution of continuity[84] is avoided: on the other hand, in water-bubbles the same thing appears subtle and ingenious, for these bubbles clump together into thin films precisely fashioned into a hemispherical shape, so that the solution of continuity is for a short time avoided.[85]

In fact, the very things that in some cases are deemed secret have in others an obvious and ordinary nature, [a fact] which will never be noticed if the experiments and thoughts of men are solely directed to the former. But generally speaking, in mechanical works, old inventions are often taken for new if someone refines or embellishes them, or unites several in one, or adapts them better for use, or makes the work larger or indeed smaller in mass or volume than it usually was, and that sort of thing.

It is therefore hardly surprising that no noble discoveries worthy of mankind have been brought to light, when men have been content and even pleased with such slight and childish tasks, even thinking themselves aiming at or indeed attaining some great end.

89

Nor should we overlook the fact that natural philosophy in every age has met with a troublesome and difficult enemy, namely superstition and the blind, excessive zeal of religion. For we see among the Greeks that those who first suggested natural causes for thunder and storms to the unaccustomed ears of men were for that reason condemned for impiety towards the gods; nor was the treatment much better that was

---

[84]Solution of continuity is the separation of the continuous parts of a body.

[85]Bacon calls instances *Clandestine* that manifest weakly a nature that is normally completely hidden. Thus he counts bubbles as Clandestine Instances of the nature of consistency, or the capacity of a body to maintain its own boundaries. The topic is elaborated *below*, in Aphorism II, 25.

meted out by some of the early fathers of Christianity to those who maintained, on most convincing grounds, which no rational man would now deny, that the earth was round, and that in consequence the antipodes must exist.

As things now stand, discourse on Nature is made harder and more perilous by the summaries and methods of exposition[86] of the scholastic theologians who, having brought theology into order as best they could, and shaped it into an art, went on to combine and mix the body of religion with the contentious and thorny philosophy of Aristotle, in an unjustifiable way.

And the treatises of those who have dared to deduce the truth of the Christian religion from the principles of philosophers, and to confirm it on their authority, tend to the same end, though in a different way, celebrating with much pomp and solemnity this union of faith and sense, as if it were a lawful marriage. They gratified men's minds with a pleasing variety of matters, but in doing so, mixed things human and divine quite improperly. And in such mixtures of theology and philosophy only that which is now received in philosophy is included; while new and possibly improved ideas are all but dismissed and banished.

Lastly, you will find that the ignorance of some divines virtually bars access to any philosophy, however improved. Some naively fear that a deeper inquiry into Nature would transgress the accepted limit of prudence, distorting what is said in the holy scriptures about the sacred mysteries against those who would pry into divine secrets, and applying them to the hidden things of Nature, which are forbidden by no interdict. Others more cunningly surmise and reflect that if intermediate causes are unknown, everything can more readily be referred to the divine hand and wand, a matter, as they think, of great importance to religion; which is nothing other than "wishing to please God through a lie".[87] Others fear from past example that developments and changes in philosophy will end in attacks on religion. Others, finally, seem to be

---

[86]This refers to the rhetorical method of exposition described in the footnote to Aphorism I, 86, *above*.

[87]Job xiii, 7: "Will ye speak wickedly for God? and talk deceitfully for him?"

anxious lest inquiry into Nature may discover something that would overthrow religion, or at least weaken it, especially among the uneducated. But these two latter fears seem to me to show an insubstantial kind of wisdom, as if men in their inmost hearts and secret thoughts distrusted and doubted the strength of religion and the sovereignty of faith over the sense, and therefore feared that they would be jeopardized by the search for truth in Nature. Whereas, if the matter is rightly considered, natural philosophy is, after the word of God, the surest antidote to superstition, and at the same time the most excellent nourishment for faith. Rightly therefore is she given to religion as a most trusty handmaid, since the one [religion] displays the will of God, the other [natural philosophy] His power. For he did not err who said, "Ye err, not knowing the scriptures nor the power of God",[88] thus blending and coupling in an indissoluble bond an insight into His will and a meditation upon His power.

It is not surprising, then, that progress in natural philosophy should be checked, when religion, the most powerful influence over men's minds, has, through the ignorance and incautious zeal of some, been drawn to take sides against her.

90

Again, in the customs and practices of schools, academies, colleges and similar institutions intended for the seats of learned men and the cultivation of erudition, everything is found hostile to the growth of knowledge. For lectures and exercises are so arranged that to think or contemplate anything other than conventional ideas hardly occurs to anyone. And if one or two should perhaps exercise their right to judge for themselves, they have to take on this task alone, getting no help from the company of others. And if they can endure this too, they will find that their hard work and independence of spirit becomes a great hindrance in their career; for the studies of men in places of this kind are confined, imprisoned one might say, in the writings of certain authors; and if anyone should disagree with them, he is immediately attacked as an

---

[88]Matthew xxii, 29.

agitator and innovator. But there is surely a great difference between affairs of state and the arts; each faces a different danger from new development and new light. In affairs of state, change, even if for the better, is suspect because of the disturbance it brings, since civil affairs rest on authority, consensus, reputation and opinion, not on demonstration; whereas arts and sciences ought to be like mines, loud on every hand with the sounds of new operations and further progress. But though that is the right course for matters to take, in practice things are different. That management of teaching that I have described and that administration and polity of knowledge usually impose a severe restraint on any progress.

91

Moreover, even if such hostility were to cease, the growth of the sciences would still be hindered by the fact that effort and hard work in that direction go unrewarded. For those cultivating the sciences and those paying for them are not the same people. For scientific advances come from great minds, whereas the prizes and rewards of science for this knowledge are in the hands of the common people, or leading citizens, who only occasionally are even moderately educated. Advances of this kind not only go unrewarded with prizes and substantial benefits, but do not even enjoy any popular esteem. For they are beyond the grasp of most people, and are easily overwhelmed and extinguished by the winds of common opinion. It is no wonder therefore if an enterprise which is not honoured does not prosper.

92

But far the greatest obstacle to the progress of the sciences and the undertaking of new tasks and new fields lies in man's despair, and in his supposition that such advances are impossible. For wise and serious men tend in these matters to lack all confidence, dwelling on the obscurity of Nature, the shortness of life, the deceptions of the senses, the weakness of judgement, the difficulties of experiments and so on. So they come to think that there are certain flows and ebbs of the sciences over the revolving times and ages of the world; at some times they grow and flourish, at others they wither and decay, so that when they have come to a certain stage and state they can go no further.

Therefore, if anyone believes or promises more, they assume that this is evidence of an immoderate and immature mind, and that such attempts, even if successful at first, would become difficult in mid-course, and end in confusion. And since thoughts of this kind occur readily to men of serious temper and outstanding judgement, we must take great care not to be led away by our affection for a good and fair object to relax or lessen our strictness of judgement. We must look constantly for what hopeful gleam of light there is, and from what quarter it shows itself and, rejecting the lighter breezes of hope, we must examine thoroughly and weigh up those which seem more steady. In fact we should call to our aid the prudence applied in state affairs, which is regularly sceptical on principle and which takes the worst view of human actions.

I now therefore have something to say about hope, especially since I am not a dealer in promises and am not going to use force or deception against men's judgement, but will lead them by the hand and of their own volition. And though the most effective way of arousing hope will be for me to bring men to particulars, especially those organized and set out in Tables of Discovery (the subject partly of the second, but much more of the fourth part of my *Instauration*), since this will be not merely the promise of the thing but, so to speak, the thing itself, nevertheless, to have everything done gently, I will proceed with my plan for the preparation of men's minds, in which preparation the revealing of grounds for hope occupies no small part. For without it the rest tends more to depress men by giving them a worse and meaner impression of things as they are than they have already, and a stronger feeling, a knowledge even, of the unhappy state of their condition, rather than to arouse any enthusiasm or spur their effort to find things out. And so my conjectures, which make what is hoped for probable, are set out and made known; just as Columbus did, before his wonderful voyage across the Atlantic Ocean, when he gave the reasons for his confidence that he could find new lands and continents beyond those known already; reasons which, although rejected at first, were later proved by experiment, and became the causes and starting points of very great things.

93

Now the beginning must come from God; for the business in hand, from the excellent quality of goodness in it, is clearly from God, who is the author of goodness and the father of light. Now in divine operations even the very smallest beginnings lead with certainty to their end. And that saying about spiritual things that "the kingdom of God cometh not with observation"[89] is found to be true in every great work of divine providence. All things glide onward calmly without commotion or sound, and the event plainly comes about before man thinks or notices that it has done so. Nor should we forget the prophecy of Daniel about the last days of the world: "Many shall pass through and knowledge shall be increased".[90] This clearly implies that it lies in destiny—that is, providence—that the passage through the world (which by its many long voyages plainly seems to be accomplished or under way) and an increase in knowledge will come at the same period of time.

94

The next argument is the greatest of all for encouraging hope, namely that drawn from the errors of time gone by and of the ways already tried. For it was a very just criticism of a badly administered government of which it was said: "The worst failing in the past ought to be our brightest hope for the future. For if you had done your duty outstandingly well and still your affairs had not much improved, then there really would be no hope left for them ever to get better. But since your affairs are in such a bad way, not from the force of circumstances but because of your own mistakes, there is good reason to hope that once those mistakes have been avoided or put

---

[89]Luke xvii, 20. The King James Bible of 1616 carries the explanatory note: "or with outward show".

[90]Daniel xii, 4. Bacon employed this text as a motto in the frontispiece to his *Novum Organum,* also reproduced in this edition. The corresponding passage in the King James Bible is "Many shall run to and fro and knowledge shall be increased"; while the modern translation of the New English Bible gives: "Many will be at their wits end, and punishment will be heavy", indicating some disagreement over the meaning of the original.

right, there can be a great change for the better".[91] Likewise, if through so many long ages past, men had kept to the right road for discovering and cultivating knowledge, and still made no progress, it would doubtless be a bold and rash belief to think that we could move further forward. But if it is the road itself that is at fault, and men's efforts have been expended quite pointlessly, it then follows that the difficulty arises, not in the things themselves, which we can do nothing about, but in human understanding and its use and application, for which there certainly is a remedy and cure. It will be best, therefore, to set out these errors, for the hindrances brought about through past mistakes are so many hopeful arguments for the future. Though I have touched on them before, I have decided also to give them now, briefly and in plain and simple language.

95

Those who have handled the sciences have been either Empiricists or Rationalists. Empiricists, like ants, merely collect things and use them. The Rationalists, like spiders, spin webs out of themselves. The middle way is that of the bee, which gathers its material from the flowers of the garden and field, but then transforms and digests it by a power of its own. And the true business of philosophy is much the same, for it does not rely only or chiefly on the powers of the mind, nor does it store the material supplied by natural history and practical experiments untouched in its memory, but lays it up in the understanding changed and refined. Thus from a closer and purer alliance of the two faculties—the experimental and the rational, such as has never yet been made—we have good reason for hope.

96

Natural philosophy has not up to now been found unblemished, but tainted and corrupted: by logic in the school of

---

[91]Demosthenes, *First Philippic,* 2.

Aristotle, by a natural theology in the school of Plato; in the second Platonic school, of Proclus and others,[92] by mathematics, which ought to mark out the boundaries of natural philosophy, not generate or give it birth. On the other hand, better things can be hoped for from a natural philosophy that is pure and unadulterated.

97

No one has yet been found of such steady and strict purpose as to decree and compel himself to sweep away common notions and speculations, and to apply his understanding, swept clear and level, to a fresh study of particulars. Thus it is that human reason, as we have it, is nothing but a medley, an unsorted collection, a mixture of chance and credulity, along with notions we imbibed as children.

But if a man of ripe years, unimpaired faculties, and a mind well purged should apply himself afresh to experience and particulars, from him we can expect better things. And on this point, I will promise myself such success as was won by Alexander the Great; and let no one tax me with vanity in this until he has heard the end of the matter, which will tend to clear me of all vanity.

For of Alexander and his achievements Æschines has said, "Assuredly we live not a mere mortal life, but for this were we born, that in after time great marvels may be told of us", as if he thought the deeds of Alexander were miracles.[93]

But in later times Titus Livius, taking a better and deeper view of the matter, said in effect that Alexander "had done no more than have the courage to despise vain fears".[94] And I think a similar judgement may be passed on me too at some

---

[92]Proclus (AD 410–485) was head of the Academy in Athens which had been founded by Plato. He was the last major Greek philosopher; his philosophy was a neoplatonic idealism, which recognized different levels of reality, which he loosely identified with various gods. His main writing was called *Elements of Theology*.

[93]Æschines (born ca. 390 BC), *Speeches against Ctesiphon*, 132.

[94]Livy (59 BC–AD 17), Book IX, 17.

future time, that I did not do great things, but merely made less of things that were believed great.

And meanwhile, as I have said already, there is no hope except in a *regeneration* of the sciences, that they may be derived by a sure method from experience and so set up afresh; which nobody, I believe, will say has been done or even thought of up to now.

98

Now the foundations of experience (since to experience we must come) have so far been either non-existent or very weak. Up to now, no search or collection has been made for a mass or store of particulars, suitable either in number or kind or certainty, nor in any way adequate to inform the understanding. On the contrary, men of learning, supine and easy-going as they are, have taken certain rumours of experience—as it were, tales and airy fancies of it—on which to base or confirm their philosophy; yet, nonetheless, they have accorded them the weight of legitimate evidence. And just as if some kingdom or state were to govern its debates and affairs, not on the strength of letters and reports sent by ambassadors or trustworthy messengers, but of the gossip of the townsfolk and the streets—that is exactly the system by which experience is brought into philosophy. We find nothing in natural history that is carefully examined, nothing that is verified, counted, weighed or measured; and what is loosely and vaguely observed must give misleading and unreliable information. And if anyone should think that this is an odd thing to say and perhaps an unfair criticism, seeing that Aristotle, so great a man himself and supported by the wealth of so great a king,[95]

---

[95]The king referred to is Alexander the Great of Macedon, who was also Aristotle's (384–322 BC) pupil. Pliny, in his *Natural History,* VIII, 17, records that Alexander "being fired with a desire to know the natures of animals and having delegated the pursuit of this study to Aristotle . . . , orders were given to some thousands of persons throughout the whole of Asia and Greece, . . . , to obey his instructions, so that he might not fail to be informed about any creature born anywhere. His enquiries addressed to those persons resulted in the composition of his famous works on zoology, in nearly 50 volumes."

could make so precise a history concerning animals;[96] and that sundry others, with more diligence but less noise, have made many additions, and others again have written copious histories and accounts of plants, metals and minerals; such a man does not seem to me to have considered and understood my present concern. For a natural history compiled for its own sake is quite unlike one collected in an organized way with the aim of informing the intellect and building a philosophy. And these two [kinds of] histories, different as they are in other matters, differ especially in this, that the former contains only the variety of natural species and no experiments of the mechanical arts. And just as in ordinary life the true personality of a person and his hidden thoughts and motives show themselves more clearly when he is under stress than at other times, so things in Nature that are hidden reveal themselves more readily under the vexations of art than when they follow their own course. There will therefore be grounds for optimism regarding natural philosophy when, and only when, natural history (which is its basis and foundation) shall have been better organized; but until that is done, hardly any.

99

Again, despite an abundance of mechanical experiments, there are very few that yield much information and help to the understanding. For the mechanic, who is in no way concerned with the investigation of truth, neither directs his mind nor turns his hand to anything unless it serves his work. Further progress in knowledge, in fact, can only be looked for with any confidence when a large number of experiments are collected and brought together into a natural history; experiments which, while they are of no use in themselves, simply help the discovery of causes and axioms. These I will call *light-bearing* experiments, to distinguish them from *fruit-bearing* ones. And experiments of this kind have one admirable property and quality—they never miss or fail. For since they are called upon, not to achieve some effect but to reveal the natural cause

---

[96]One of Aristotle's books is entitled *History of Animals*.

of something, whichever way they turn out, they answer their purpose equally well: they settle the question.

100

And not only must we look for and acquire a greater number of experiments, and ones of a different kind from those used hitherto, but also a quite different method, order and procedure must be introduced for the continuation and furtherance of experience. For experience that is aimless and takes its own course is, as I said above [in Aphorism I, 82], a mere groping in the dark, stupefying men more than giving them information. But when experience proceeds in accordance with a definite rule, in due order and without interruption, we can hope for some improvement in knowledge.

101

But even after such an abundance of material from natural history and experience, as is needed for the work of the understanding or of philosophy, is ready at hand, the understanding is still by no means capable of handling this material offhand and from memory, any more than one should expect to be able to manage and master from memory the computation of an astronomical almanac. Yet up to now thinking has played a greater part than writing in the business of invention, and experience has not yet become literate. But no adequate inquiry can be made without writing, and only when that comes into use and experience learns to read and write can we hope for improvement.

102

Moreover, since there is such a great number of particulars, an army of them you might say, and an army so scattered and diffuse as to distract and confuse the understanding, there is little to be hoped for from the skirmishings and aimless movements to and fro of the understanding, unless all those particulars pertaining to the subject under inquiry are disposed and arranged by appropriate tables of discovery—well organized and, as it were, living—and the mind is brought to the well-prepared and digested assistance which these tables afford.

103

Now after this copious supply of particulars has been ranged in a correct and orderly fashion before our eyes, we should not pass on straight away to the search for and discovery of new particulars, or works: or at least if we do, we should not rest there. Of course I do not deny that when all the experiments of all the arts have been collated and digested and brought within one man's notice and judgement, the mere transferring of the experiments of one art to others may result in many new discoveries of service to the life and state of man, by means of that experience that I call literate. And yet we cannot hope for very much from that. Much more, though, [is to be hoped for] from the new light of axioms derived from those particulars by a certain course and rule, which in turn will point to new particulars. Such a road is not level, but rises and falls; first ascending to axioms, then descending to works.

104

However, the understanding must not be allowed to leap and fly from particulars to remote and nearly the most general axioms (such as the so-called first principles of arts and of things), and from their [supposed] unshakable truth, to prove and deliver intermediate axioms. This is what has happened up to now, the understanding being inclined thereto instinctively, and also long trained and accustomed to it by syllogistic demonstrations. But there will be hope for the sciences when, and only when, ascent is made by the right kind of ladder, through an uninterrupted, connected series of steps, from particulars to lesser axioms, then to intermediate axioms, one above the other, and last of all to the most general. For the lowest axioms are little different from bare experience, while the highest and most general (which we have) are conceptual and abstract, without any solidity. It is the intermediate axioms that are the true and solid and living ones, on which the affairs and fortunes of mankind are built. And above these, finally, are those most general axioms, such, that is, as are not abstract but are really limited by these intermediate ones.

So it is not feathers we must provide for the human understanding so much as lead and heavy weights, to restrain all leaping and flying. This has never yet been done, but when it is, we may have better hopes for knowledge.

105

Now in establishing an axiom, another form of *induction* must be devised than that in use hitherto; and it should be used, not only for testing and discovering so-called first principles, but also lesser and intermediate axioms, in fact, all axioms. For induction that proceeds through simple enumeration[97] is childish, its conclusions are precarious, and open to danger from a contradictory instance, and it generally makes its pronouncements on too few things, and on those only that are ready to hand. But *induction* that will be of any use for the discovery and demonstration of the arts and sciences must analyse Nature by proper rejections and exclusions, and then, after a sufficient number of negatives, come to a conclusion on the affirmative instances. None of this has yet been done, or even attempted, except only by Plato, who does indeed use this form of induction to some extent in examining definitions and ideas. But in order to equip this induction or demonstration well and in the prescribed manner, we need very many things which no mortal has yet thought of; so much so, that more hard work will have to be devoted to it than has been expended hitherto on the syllogism. And with the aid of this induction we can not only discover axioms but also define notions. And truly, it is in this *induction* that our best hope lies.

106

Now in establishing axioms by means of this induction, we must also examine and check whether the axiom so established is only fitted to and made to the measure of those

---

[97]See footnote to Aphorism I, 69, *above.*

particulars from which it is derived, or whether it is larger and wider. And if it is larger or wider, we must look to see whether it confirms its largeness and wideness by indicating new particulars, as a kind of collateral security; lest we either stick fast in things already known, or perhaps weakly grasp at shadows and abstract forms, not solid and actual material things.[98] When these things come into use, then at last we shall see a gleam of real hope.

107

Here too should be remembered what I said earlier [in Aphorism I, 80] about extending the scope of natural philosophy and leading the particular sciences back to it, so that there is no severing of the branches of knowledge from the stem; for unless this is also done there will be less hope for progress.

108

So much then for dispelling despair and creating hope by the dismissal or correction of the errors of earlier times; now we must see what other grounds for hope there may be. This one comes to mind—if many useful discoveries have been made by some chance or through some favourable circumstance, by men who were not looking for them and were engaged on some other matter, then no one can doubt that much more would be discovered by men who were actively engaged in looking for them, and doing so in a methodical, not

---

[98]Spedding has drawn attention to a helpful parallel passage in Bacon's own English, in his *Valerius Terminus* (abridgement of chapter 12): "That the discovery of new works and active directions not known before, is the only trial to be accepted of; and yet not that neither, in case where one particular giveth light to another; but where particulars induce an axiom or observation, which axiom found out discovereth and designeth new particulars. That the nature of this trial is not only upon the point, whether the knowledge be profitable or no, but even upon the point whether the knowledge be true or no; not because you may always conclude that the Axiom which discovereth new instances is true, but contrariwise you may safely conclude that if it discover not any new instance it is in vain and untrue."

an impulsive or desultory, way. For although it might happen once or twice that a man has the good fortune to stumble on something that previously had escaped his great efforts and tireless searching, nevertheless, upon the whole, the opposite is surely found to be the case. Many more and better results, therefore, can be expected, and more frequently too, by using reason and effort and direction and purpose, than by relying on chance and animal instinct and the like, which until now have been the source of our discoveries.

109

And there is another ground for hope, in that some of the inventions already made have been of such a kind that, before they were invented, it would hardly have occurred to anyone to have the least idea about them; they would have derided them as impossible. For men usually guess at new things in the light of things that happened before, their imagination being preoccupied and coloured by them. This way of forming opinions is very prone to error, since many of the waters we seek from the springs of Nature do not flow along familiar channels.

It is as if before the invention of cannon, someone had described them by their effects, saying that there was a new invention, by which the greatest walls and fortifications could be shattered and struck down from afar. Men no doubt would be thinking about the many different ways in which the power of catapults and other machines could be multiplied by weights and wheels and similar devices for ramming and hurling; but the idea of a fiery blast expanding and exploding so suddenly and violently, would scarcely ever have occurred to any man's imagination or fancy. He would never have seen anything like it, except perhaps in an earthquake or thunderbolt, which would have been straightway dismissed as marvels of Nature, quite impossible for men to imitate.

In the same way, if before the discovery of silk, anyone had put out a story that a kind of thread had been discovered for use in clothing and furniture, which far outclassed linen or woollen thread in fineness and yet in strength too, as well as in beauty and softness, men would think at once of some silky sort of vegetable matter, or of the finer hairs of some animal, or the feathers and down of birds; certainly they would never ever have thought of a textile made by a tiny worm, and in such abundance, and renewing itself each year. In fact if anyone had said anything about a worm, he would no doubt have been laughed at, as if he were dreaming of a new kind of spider's web.

Likewise again, if someone before the invention of the compass had reported that an instrument had been invented by which the quarters and points of the heavens could be exactly found and distinguished, men's imagination would at once have been stirred to think of more exquisitely made astronomical instruments of many different kinds; but that anything could have been discovered whose movements would agree so well with the motions of the heavenly bodies, and yet itself not be one of them but only a stone or metal substance, would have been thought absolutely unbelievable. Yet these things and others like them lay hidden from men through long ages of the world, and were not discovered by philosophy or the arts of reasoning, but by chance and favourable circumstances. They are, as I have said, so utterly different and remote from anything previously known that no preconception could possibly have led to them.

There is therefore every reason to hope that there are still many very useful things, which have not so far been discovered, hidden from us in the bosom of Nature, having no affinity or parallel with things already discovered, but quite off the beaten track of our imagination. No doubt they too will, at some future time, after many turnings and revolutions of the centuries, come forth, just as those earlier ones did; but with the method I am now discussing they can be expected soon, all together and quickly.

110

But we also see other discoveries that prove that mankind can actually step over or pass by notable inventions, even when they lie at our feet. For however much the inventions of gunpowder, silk, the compass, sugar, paper or such things may appear to depend on certain properties of things and Nature, there is surely nothing in the craft of printing that is not open and almost obvious. Nevertheless, men never noticed that while it is more difficult to assemble type than to write letters by hand, there is this difference, that type once set can provide an infinite number of copies, while letters written by hand yield only one. Or perhaps again they did not notice that ink could be so thickened as to colour without running, particularly when the type lay face uppermost and the impression was made on it from above, so that for many centuries they did not have this most elegant invention which does so much to propagate learning.

In this business of invention, the human mind is often so foolish and awkward that first it doubts and then despises itself. At first, it seems incredible to it that any such thing can be invented, but after it has been, it seems again incredible that men should have missed it so long. And this very thing is a good cause for hope, namely, that there is a great mass of inventions remaining which could be brought to light, not only by means of processes still unknown, but also by transferring, arranging and applying those already known, using that literate experience of which I have spoken [in Aphorisms I, 101 and 103].

111

Nor should we overlook this hopeful sign. Let men consider, if they will, the vast intellectual effort and time and resources that have gone into matters and studies of far less use and value, only a small part of which, if turned to sensible, solid purposes, would find no difficulty it could not overcome. This I think fit to add, because I frankly concede that a collection of natural and experimental history of the sort I have in mind, the sort we ought to have, would be a great and, as it were, a royal task, and one involving much labour and expense.

112

No one however should be alarmed by the great number of particulars, but think them rather a reason for hope. For the particular phenomena of the arts and of Nature are only a handful compared to the fanciful speculations of the intellect, when it is separated and removed from the evidence of things. But the end of this road is in open country, and is not far off; the other road has no ending, just infinite entanglement. For men up to now have spent hardly any time with experience, and have barely touched it; instead they have squandered endless time on intellectual ponderings and commentaries. Now if there were someone among us who could answer our questions concerning the operation of Nature, the discovery of all causes and sciences would be a matter of a few years.

113

Moreover, I think that men can take some hope from my own case, and I say this not to boast but because it is a useful remark. Anyone who is despondent should consider me, a man of all men of my time the most occupied with affairs of state, not in very good health (which costs me much time), altogether a pioneer in this subject, following no man's footsteps, discussing these matters with no living soul, who has yet brought these matters some way, as I believe, by diligently forging ahead along the true road and submitting the mind to things. And then let him consider how much we can expect from men with abundance of leisure, collaborating with others, and over a period of years, after these directions of mine. This is particularly so since my way can be trodden not only by one man at a time, as is the case with that rational method,[99] but one where the efforts and labour of men, especially in the collecting of experience, can best be distributed and then brought together. For men will only begin to know their full strength when, instead of great numbers working on the same things, we have some responsible for one thing, some for another.

114

Finally, even if the breath of hope that is wafted to us from that *new continent* were fainter and harder to detect than it is,

---

[99]Bacon is here presumably referring to the "Sophistical or rational" school of philosophy already discussed in Aphorisms I, 63 and 64.

I am convinced that the attempt must be made, unless we wish to be found utterly feeble-spirited. For the risks of not trying and of not succeeding are unequal; in the one case we throw away an immense good, in the other just a little human labour. In fact, it is clear to me, from what I have said and also from what I have left unsaid, that there is abundant ground for hope, not only to encourage the energetic man to make the attempt, but also to bring a man of prudent and sober mind to believe.

115

Now I have said enough about dispelling the despair that has been one of the most potent causes of delay and hindrance to the progress of the sciences. I have finished, also, what I have to say about the signs and causes of the errors, the lack of enthusiasm, and the ignorance that now prevail, especially since the more subtle causes, which are overlooked in popular judgement or observation, should be referred to what I have said about the idols of the human mind.

Here also I must end the destructive part of my *Instauration,* which has been effected by three refutations, namely, the refutation of *Natural Human Reason* left to itself; the refutation of *Demonstrations;* and the refutation of *Theories,* or of accepted philosophies and doctrines. The refutation of these has been, as it could only be, by signs and the evidence of causes, since no other confutation was open to me, disagreeing as I do with others both on principles and on methods of demonstration.

It is time therefore to move on to the art itself and the rule of the *Interpretation of Nature;* but there remains something to be attended to. For while in this first book of aphorisms, I have set myself to prepare men's minds as much to understand as to accept what is to follow, now that I have cleansed and swept and smoothed the floor of the mind, it remains for the mind to be brought into the right position, to give it a favourable aspect, as you might say, towards what I am going to put before it. For in approaching something new, it is not only the strong preoccupation with old opinions that brings on prejudice, but also a false preconception or prefiguring of the new thing which is being presented. I will therefore try to win good and true opinions about the things I am going to put forward, although only for the time being and, like an interest-bearing loan, until the thing itself is fully known.

116

First of all, then, I must ask men not to imagine that I want to found a new sect of philosophy, like the ancient Greeks or some of the moderns, Telesio, Patrizi or Severinus.[100] This is not what I am doing, nor do I think that it matters much to the fortunes of mankind what abstract views about Nature and the first principles of things a man may hold. For no doubt many old ideas of this kind can be revived or similar new ones introduced, just as it is possible to suppose many theories of the heavens which all agree well enough with the phenomena but still differ from each other.[101]

I, for my part, have nothing to do with such unprofitable conjectures. On the contrary, I intend to find out whether I can in fact lay down firmer foundations for the power and grandeur of man, and extend their limits more widely. And although my findings are few and only in certain special subjects, they are, I believe, far truer and safer, and also more fruitful, than those in use hitherto (and these I have assembled into the fifth part of my *Instauration*); nevertheless I am not proposing any universal or comprehensive theory. I do not think the time has yet come for such a thing. Neither can I hope to live long enough to complete the sixth part of the *Instauration* (which is

---

[100]Bernardino Telesio of Cosenza (1509–1588) was to some degree admired by Bacon, who called him the "best of the novellists [i.e., innovators]". He was a vigorous critic of Aristotle; he adopted the physical theories of Parmenides and opened a famous school in Naples. His principal work was *De Rerum Natura,* which Bacon studied closely. Francesco Patrizi (1529–1597) held a chair of philosophy at the University of Ferrara; he wrote *Nova de Universis Philosophia* (1591), a work which attempted to combine Platonic and Aristotelian philosophies and which Bacon drew on in his studies of the tides. Peter Severinus (1540–1602) was a Danish physician who composed a number of philosophical and medical works, largely following Paracelsian doctrine.

[101]This point is also made in Aphorism I, 62, *above,* and explained in a footnote there.

intended for the philosophy discovered by the legitimate interpretation of Nature). I shall be content if I can work soberly
and usefully in the intermediate stages, and meanwhile sow
for men after me the seeds of a purer truth, and play my part in
the beginning of great things.

117

And just as I am not the founder of a sect, so I do not make
any lavish promises of particular works. It may be objected
that I, who so often talk of works and refer everything to them,
should be showing some works myself by way of an earnest. My
way and method, however (as I have often clearly stated and
would like to state again), is not to extract works from works,
nor experiments from experiments as the empiricists do, but
from works and experiments to extract causes and axioms, and
again from those causes and axioms to extract new works and
experiments, as a legitimate interpreter of Nature.

And although in my tables of discovery, which comprise
the fourth part of the *Instauration,* and also among the
examples of particulars, which I have enumerated in the
second part [i.e., *Novum Organum*], as well as in my remarks
on history, described in the third part of the work, anyone even
moderately perceptive and intelligent will see everywhere
indications and outlines of many noble works; nevertheless, I
frankly confess that my present knowledge of natural history,
whether from books or from my own investigations, is neither
full nor certain enough to satisfy the requirements of a
legitimate interpretation.[102]

Anyone therefore who is more apt and better prepared for
mechanical matters, and is clever at hunting down works
merely by a frequent use of experiments, is free to employ that
diligence to pluck out from my history and tables any number
of things that he can find on his way, and apply them to works
and so receive some interest, as it were, before he lays his hand
on the capital. But for my part, having higher aims in mind, I
condemn all hasty and premature delay on things of that kind,

---

[102]The various parts of Bacon's *Great Instauration* are listed above in
The Plan of the Work.

being, as I often say, like Atalanta's apples. I have no childish longing for golden apples, but stake all on the victory of art over Nature in the race. Nor do I hurry to reap moss or the green corn, but wait for the harvest in its season.

118

It will also happen, no doubt, that someone, after reading my natural history and tables of discovery, will find in those very experiments some things that are not quite certain, or downright false, which may make him think that my discoveries depend on foundations and principles that are false and doubtful. But this is not important, for such things are bound to happen at first. It is only as if in writing or printing, one or two letters perhaps were wrong or misplaced, which does not impede the reader much, since the mistakes are easily corrected from the meaning. In the same way, men should realize that there may be many experiments in my natural history that are wrongly believed and accepted, which will soon, by the discovery of causes and axioms, be easily deleted and rejected. On the other hand, it is true that if the mistakes in any natural history are important, frequent and continual, they cannot possibly be corrected or amended by any happy contrivance of mind or art. If therefore in my natural history, which has been tested and collected with such diligence, strictness and almost religious care, there still lurks now and then among particulars some mistake or inaccuracy, what should be said of common natural history, which compared with mine is so careless and facile? Or of the philosophy and sciences built upon such sands (or rather quicksands)? No one therefore should be troubled by these mistakes I have described.

119

In my natural history and experiments, many things will also be found trivial and commonplace, many that are base and ignoble, many again that are exceedingly subtle and merely speculative, and of no apparent use; and things of this kind are liable to deflect and discourage men's interest.

And as for those things that seem commonplace, men

should bear in mind that up to now they have been accustomed to do no more than ascribe the causes of things of rare occurrence to things that occur frequently, but never to investigate the causes of the latter, simply taking them for granted.

Thus they do not seek the causes of weight, of the rotation of the heavenly bodies, of heat, of cold, of light, hardness, softness, rarity, density, liquidity, consistency, the living and inanimate states, homogeneity, heterogeneity nor, finally, of anything with an organic structure; but taking them as obvious and manifest, they dispute and pronounce judgement on things of less frequent and familiar occurrence.

I, on the other hand, know well that no judgement can be passed on what is uncommon or remarkable, much less on what is newly brought to light, unless the causes of common things, and the causes of those causes, are properly examined and found, and therefore of necessity I am bound to admit the very commonest things into my history. In my opinion, in fact, nothing has hindered philosophy more than the failure to give time and attention to things of familiar and frequent occurrence that are accepted in passing, without any inquiry into their causes: for information is less often needed about things unknown than is attention to things known.

120

And as for things that are base, or even filthy, such as one has to apologize for mentioning (as Pliny says),[103] these must be admitted into natural history no less than things of the utmost splendour and price. Nor is natural history polluted thereby, for the sun enters impartially into palaces and sewers, yet is not polluted. For myself, I am not erecting or

---

[103]Pliny the Elder (AD 23 or 24–79) wrote an encyclopaedic *Natural History,* containing a vast array of factual information on a huge range of subjects. In the last letter that Bacon is known to have written, he expressed a certain affinity for Pliny, who, he fancifully claimed, "lost his life trying an experiment about the burning of the mountain Vesuvius", just as Bacon had nearly (as he thought) done in his experiment on the conservation of flesh by freezing.

The remarks of Pliny's to which Bacon is alluding occur at the beginning of the first book of his *Natural History.*

dedicating some capitol or pyramid to the pride of man, but
laying a foundation in the human understanding for a holy
temple, modelled on the world. I therefore follow that model,
for what is worthy of existence is worthy of being known,
knowledge being the image of existence. And base things exist
just as much as splendid things. And for that matter, just as
some putrid substances like musk or civet yield the best
scents, so base and sordid details sometimes provide excellent
light and information. But I have said more than enough, since
this kind of fastidiousness is obviously childish and effemi-
nate.

121

There is another point we must consider much more
carefully, namely that there are many items in my history that
will seem to common comprehension, or even to an intelligent
man who has been conditioned by the present state of affairs,
to be of curious and useless subtlety. On this, therefore, before
anything else, I have said and must say again, that at the
beginning and for some time, I look only for *light-bearing*
experiments, not *fruit-bearing* ones, following, as I have often
said, the example of the divine creation, when on the first day,
He made light only, and devoted a whole day to that alone,
without introducing any material work in that time.

If, therefore, anyone should think that such things are of
no use, he should consider whether he also thinks light to be of
no use, because it is not a solid or material thing. To tell the
truth, well examined and definite knowledge of simple natures
is like light, in that it provides an entrance to all the inmost
parts of Nature's works, and by its power embraces and brings
in its train whole throngs and troops of works, and the sources
of the noblest axioms; yet in itself it is not of great use. So too
the letters of the alphabet have in themselves and individually
no meaning or use, yet they are the prime material for the
composition and organization of all language. Similarly, the
seeds of things are of great power, although they are themselves of no use except in their development. And the scattered
rays of light itself confer none of their benefit, unless they
converge.

And if some are put off by speculative subtleties, what

shall I say about the schoolmen, who were immensely addicted to subtleties? Theirs were subtleties spent on words, or at least on common notions (which is much the same thing), not on things or Nature, and as such were devoid of any utility, both in their origin, and in their consequences. Nor were they of the kind that have no immediate use, but boundless use in their consequences, as the ones I am speaking about are. Men should be certain of this, that all subtlety of disputation and intellectual discourse, if it is only applied after axioms have been discovered, comes too late, and in the wrong order; and that the right and proper time for subtlety, or at least the principal time, is when it is spent in weighing experience and founding axioms upon it; for that other subtlety merely snatches and catches at Nature without ever taking firm hold and capturing it. Certainly what is said about opportunity or fortune is most true if applied to Nature, namely that "it has a forelock, but is bald behind".[104]

As the last word on the subject of contempt for including things in natural history that are commonplace or base or exceedingly subtle and in their origin of little use, we may take as an oracle the reply of that poor woman who said to a haughty king who had rejected her petition as not worth his attention and beneath his dignity: "Then stop being a king!"[105] For it is most certain that Nature can never be won or governed by anyone who regards such things as too paltry and insignificant, and is unwilling to concern himself with them.

122

It may be thought rather surprising and harsh of me to sweep aside all at once, with a single impetuous stroke, all sciences and their authors, without calling on any of the ancients for aid and comfort, but relying on my own strength alone.

I know that if I had wished to proceed with less honesty, I

---

[104]The meaning of this ancient proverb is preserved in the current wisdom that one should take time by the forelock.

[105]This story is told of King Philip of Macedon by Plutarch in his *Sayings*, III (179), who adds that the King was so amazed at her words that he proceeded to hear not only her case but those of others.

could easily have gained assent and respect by citing the ancient times before the days of the Greeks (when the natural sciences may have flourished more, though with less fanfare, not yet having arrived at the trumpets and pipes of the Greeks), or even by citing, in part at least, some of the Greeks themselves; in the manner of those parvenus who fashion and feign for themselves a noble lineage, tracing it through favourable genealogies from some ancient house. For my part, though, I rely on the evidence of things and will have no truck with any sort of fiction or imposture; nor do I think it matters any more to the business I am on whether our present discoveries were once known to the ancients and have sunk and surfaced again through the chances and changes of events along the centuries, than it matters to mankind whether the New World is that famous island of Atlantis,[106] and so known to the ancient world, or whether it has been discovered now for the first time. For the discovery of things should be searched for by the light of Nature, not fetched back out of the darkness of antiquity.

As for that wholesale censure [expressed in the opening lines of this aphorism], on due consideration, it will be found quite certain to be both more probable and more modest than if it were partial. For if there had not been errors deep-rooted in the primary notions, there would inevitably have been some true discoveries that would have put right mistaken ones. But since the errors were fundamental, and such as arise from carelessness and oversight rather than from wrong or faulty judgement, it is not surprising that men have not won what they have not desired, nor reached a goal that they had not set before them, nor completed a journey that they had not begun or persisted with.

And as for the criticism that my action amounts to arrogance, certainly, if anyone claims to be able to draw a straighter line or a more perfect circle than another by steady hand and sharp eye alone, this implies a comparison of skill; but if

---

[106]Atlantis is the name of a possibly mythical island in the Atlantic Ocean, said to have been a powerful kingdom before being overwhelmed by the sea. It is mentioned in Plato's *Critias* and also in his *Timaeus*. Bacon's work, the *New Atlantis*, described a utopian society dedicated to the pursuit of knowledge.

he asserts only that using a ruler or a pair of compasses, he can draw a straighter line or more perfect circle than anyone who simply uses eye and hand, he makes no great boast. And what I say here applies not only to this first and pioneering attempt of mine, but to all who will devote themselves to this work after me. For my method of discovering knowledge places men's natural talents almost on a level, and does not leave much to their individual excellence, since it performs everything by the surest rules and demonstrations. These contributions of mine therefore, as I have often said, come more from good fortune than from my particular ability, and are rather the birth of time than of innate ability. For certainly chance plays no less a part in men's thinking than it does in their works and deeds.

123

I can say then of myself, since it marks the distinction so well, what has been said in jest: "It is impossible they should agree, since one drinks water and the other drinks wine."[107] For other men, both in the past and nowadays, have drunk a crude liquid in their sciences, like water either welling up spontaneously from their understanding or drawn up by wheels from a well through dialectic. I, on the other hand, offer as a drink a wine strained from countless grapes, and those ripe and in season, gathered in bunches, collected together, then crushed in the press and finally purified and clarified in the vat. No wonder then that they and I do not agree.

124

Again, it will doubtless be thought that the goal or target of the sciences (the very point wherein I find fault in others) which I myself have set up is neither true nor the best; that in fact, the contemplation of truth is a higher and more worthy

---

[107]"Then Philocrates rose, and said, in a very supercilious manner: 'No wonder Demosthenes and I disagree, men of Athens. He drinks water; I drink wine'." Demosthenes, *On the False Embassy*, 355.

aim than any usefulness or magnitude of works, and that this long and painstaking time spent on experience and material things and on the flux of particular events will fix the mind on the ground, or rather hurl it into a hell of confusion and chaos, thus banishing and driving it away from the serene tranquillity of abstract wisdom, as from a much holier state. But I would readily agree with that line of argument; and indeed this very thing which they approve of, and so much prefer, is what I am above all concerned with. For what I am establishing in the human understanding is a true model of the world, as it is found to be, not what anyone's own reasoning shall have dictated to him. And this cannot come about unless the world is most carefully dissected and anatomized. But I say that those foolish and aping imitations of worlds which men's fancies have created in their philosophies must be utterly put to flight. Men must realize, therefore, as I said earlier [in Aphorism I, 23], how great a difference there is between the idols of the human mind and the ideas of the divine mind. The former are no more than arbitrary abstractions; the latter are the Creator's true stamp upon created things, printed and defined on matter by true and precise lines. In this respect, therefore, truth and utility are the very things themselves (*ipsissimae res*);[108] so works themselves are of greater value as pledges of truth than as comforts of life.

125

Again, it may perhaps be thought that I am only doing what has been done already, and that the ancients themselves

---

[108]This rather perplexing phrase has engendered much discussion, of which Rossi's is the most authoritative. Spedding's translation, "Truth . . . and utility are . . . the very same thing", is inaccurate. Like Rossi, we take the phrase to mean that truth and utility are the essence of the matter. Bacon uses the same phrase in Aphorism II, 13, to describe the essence or "form of a thing"; it is, he says, "the very thing itself (*ipsissima res*)"; and in Aphorism II, 20, Bacon says that "the very essence of heat, or the substantial self of heat (*ipsissimus calor, sive quid ipsum caloris*), is motion and nothing else". See Paolo Rossi, *Philosophy, Technology, and the Arts in the Early Modern Era,* trans. S. Attanasio (New York: Harper & Row, 1970).

took the same road as I; that I too, after all my toil and moil, shall probably come at last to one or other of those philosophies that prevailed among the ancients. For they too, in the first stages of their studies, prepared a vast number of examples and particulars, and digested them by subject and specific topic in notebooks, and proceeded from them to compose their philosophies and arts. And afterwards, when they had mastered the matter, they made them public, adding a few examples here and there by way of illustration and to lend credibility. They thought it unnecessary and inconvenient to publish their summaries of particulars and memoranda and notebooks; like builders removing all scaffolding and ladders out of sight, once the building is up. There can be no doubt that this was what was done. But anyone who has not entirely forgotten what I said earlier will easily answer this objection, or rather scruple. For the ancients themselves openly avowed the form of their inquiry and discovery, and their writings make no secret of it. It was in fact simply this: out of a few examples and particulars, with the addition of common notions and perhaps some portion of the most popular received opinions, they flew to the most general conclusions or principles of the sciences, with respect to whose fixed and immovable truth, through intermediate propositions, they extracted and proved inferior conclusions, and from these they constructed their art. And then, if any new particulars and examples were brought forward which would conflict with their opinions, they subtly fitted them into their system by distinctions or explanations of their rules, or else crudely removed them by provisos [i.e., by adding certain limiting clauses to their laws]; while for any particulars that were not conflicting, they laboured long and hard to find causes that agreed with their principles. But that was not the natural history and experience that it should have been—far from it; and that flight straight to the greatest generalities ruined everything.

126

It will also be thought, because of my injunction against uttering pronouncements and laying down fixed principles

until, through intermediate steps, the most general propositions have been properly reached, that I support a kind of
suspension of judgement, and reduce the matter to *Acatalepsy*
[the doctrine that the world is incapable of being understood].
What in fact I have in mind and propose is *Eucatalepsy* [the
doctrine that a good understanding is possible]; for I do not
disparage the sense, but help it; I do not disdain the understanding, I govern it. And it is surely better to know what one
needs to know, and yet to think one does not know everything,
than to think one knows everything and yet know nothing of
what is needed to be known.

127

It may also be asked, in doubt rather than criticism,
whether I am speaking of natural philosophy only, or whether
I mean that the other sciences—logic, ethics, politics—should
also be carried on by my method. I would answer that I
certainly do think my words have a universal application; and
just as common logic, which governs by means of the syllogism,
applies to all the sciences—not just to natural science—so my
logic, which proceeds through *induction,* also embraces all
things. For I am compiling a history and tables of discovery
about anger, fear, shame and the like, and also about political
matters, and no less about the mental actions of memory,
composition and division,[109] judgement and the rest; about all
these, just as much as about hot and cold, or light, or
vegetation or the like. But since my method of *interpretation,*
once the history has been prepared and put in order, addresses
not only the operations and discourse of the mind, as common
logic does, but the nature of things as well, I therefore so guide
the mind as to enable it to apply itself to the nature of things in
every appropriate way. And for that reason I propose many
different rules in the doctrine of *interpretation,* which to some
extent adapt the method of discovery, according to the character and condition of the subject under investigation.

---

[109]"Composition and division" are mentioned above in Aphorism I, 58,
and obliquely referred to in Aphorism I, 55.

128

On one point there should be no doubt at all, namely whether I wish to demolish and destroy the philosophy and arts and sciences which are now in use. On the contrary, I am very glad to see them used, cultivated and honoured. For I have no wish to prevent those arts and sciences that now flourish from providing food for argument, adornment for conversation, employment for professors and from being a source of profit to those in business; in short, from being accepted by common consent, like a kind of coinage. But I must make it clear that the things I am introducing will not be very suitable for such purposes, since they cannot be brought down to the common man's comprehension, except through their effects and works. But my published writings, and especially my books *On the Advancement of Learning,* will confirm the sincerity of my profession of affection and goodwill towards the received sciences, so I will make no further effort to win that argument with words. I offer this clear and firm warning, however, that by the methods now in use there will never be any great advance in the doctrines and study of the sciences, nor can those sciences be made to produce any great works.

129

It remains for me to say a few words about the excellence of the end I have in view. If I had said them at the beginning, they could have seemed more like wishes, but now that hope has been raised and unfair prejudices removed, they will perhaps have greater weight. And if I had myself completed and entirely accomplished everything, and without calling in any others from time to time to help and share the work, I would still have avoided such remarks, for fear they should be taken as a proclamation of my own merits. But since I want to encourage the efforts and rouse and kindle the spirits of others, it is fitting that I should put certain thoughts before men's minds.

In the first place, it is apparent that the bringing in of notable discoveries holds the first place by a long way among the actions of men; this was the judgement of ancient times, for they accorded divine honours to inventors, while to those who rendered distinguished service to the state (such as founders of cities and empires, legislators, those who rescued their countries from long-standing evils or were victorious over tyrants) they decreed merely the honours of heroes. And certainly, if one compares these things rightly, one will find this a fair judgement of that earlier time. For the benefits from discoveries can extend to the whole human race, civil benefits only to those in certain places. The latter, too, do not endure beyond a few generations, the former almost for all time. Moreover, a change for the better in affairs of state often comes about in violence and upheaval, but discoveries bring blessings and benefits without harm or unhappiness to anyone.

Discoveries, in fact, are like new creations, imitations of divine handiwork; as well the poet sang:

> 'Twas glorious Athens first gave wretched men
> In times of old the seeds that bore rich fruit.
> And RE-CREATED life and laid down laws.[110]

And it seems worth noticing that Solomon who, with all his empire and his gold, the magnificence of his works, his court, his household, his fleet and the splendour of his fame, stood at the summit of men's admiration, yet gloried in none of these, when he wrote that "the glory of God is to conceal a thing; the glory of a king is to search it out".[111]

Again, consider if you will the difference there is between the life of men in the most civilized province of Europe, and in the most savage and barbarous part of New India [i.e., America], and reflect that the difference is so great as truly to justify the saying "Man is a god to men", not only for the help and benefits he can bring, but also by comparing their conditions. And this difference comes not from soil, nor climate, nor bodily strength, but from the arts.

Again, it is worth noticing the great power and value and consequences of discoveries, in none more obvious than those three that were unknown to the ancients, and whose begin-

---

[110]These lines slightly misquote Lucretius (*On the Nature of Things,* VI, 1–3).

[111]Proverbs xxv, 2.

nings, although recent, were obscure and unsung, namely, the arts of *printing, gunpowder* and the *compass.* For these three have changed the whole face and condition of things throughout the world, in literature, in warfare and in navigation. From them innumerable changes followed, so much so, that no empire, no sect, no star has been seen to exert more power and influence over the affairs of men than have these mechanical discoveries.

Moreover, it is not irrelevant to distinguish three kinds, three stages as it were, in human ambition. The first is shown by those who seek to extend their own power in their own country, which is a common and unworthy kind. The second, by those who strive to extend their country's power and dominion among mankind, which sort has certainly some dignity, but is no less covetous. But the man who labours to establish and extend the power and dominion of the human race itself over the whole universe displays an ambition (if ambition it can be called) that is without doubt healthier and more noble than the others. But the dominion of man over things rests solely in the arts and the sciences. For Nature is not ruled unless she is obeyed.

And again, if the usefulness of just one particular invention has so impressed men that they deemed superhuman the man who could secure the devotion of the entire human race through some benefit he brought, how much loftier will it seem to discover something that will enable all other discoveries to be readily made? And yet, to tell the whole truth, just as it is thanks to light that we can go our ways and practise our arts, read, and recognize each other, while actually seeing the light is more excellent and beautiful than all its manifold uses; in the same way, surely, the very contemplation of things as they are, without superstition or imposture, error or confusion is in itself more praiseworthy than all the fruit of inventions.

Lastly, if objection is made to the corruption of the sciences and arts to evil purposes or to luxury and the like, not much notice should be taken of that, for as much could be said of all earthly goods, of cleverness, courage, strength, beauty, wealth, light itself and the rest. Let the human race only recover its God-given right over Nature, and be given the necessary power; then right reason and sound religion will govern the exercise of it.

130

It is now time for me to propound the art of interpreting Nature: although I believe I am offering in this art precepts of the utmost usefulness and truth, yet I do not claim that it is absolutely necessary (as if nothing could be done without it), nor that it is perfect. For it is my opinion that if men had at hand a just history of Nature and experience, and worked assiduously with it, and could impose these two rules of conduct on themselves—one, to lay aside received opinions and notions, and the other, to restrain the mind for a time from the highest generalities and those next to them—they would be able, by their own native intellect, without any other art, to adopt and fall in with my form of interpretation. For once the obstacles are out of the way, interpretation is a true and natural operation of the mind; but with my precepts, everything will assuredly be in better readiness and much more dependable.

I do not affirm, however, that nothing can be added to these precepts; on the contrary, I, who consider the mind not only in its natural capacity but in its connection with things, cannot but believe that the art of discovery may grow with the number of new discoveries.

The Second Book of Aphorisms Concerning the Interpretation of Nature or the Kingdom of Man

APHORISM

1

It is the task and purpose of human power to generate and superinduce a new nature or new natures on a given body. It is the task and purpose of human knowledge to discover the form of a given nature, or its true specific difference, or nature-engendering nature,[112] or source of emanation (for these are the terms I have which come closest to the thing). And subordinate to these primary tasks there are two others, secondary and of an inferior character; subordinate to the former, the transformation of one material substance into another, within the bounds of *possibility;* subordinate to the latter, the discovery, in every instance of generation and motion, of the *latent process* operating continuously from the manifest efficient and the manifest material [causes] to the resulting form; and likewise the discovery of the *latent schematism*[113] of bodies at rest and not in motion.

---

[112]"Nature-engendering nature" is Ellis's translation of *natura naturans,* literally, "nature naturing". It is the internal state of a body that is responsible for a corresponding observable nature. In Spinoza's philosophical system, the phrase came to mean God, as the immanent cause of the universe.

[113]"Latent process" is explained by Bacon in Aphorisms II, 5 and 6, *below.*

By "latent schematism" Bacon means a body's hidden, inner structure, or arrangement of parts; in Aphorism II, 39, he says that latent

2

In what an unhappy state human knowledge of today finds itself is clear even from common maxims. It is correctly laid down that "To know truly is to know through causes".[114] And these causes are rightly divided into four kinds: the material, the formal, the efficient and the final.[115] But of these the final cause, so far from assisting the sciences, actually corrupts them, except for those concerned with human actions; the discovery of the formal cause is a forlorn hope; while efficient

---

CONTINUED FROM PAGE 133

schematism may be seen through a microscope. Bacon often also speaks just of the "schematisms" of a body or of matter, by which he seems to mean its manifest physical properties as they arise out of its inner structure. They are, he says in Aphorism II, 40 (4), "related to dissimilarities of the parts contained in the same body, and to their arrangements and dispositions". In the *De Augmentis*, III, iv, Bacon lists some schematisms of matter:

> Abstract physics may most rightly be divided into two parts—the doctrine concerning the Schematisms of Matter and the doctrine concerning Appetites and Motions. Both of these I will quickly enumerate, and thence may be derived some shadow of the true Physics of Abstracts. The Schematisms of Matter are: dense, rare; heavy, light; hot, cold; tangible, pneumatic; volatile, fixed; determinate, fluid; moist, dry; fat, crude; hard, soft; fragile, tensile; porous, close; spirituous, jejune; simple, compound; absolute, imperfectly mixed; fibrous and full of veins, simple of structure or uniform; homogeneous, heterogeneous; specific, non-specific; organic, inorganic; animate, inanimate. Further I do not go.

We have followed Graham Rees's suggestion to translate *schematismus* simply as "schematism", though "constitution" would also do. (Rees, "Bacon's philosophy: some new sources", in *Francis Bacon: Terminologia e Fortuna nel XVII Seculo,* ed. M. Fattori, Edizioni dell' Ateneo, Rome.)

[114]Aristotle, *Posterior Analytics,* I, ii.

[115]Aristotle's four types of "cause" were intended to provide answers to four kinds of question. The material cause is that out of which a thing is made; the formal cause is the structure of its constituents which makes it what it is, its essence, in other words; the efficient cause is the initiator of a change, and comes closest to the current concept of a cause; and the final cause is the end or goal towards which the thing is working. The idea behind this classification is that Nature operates like a craftsman who starts off with certain raw materials producing a definite form or shape and guided by a plan.

and material causes (of the kind that are sought and accepted, that is, causes remote and removed from the *latent process* leading to the form) are perfunctory and superficial, and contribute almost nothing to true and active knowledge. Not that I have forgotten that I earlier noticed [in Aphorism I, 51], and corrected as an error of the human mind, the view that forms are the primary essences. For although nothing truly exists in Nature except separate bodies performing separate pure actions, in conformity with a law; in philosophy, on the other hand, that very law and the search for, discovery, and explanation of it, are the foundation of knowledge as well as of operation. And this *law,* and its clauses, I call by the name of forms, chiefly because that term has come into common and familiar use.

3

If someone knows the cause of any nature, such as whiteness or heat, in certain objects only, his knowledge is imperfect; and if anyone can superinduce an effect on certain materials only (among those that are susceptible to such an effect), his power likewise is imperfect. But if someone knows only the efficient and material cause (causes which are variable, and only vehicles, and causes that convey the form in certain cases),[116] he can make new discoveries on a substance to some extent similar and suitably prepared, but he does not move the more deeply fixed boundaries of things. But the person who knows forms embraces the unity of Nature in substances utterly different from each other, and can therefore uncover and produce effects that have never been produced before, such as neither the vicissitudes of Nature, nor tireless experimenting nor mere chance would ever have brought into being, and which men would never have thought of. For this reason, both truth in contemplation and freedom in operation follow from the discovery of forms.

---

[116]Thus to take an example that Bacon himself uses, fire is an efficient cause of hardening in clay, but it is not an invariable cause of hardening, since it produces softening in wax.

4

Although the roads to human power and human knowledge are closely linked and more or less the same, yet because of the harmful and inveterate habit of dwelling on abstractions, it is much safer to begin and raise up sciences from those foundations that relate to the active part, and let that part indicate and determine the contemplative part. If therefore someone wanted to generate and superinduce any nature on a given body, we must see what kind of precept, direction or guidance he would most wish for; and express that in language that is simple and not at all abstruse.

If, for example, one wished to superinduce on silver the yellow colour of gold, or an increase in weight (within the laws of matter), or transparency on any stone that is not transparent, or toughness on glass, or vegetable life on a non-vegetable body, we must consider, I say, what precept or guidance one would most wish to be given.

First of all, no doubt, one will want to be shown something that will not fail in operation, nor disappoint in experiment. In the second place, one will wish for such a rule as does not restrict one to certain means or particular methods of operation. For one may perhaps not have such means, nor possess the opportunity and ability to create or procure them conveniently. And if there are other means or methods, besides that advised, for producing the required nature, they may be among those which are in the operator's power to use, but from which he is nevertheless barred, by reason of the narrowness of the rule given him, so that he fails to obtain a result. And in the third place, he will want to be shown something which is not just as difficult as the very operation he is investigating, but comes nearer to what is practicable.

Thus for a true and complete rule of operation, the proposition will be as follows: *it should be certain, free,*[117] *and inclining to or having relation to action.* And this also holds good for the discovery of the true form. For the form of any nature is such that when it is there, the given nature infallibly follows. It is

---

[117]The rule of operation should be "free" in the sense intended in the second point of the previous paragraph, and in the previous aphorism, namely, of not being unnecessarily restrictive.

therefore always present when that nature is present, and universally implies it, and is in it in all cases. Again, the form is such that, once it is removed, the given nature invariably flees also. It is therefore always absent when that nature is absent, and always implies its absence, and is in it alone.[118] Finally, the true form is such that it derives the given nature from some source of being that is inherent in more natures, and is (as they say) better known to Nature (*notior naturae*)[119] than the form itself. So for a true and perfect axiom of knowledge the proposition or precept would be as follows: *that another nature be discovered which is interchangeable with the given nature, and yet is a limitation of a more general nature (naturae notioris), as of a true genus.* These two propositions, the active and the contemplative, are the same things, and what in operation is of the most use, that in knowledge has the most truth.

5

Now the precept or axiom concerning the transformation of bodies is of two kinds. The first regards a body as a troop or collection of simple natures; thus in gold the following occur together: that which is yellow; that which is heavy, up to a certain weight; that which is malleable or ductile, to a certain extent; that which is not volatile, and is not consumed by fire; that which becomes fluid, to a certain degree; that which can be separated and dissolved by certain means; and so on, through all the natures that are united in gold. An axiom of this kind therefore derives the thing from the forms of simple natures. For whoever knows the forms of yellowness, weight, ductility, fixity [i.e., non-volatility], fluidity, solutions,[120] and

---

[118]This sentence is rather compressed: "It [i.e., the form] is therefore always absent when that nature is absent, and [the absence of the form] always implies its [i.e., that nature's] absence, and is in it [i.e., in that nature] alone."

[119]On the meaning of *notior naturae,* see footnote 12.

[120]"Solutions" refers to the aspect of gold just mentioned that it "can be separated and dissolved (*solvatur*) by certain means", presumably with acids.

so on, and the means of superinducing them, and their degrees and measures, will see and ensure that these natures may be combined in a certain body, and from this, transformation into gold would follow. And this kind of operation pertains to primary action. For the principle of generating a single simple nature is the same as that of generating many, except that we are more hampered and restricted in dealing with several natures because of the difficulty of uniting so many, which do not readily combine, except in the natural and ordinary course of things. It has to be said, however, that this method of operation (that looks at simple natures, albeit in a concrete body) proceeds from those things that in Nature are immutable and eternal and universal, and opens up for human power broad paths, such as the comprehension of man (as things now stand) can scarcely grasp or imagine.

Now the second kind of axiom, that concerned with the discovery of the *latent process,* does not proceed through simple natures but through concrete bodies, as they are found in the ordinary course of Nature. As for example, when inquiry is made into the generation of gold, or any other metal or stone; from what beginnings it came, how and by what process, from its first seeds or earliest rudiments down to the perfect mineral; or similarly, by what process plants are generated, from the first coalescence of juices in the earth, or from seeds, to the fully-formed plant, with all the successive motions and diverse and continued efforts of Nature; similarly, how animals are generated and develop through the stages from copulation to birth; and likewise concerning other bodies.

This inquiry however does not only have in view the generation of bodies, but also other motions and operations of Nature. As for example, when inquiry is made into the whole series and continued action in nutrition, from the first reception of food to its complete assimilation; or likewise into voluntary motion in animals, from the first impression on the imagination, and the continued efforts of the spirit, through to the bendings and movements of the limbs; or the development from the movement of the tongue and lips and other organs through to the utterance of articulate sounds. Thus these inquiries also consider natures that are concrete, or conjoined and in a structure; and they are directed to what we may call Nature's particular, special patterns of behaviour, not to her fundamental, general laws, which constitute forms. On the other hand, it must be confessed that this course seems the quicker and nearer at hand, and to offer better hope than that primary one.

In the same way, the operative part, which corresponds to this contemplative part, starts from the ordinary things that are found in Nature and extends its operation to those things that are nearest, or at least not far removed from them; but deeper, radical operations on Nature depend entirely on primary axioms. And where man has not the ability to operate, but only to gain knowledge, as in the case of the heavenly bodies (for it is not given to man to operate on them or change or transform them), even then, inquiry into the fact itself, or the truth of the thing, no less than knowledge of causes and consents[121] must be carried back to those primary and universal axioms concerning simple natures, such as the nature of spontaneous rotation, of attraction or magnetism, and of many other things of a more general kind than the heavenly bodies themselves. Certainly, no one can hope to determine whether it is the earth or the heavens that are rotating in diurnal motion, unless he first understands the nature of spontaneous rotation.[122]

6

Now this *latent process* of which I speak is very different from anything that the minds of men, beset as they now are, can easily conceive. For I am not thinking of certain visible measures or signs or steps of a process in bodies, but entirely of a continuous process that is largely hidden from the sense.

For example, in all generation and transformation of

[121]"Consents" between bodies, or parts of bodies, are sympathetic responses in the one when an alteration occurs in the other.

[122]Spontaneous rotation is the subject of one of Bacon's inquiries in Aphorism II, 36 (*3*) and Aphorism II, 48 (*17*). Bacon was not in fact well disposed to the idea that the earth had a diurnal motion, as he indicates, for example, in Aphorism II, 46, and in other writings of his. Bacon's view of the matter is discussed in Urbach, *Francis Bacon's Philosophy of Science,* pp. 129–34.

bodies, what is lost and given off, what remains, and what is added, must all be investigated, as also what is expanded, what contracted; what is united, what separated; what is continued, what cut off; what impels, what impedes; what dominates, what yields; and much else.

And these facts are not only to be sought in the generation or transformation of bodies; but also in all other alterations and motions, a similar inquiry must be made into what occurs before, what after; what is quicker, what is slower; what produces motion, what checks it; and things of that kind. But all these things are quite unknown and untouched by the sciences, entangled as they are in the most stupid and downright useless web of so-called learning. For seeing that every natural action proceeds through the smallest particles, or at least those too small to be perceived by the sense, no one should expect to control or alter Nature unless he has properly understood and noted them.

7

Similarly, the investigation and discovery of the *latent schematism* in bodies is also a new thing, no less than the discovery of the *latent process* and the form. Indeed, so far, we are plainly only treading the outer courts of Nature and not preparing the way into her inner chambers. Yet no one can bestow a new nature on a given body, or successfully and appositely transform it into a new body, unless he has a good knowledge of the body that is to be altered or transformed. For otherwise he will run into fruitless methods, or at least difficult and perverse ones, unsuited to the nature of the body on which he is working. It is clear therefore that a way to this must also be opened and constructed.

In the anatomy of organisms such as man and animals, some sound and profitable work has certainly been done, work which seems to be a subtle undertaking and a good examination of Nature. But this kind of anatomy is concerned with what can be seen or perceived by the sense, and has its place in organisms alone. Certainly it is simple and straightforward, compared with the true anatomy of the schematism hidden within bodies that are regarded as uniform, especially in things that have a specific character, and in their parts, like iron or stone; or in the parts of uniform structure of a plant or animal, like a root, leaf, flower, flesh or blood or bone, etc. And even in this field men's industry has not been altogether lacking, as is shown by the separation of uniform bodies by distillations and other methods of resolving them, so that the complex nature of a compound may become apparent by combining its homogeneous parts. This also is a useful exercise, and conduces to our object, though more often it is deceptive, in that many natures that have really been newly superinduced and imparted by fire or heat or other means of opening[123] are thought to be caused by separation, as if they existed before in the compound. But these things too are only a small part of the work of discovering the true schematism in a compound, which is a far more subtle and exact thing, and something which the actions of fire throw into disorder rather than elicit and bring to light.

The separation and resolution of bodies must, therefore, be performed, certainly not by fire, but by reasoning and true *induction,* with the help of experiments, and through comparison with other bodies, and the reduction to the simple natures, and their forms, that occur together and are interwoven in the compound; we must pass, it is clear, from Vulcan to Minerva,[124] if we intend to bring to light the true structures and schematisms of bodies, on which depend every hidden and, as they say, specific property and virtue in things, and from which also the rule governing every powerful alteration and transformation is derived.

For example, we should try and find out how much spirit there is in every body, and how much tangible essence; and as to that spirit, whether it is abundant and swelling, or meagre and scanty, tenuous or denser, more akin to air or to fire, active or inactive, weak or strong, in advance or in retreat, cut off or continuous, in agreement with external and surrounding objects, or in disagreement, and so forth. And we should make similar inquiries into the tangible essence (which admits of no

---

[123]"Opening", "separation" and "solution" (here translated "resolution") are closely related terms, indicating the breaking down of a substance into parts, for instance by distillation. See footnote 240 on page 236, *below.*

[124]Vulcan was the Roman God of Fire, Minerva the Goddess of Wisdom.

fewer differences than the spirit), into its surface texture, its fibres and its whole structure; and also into the disposition of the spirit through the bodily mass, with its pores, passages, veins and cells and the rudiments and first efforts of the organized body. But in these inquiries too, and for that matter in any discovery of latent schematism, a true and clear light is shed by the primary axioms, which effectively dispels all obscurity and subtlety.

8

In this way we shall be led, not to the atom, which presupposes a vacuum and immutable substance (both of which are false) but to real particles, such as are found.[125] Nor again is there cause for alarm at the subtlety of the inquiry, as if it were inexplicable; on the contrary, the closer the inquiry comes to simple natures, the more intelligible and clear will everything become; the business will be transferred from the complicated to the simple, from the incommensurable to the commensurable,[126] from the irrational to the rational [numbers or quantities], from the indefinite and doubtful to the definite and certain, as happens in the letters of the alphabet and the notes of a harmony. Now the study of Nature proceeds best when physics is bounded by mathematics. And no one should be afraid of large numbers or of fractions. For in things

[125]In his *Thoughts on the Nature of Things*, Bacon distinguished an atomism "which presupposes a vacuum" from one which simply asserts that matter is composed of indivisible particles; the latter, he said, may be "safely and securely laid down". He drew the further distinction between an atomism in which the ultimate particles were similar and one in which they had different shapes and sizes. It was the latter version of atomism that was, according to Bacon, based on a denial of the universal transmutability of substances, and which Bacon saw no reason to adopt. All in all, Bacon does not seem to be rejecting atomism *tout court* here, just one form of that doctrine. (There is detailed discussion of these points in Urbach, *Francis Bacon's Philosophy of Science.*)

[126]In Aphorism I, 66, Bacon speaks disapprovingly of the practice of seeking explanations in terms of "subtle and incommensurable mixtures" of primary qualities, by which he meant the qualities moist, dry, hot and cold, of Aristotelian physics. The incommensurables mentioned here are perhaps those same primary qualities.

that are dealt with by number, it is as easy to posit or conceive a thousand as one, or a thousandth part of one as the whole number one.

9

From the two kinds of axioms set out above, there arises a fitting division of philosophy and the sciences, adapting the received terms (which come nearest to expressing the matter) to my meaning. Namely, that the investigation of *forms,* which are (by reason, certainly, and in accordance with their law)[127] eternal and unchanging, constitutes metaphysics, while inquiry into the *efficient,* and *material* causes, and the *latent process* and the *latent schematism* (which all have regard to the common or ordinary course of Nature, not fundamental and eternal laws) constitutes physics. And subordinate to these there are, similarly, two practical divisions; for physics, the mechanical arts; for metaphysics—because of its broad paths and its greater command over Nature—magic (in the purified sense of the word).[128]

10

Having thus set up the goal of my teaching I must now go on to the precepts—and that in the most direct and straightforward order. Now the directions for the interpretation of Nature are of two separate kinds: the first for eliciting or

---

[127]Ellis suggests that this obscure remark is a saving clause indicating that God could, if He chose, change the forms. We think it more probably means that forms were, by their very nature, eternal.

[128]This parenthetic comment is clarified by Bacon in his *De Augmentis,* III, v: "I must here stipulate that magic, which has long been used in a bad sense, be again restored to its ancient and honourable meaning. For among the Persians magic was taken for a sublime wisdom, and a knowledge of the universal consents of things; and so the three kings who came from the east to worship Christ were called by the name of Magi. I however understand it as the science which applies the knowledge of hidden forms to the production of wonderful operations; and by uniting (as they say) actives with passives, displays the wonderful works of nature". These remarks closely resemble those of John Baptista Porta in book I, ch. 2 of his *Natural Magic.*

devising axioms from experience, the second for drawing or deriving new experiments from axioms. The former again is divided three ways, that is, into three provisions: that for the sense, for the memory, and for the mind or reason.

First of all, a sufficient and suitable *natural and experimental history* must be compiled. That is fundamental to the matter. For there must be no imagining or supposing, but simply discovering, what Nature does or undergoes.

But this *natural and experimental history* is so various and scattered that it would confuse and distract the understanding, unless it is set out and presented in a suitable order, for which purpose *tables* and *arrangements of instances* should be drawn up, and put together in such a manner and order as to enable the understanding to deal with them.

Even if this is done, the understanding acting freely and spontaneously is still inadequate and unfitted to the work of forming axioms unless guided and guarded. In the third place, therefore, we must employ a legitimate and true *induction,* which is the very *key of interpretation.* I must therefore begin with this third provision, and then go back to the others.

11

The investigation of forms proceeds in this way. For a given nature, there must first be made a *presentation*[129] *to the understanding* of all known *instances* which agree in the same nature, though in the most dissimilar materials. And such a collection must be compiled as a simple account, with no premature speculation or any great refinement. For example, take the investigation of the form of heat.

INSTANCES AGREEING IN THE NATURE OF HEAT

1. The rays of the sun, especially in summer and at midday.
2. The sun's rays reflected and condensed, as between

---

[129]The term in the Latin is a legal one indicating the action of formally presenting oneself in a court of law as a party to a cause.

mountains or by walls, and especially in burning-glasses.[130]

3. Fiery meteors.[131]
4. Burning thunderbolts.[132]
5. Eruptions of flames from cavities in mountains, etc.
6. All flame.
7. Ignited solids.[133]
8. Natural hot springs.
9. Boiling or heated liquids.
10. Hot vapours and fumes and the air itself, which acquires a very fierce and glowing heat if it is shut in, as in reverberatory furnaces.[134]
11. Certain weathers that are fine and cloudless by virtue of the very constitution of the air, irrespective of the time of year.
12. Air shut up underground in some caverns, especially in winter.
13. All hairy substances, such as wool, the hides of animals, and down, have some warmth.
14. All bodies, whether solid or liquid, dense or rare (like air itself), when brought close to fire for a time.
15. Sparks produced from flint and steel through violent percussion.
16. Any body that is rubbed hard, such as stone, wood, cloth, etc.; so much so, that wagon-shafts and wheel axles sometimes catch fire; indeed, the way the West Indians kindled fire was by friction.

---

[130]A burning-glass may be either a convex lens, or a concave mirror, both of which have the power of focusing the sun's rays on an object.

[131]Meteors were any kind of atmospheric phenomenon. Fiery meteors refers in particular to shooting stars, lightning, etc.

[132]The electrical nature of lightning was not understood in Bacon's day and the term *thunderbolt* reflects the ancient belief that the damage it causes was produced by a bolt or dart discharged by the gods.

[133]When Bacon talks of a body being "ignited", he does not mean that it has been kindled into a flame but—in accordance with seventeenth century usage—that it has been heated by fire and made intensely or glowing hot.

[134]A reverberatory furnace is one constructed in such a manner that the flame is forced back on the substance exposed to it.

17. Green and damp vegetation simultaneously confined and bruised, as for example, roses crushed in
baskets; so much so, that hay, if stored wet, often
catches fire.

18. Quicklime, when sprinkled with water.

19. Iron, when first dissolved by strong solvents[135] in a
glass vessel, even without being placed near fire;
similarly tin, but not so intensely.

20. Animals, especially and continuously through their
inner parts; although in insects the heat is not
perceptible to the touch, because of the smallness
of their bodies.

21. Horse dung, and similar fresh animal excrements.

22. Strong oil of sulphur and of vitriol has the effect of
heat in burning linen.[136]

23. Oil of marjoram and of similar herbs has the effect
of heat in burning the bones of teeth.

---

[135]We have followed the *Oxford English Dictionary* in translating *aquae
fortes* (literally: strong waters) as strong solvents. From Instance 25, under the Table of Deviation, II, 12, *below,* it is clear that Bacon included in
the term both aqua regia (a mixture of nitric and hydrochloric acids) and
aqua fortis (nitric acid). In his *Sylva Sylvarum,* 495, Bacon mentions that
strong waters can be made from Sundew, a plant discussed in Aphorism
II, 50 (3), *below.*

[136]Oil of vitriol is generally agreed to be concentrated sulphuric acid,
and oil of sulphur is usually, but somewhat more tentatively, identified
with the same acid. Thus Fowler (1878, p. 357) conjectured that Bacon is
exploiting the rhetorical device of using both terms to refer to the single
acid. However, in his table indicating the densities of various substances,
Bacon lists the two oils separately and finds the density of oil of vitriol to
be a little less than that of ivory and rather more than that of oil of
sulphur, to which is ascribed the same density as chalk. (*History of Dense
and Rare, Works,* V, p. 341)
Paracelsus gave the following recipe for oil of vitriol: "Take as much
vitriol (metal sulphate) as you will, and distil it by descent. It renders a
bright green oil, and is called milk of mercury. But it must have a large
fire; it is like in its nature to balsam", and in another method of preparing
oil of vitriol, a milky white fluid is said to be obtained. Paracelsus prepared oil of sulphur by putting a liquefied mixture of sulphur, tartar and
glass gall (the latter being a whitish scum thrown up by fused glass) into
a strong salt solution. (*A Manual of Paracelsus the Great,* in *The Hermetical and Alchemical Writings of Paracelsus,* II, p. 349)

24. Strong, well-rectified spirit of wine [i.e., alcohol]
has the effect of heat, in that the white of an egg
dropped into it hardens and becomes white, almost
like cooked eggwhite; and bread put in it becomes
dry and crusty like toast.

25. Aromatic and hot plants, like dracunculus, old nasturtium,[137] etc., although not warm to the hand
(whether whole or powdered), yet if chewed a little,
feel hot and almost burning on the tongue and
palate.

26. Strong vinegar, and all acids, on all parts of the
body where there is no epidermis, like the eyes, the
tongue, or any other part that has been injured
and deprived of skin, cause pain not very different
from that induced by heat.

27. Even keen and hard frosts bring a certain burning
feeling—"Nor burns the North Wind's piercing
cold".[138]

28. Other instances.

This table I call the *Table of Existence and Presence.*

12

Secondly, we must make a presentation to the understanding of instances that lack the given nature, for the form, as I
have said [in Aphorism II, 4], should be absent when the
nature is absent no less than be present when the nature is
present. But to list all these would be endless.

The *negatives* should therefore be subjoined with the

---

[137]Dracunculus is a member of the Arum family, whose hotness was
well known in the sixteenth and seventeenth centuries and was remarked
on, for example, in the standard herbal by Gerarde; Gerarde also says of
nasturtium that it "is sharpe and biting to the tongue; and therefore is
very hot and drie . . . the seed is much more biting than the herbe, and is
hot and drie almost in the fourth degree". Bacon commended young nasturtium as a tonic for the blood (*History of Life and Death*, v (21)).

[138]Bacon is slightly misquoting from Virgil's *Georgics*, I, 93: "Lest the
thin rains or the fierce power of the violent sun or the North Wind's
piercing cold burn them".

affirmatives, and absences investigated only in those objects which are most akin to those in which the given nature is present and apparent. This I call the *Table of Deviation,* or *Absence in Proximity.*[139]

Instances in Proximity, where the Nature of Heat Is Absent

To the first *affirmative* instance, the first *negative* or subjoined instance. 1. The rays of the moon and of stars and comets are not found warm to the touch. In fact the sharpest frosts are observed when the moon is full. But the larger fixed stars, when the sun approaches them or is near them, are thought to increase and intensify the sun's heat, as happens when the sun sits in Leo and in the dog-days.[140]

Subjoined to the 2nd 2. The sun's rays do not give out heat in the middle region of the air, as they call it,[141] and the reason which is commonly given for this is not a bad one, namely, that this region is neither close enough to the body of the sun, from which its rays emanate, nor to the earth, from which they are reflected. And this is clear from the summits of mountains (unless they are very high), where snows last perpetually. It has however been noticed by some that on the summit of the Peak of Tenerife and also in the Peruvian Andes, the mountaintops themselves are bare of snow, which lies only somewhat lower down.[142] Moreover, the air itself on those same

---

[139]Absence in Proximity: that is, absence of the nature in question in substances that bear a close affinity or kinship to another in which that nature does exist.

[140]The dog-days occur around the time of the solar rising of either Sirius, the greater dog-star, or Canicula, the lesser dog-star. This period was reputed from ancient times to be the hottest and most unwholesome of the year. Seneca, in his *Natural Questions,* VII, 27, asks, "Why is it that in Leo the sun is always blazing and scorches the earth with its heat . . . ?"

[141]The regions of the air occupied the space between the moon and the earth, as Bacon says in his *Aphorisms on the Composition of the Primary History,* Aphorism 4, *below.* The middle region of the air is evidently at mountaintop height.

[142]The Peak of Tenerife is a spectacular cone-shaped mountain whose base occupies nearly two thirds of the island of Tenerife and which rises to over 12,000 feet above sea level. In Bacon's time the Peak was proverbial for its height and size.

summits is not felt to be very cold, but only thin and keen, to such a degree that in the Andes it pricks and hurts the eyes through its excessive sharpness, and even pricks the mouth of the stomach and induces vomiting. And it was observed by the ancients that at the summit of Olympus the thinness of the air was such that those who climbed it had to take with them sponges soaked in vinegar and water, and repeatedly apply them to their mouth and nostrils, the air being too thin for respiration. And on that summit, it was even reported, so great was the calmness and stillness of the air, free from rain and snow and wind, that letters traced by a finger by those making sacrifice in the ashes of the burnt offerings on the altar of Jupiter remained there quite undisturbed the following year. And even today, men climbing to the summit of the Peak of Tenerife do so by night and not by day, and soon after sunrise are warned and urged by their guides to hasten down, apparently because of the danger that they might faint and suffocate from the thinness of the air.[143]

To the 2nd 3. The reflection of the sun's rays in the regions of the polar circles is found to be very weak and ineffectual in producing heat; so much so, that the Netherlanders, who spent the winter in Nova Zembla, when in early July they expected their ship to be freed from the mass of ice that hemmed her in, were disappointed in their hopes and had to take to their boats.[144] The direct rays of the sun, therefore, do not seem to

---

[143]This was reported by José de Acosta in Book III of his celebrated work *A Natural and Moral History of the Indies,* 1590. Bacon refers explicitly to Acosta in Aphorism II, 36, *below.*

[144]The incident described relates to the Dutch navigator, Willem Barents, who in 1596 made his third expedition to Nova Zembla, or 'New Land', an Arctic island off the coast of European Russia discovered in the mid-sixteenth century. The two ships under Barents's command separated, and his own, after rounding the north of Nova Zembla, stuck fast in the ice and was forced to winter in the north. Because his ship was still ice-bound the following summer, most of the crew abandoned her, leaving in two open boats on 13 June (not July); most of those who fled survived, but Barents himself died on 20 June 1597. These events were related by Gerrit de Veer in his work *The Three Voyages of Barents,* 1598, and were confirmed by the discovery in 1871 of the house where Barents holed up, and by the further discovery in 1875 of his notebooks, which had been preserved in the snow.

have much strength, even on level ground, nor when they are reflected, unless they are multiplied and combined, as happens when the sun is nearly at its perpendicular. For then the incidence of the rays makes more acute angles, so that the lines of the rays are closer together; whereas, on the other hand, when the sun shines very obliquely, the angles are very obtuse, so the lines of the rays are further apart. But it should be noted as well that there may be many actions of the sun's rays, and those also arising from the nature of heat, which are not proportioned to our sense of touch; so that while they produce no heat as far as we are concerned, in respect of some other bodies they may have that effect.

To the 2nd   4. Have an experiment of this kind performed. Take a lens made in the opposite way to a burning-glass [so that it is concave] and place it between your hand and the sun's rays, and note whether it reduces the heat of the sun, in the way that a burning-glass increases and intensifies it. For it is clear that optic rays make images appear larger or smaller according as the glass is made thicker in the middle or at the edge. Observe therefore whether there is the same effect with heat.

To the 2nd   5. Try carefully an experiment to see whether the moon's rays passing through the most powerful and well-made burning-glasses can be received and so collected to produce even the smallest degree of warmth. And if this degree of warmth is too slight and weak to be felt, recourse should be had to those glass vessels which indicate the hot or cold state of the air.[145] Thus, let the rays of the moon fall through a burning-glass and strike the top of the glass vessel, then mark whether the water level falls as a result of the warmth.

To the 2nd   6. Let a burning-glass also be used on a hot object that does not emit rays or light, like iron or stone when they are heated but not ignited, or on boiling water, and the like, and mark whether there is any increase of heat, as there is with the sun's rays.

---

[145]The glass vessels Bacon is referring to are the primitive air thermometers which he elsewhere calls graduated or calendar glasses and which he describes very fully under Instance 38 of the Table of Comparison, Aphorism II, 13, *below.*

To the 2nd 7. Try also a burning-glass with an ordinary flame.[146]

To the 3rd 8. Comets (if we may reckon them also among meteors)[147] are not found to have any lasting or obvious effect in increasing the warmth of the season, although droughts are fairly often observed to follow them. Moreover beams and columns of light and chasms and the like appear more often in the winter-time than in summer, and most of all in times of the severest frost, but accompanied by droughts.[148] Thunderbolts and lightning and thunder, on the other hand, rarely occur in the winter, but during the time of great heat. But falling stars, as they are called, are commonly thought to consist of some bright and glowing viscous substance rather than to be of a strongly fiery nature. However, this should be further investigated.

To the 4th 9. There are some lightning flashes that give light but do not burn, but these always occur without thunder.[149]

To the 5th 10. Volcanic eruptions, some with flames, are found

---

[146]This experiment and others similar to those mentioned in the previous paragraph had in fact already been described by Porta in his *Natural Magic,* book 2, ch. 4.

[147]Whether comets were meteors is discussed by Seneca, in book VII of his *Natural Questions.*

[148]Aristotle discussed the same phenomena in his *Meteorology,* 342a 34–35: "Sometimes on a clear night a number of appearances can be seen taking shape in the sky, such as 'chasms', 'trenches' and blood-red colours". And Seneca in his *Natural Questions* I, 14.1, describes chasms as occurring when "some area of the sky settles and, gaping in hiding (so to speak), sends out flame". Pliny, *Natural History,* II, 97 : "There also occurs a yawning of the sky itself, called chasms and also something that looks like blood, and a fire that falls from it to the earth, the most alarming possible cause of terror to mankind, as happened in the third year of the 107th Olympiad [349 BC], when King Philip was throwing Greece into turmoil".

The phenomena in question appear to be those of the Aurora Borealis, which, though much more common further north, is sometimes seen in the Mediterranean. However, the Aurora Borealis is not more active in winter than in summer, but goes through a maximum in October and March, and a minimum in June and January.

[149]The lightning referred to here appears to be that known as heat-lightning, which is the diffuse illumination observed when the lightning flashes are too distant for the thunder to be heard.

no less often in cold regions than in hot, as in Iceland and Greenland. In cold regions too the trees are often more inflammable and resinous and contain more pitch, like firs, pines and others, than in warm regions. But there has not been enough inquiry into the situation and the kind of soil where such eruptions usually occur for us to be able to subjoin a negative to this affirmative instance.

To the 6th 11. Flames are always either more or less hot, and there is no negative to be subjoined at all; and yet the so-called *ignis fatuus*,[150] which sometimes even settles on a wall, is said to have little heat, perhaps as much as the flames of spirit of wine, which are mild and gentle. But milder still seems to be the flame that, according to some trustworthy and serious accounts, appeared round the heads and hair of boys and girls, not singeing their hair at all, but gently flickering about them. And it is a most assured fact that a certain coruscation can sometimes be seen round a sweating horse on a journey by night in clear weather, without any obvious sign of heat. And a few years ago it was widely spoken of as if it was a miracle, that the apron of a certain girl gave off sparks when moved or rubbed slightly; which happened perhaps because of the alum or other salts used in the dye, adhering rather thickly to it and forming a crust, which was then broken by the rubbing. It is also most certain that all sugar, whether refined (as they call it) or raw, so long as it is somewhat hard, gives off sparks when broken or scraped with a knife in the dark. Similarly, sea and salt water are sometimes found to give off sparks when struck hard by oars. And in tempests also the sea foam sparkles when violently agitated at night; a sparkling which the Spaniards call *sea lung*.[151] Also no adequate inquiry has been made into

---

[150]*Ignis fatuus,* literally, "foolish fire", is a pale flame that occurs sometimes over marshes, and is generally reckoned to be due to the spontaneous ignition of gases, particularly methane, from decomposing plant and animal matter. The flame is also known as "will-o'-the wisp".

[151]Fowler cites a passage from Charles Darwin's *A Naturalist's Voyage Round the World,* 1845, Ch. 8, which nicely describes this phenomenon: "While sailing a little south of the Plata on one very dark night, the sea presented a wonderful and most beautiful spectacle. There was a fresh breeze, and every part of the surface, which during the day is seen as foam, now glowed with a pale light. The vessel drove before her bows two

what sort of heat is possessed by that flame, which sailors of old used to call *Castor and Pollux* and modern sailors call *St. Elmo's Fire.*[152]

To the 7th 12. Everything ignited so that it turns a fiery red, albeit without a flame, is always hot, and there is no negative to be subjoined to that affirmative. But the thing which comes nearest to it seems to be rotten wood, which glows at night and yet has no perceptible heat; and the rotting scales of fish also shine at night, but are not found warm to the touch, nor again is the body of a glow-worm, or the fly called *Lucciola,* warm to the touch.

To the 8th 13. No adequate inquiry has been made into the situation or the nature of the soil where hot springs emerge, so no negative instance may be subjoined.

To the 9th 14. To warm liquids is subjoined the negative instance of liquid itself in its own nature. For no tangible liquid is found to be naturally hot and to remain so indefinitely; it may merely have heat superinduced upon it for a time, as a nature foreign to it; so that the liquids hottest in their power and effect, like spirit of wine, chemical oils of spices, even oils of vitriol and sulphur and such like, which after a short time burn, are cold at the first touch. But water from hot springs, once taken up in any vessel and separated from its source, cools just like water that has been heated by fire. On the other hand, an oily body is less cold to the touch than an aqueous one, as oil is less cold to the touch than water, and silk less than linen. However, this belongs to the *Table of Degrees of Cold.*

---

billows of liquid phosphorus, and in her wake she was followed by a milky train. As far as the eye reached, the crest of every wave was bright, and the sky above the horizon, from the reflected glare of these livid flames, was not so utterly obscure as over the vault of the heavens." The phosphorescence is due to living creatures whose natural phosphorescence is stimulated by the movement of the water.

[152]St. Elmo's Fire is the ball of light which is sometimes seen on a ship during a storm, especially about the masts or yard-arms. The phenomenon was remarked on by Seneca (*Natural Questions,* I, 1. 13–16): "In a great storm, stars of a sort appear, settling on the sails. Sailors in danger then believe they are being helped by the divine power of Pollux and Castor". Pliny the Elder also describes the phenomenon in his *Natural History,* II,101.

To the 10th   15. Similarly, the nature of vapour itself, as we find it, is subjoined as a negative to hot vapour. For exhalations from oily substances, though readily inflammable, are yet not found to be hot, unless they have recently been exhaled from a hot body.

To the 10th   16. In a similar way, the negative instance of the nature of air itself is subjoined to hot air. For we do not find air to be hot, unless it is enclosed, or subjected to friction,[153] or plainly heated by the sun or fire or some other hot body.

To the 11th   17. Here may be subjoined the negative of unseasonably cold weather, which we find occurring when East or North winds blow; just as we have weather of the opposite kind, when the South or West winds blow. Likewise, a tendency to rain, especially in winter-time, comes with mild weather, while frost, on the other hand, comes with cold.

To the 12th   18. Here I subjoin the negative of air enclosed in caverns in summer time. But much more careful investigation is needed of enclosed air. For in the first place, there is room for doubt as to the nature of air in itself with regard to heat and cold. For air clearly receives heat from the influence of the heavenly bodies; and cold perhaps from exhalations from the earth; and again in the so-called middle region of the air, from cold vapours and snow. So no judgement can be reached about the nature of air through air that is outside and in the open, but a truer judgement might be made about air that is enclosed. It is however necessary for the air to be enclosed in such a vessel and material as will not itself impart either heat or cold from a power of its own to the air, nor will readily admit the influence of the air outside it. An experiment should therefore be performed using an earthenware jar wrapped round with many layers of leather to protect it from the outside air, and holding the air tightly closed there for three or four days. After the vessel has been opened, the air should be tested either by hand or by applying a graduated glass.[154]

---

[153]Friction with the air is also mentioned under Instances 21 and 22, *below*.

[154]This graduated glass, which was a primitive thermometer, is described below under Instance 38 of the Table of Comparison, Aphorism II, 13.

To the 13th 19. Similarly, it is not certain whether the warmth in wool and furs and feathers and the like, comes from some very small amount of heat inhering in them, in that they have been taken from animals; or whether it comes from a certain greasiness and oiliness, which is of a nature akin to warmth; or simply from the confinement and separation of air, as I said in the preceding paragraph. For all air that is cut off from contact with the outer air seems to have some warmth. An experiment should therefore be made with fibrous substances made of linen, not of wool or feathers or silk, which come from animals. It should also be observed that all powders (which clearly include air) are less cold than the whole bodies from which they come, in the same way that we find foam, since it contains air, less cold than the liquid from which it comes.

To the 14th 20. No negative is subjoined to this. For no known substance, either tangible or spirituous, fails to become hot when placed near fire. But they do differ in this, that some things, like air, oil and water, become hot more quickly, others more slowly, like stone and metals. But this belongs to the *Table of Degrees.*

To the 15th 21. No negative is subjoined to this instance, except that it should be carefully noted that sparks are produced from flint and steel or any other hard substance only when some minute pieces are struck off the substance of the stone or the metal, and it is not friction with the air that of itself creates sparks, as is commonly thought. Also, the sparks themselves, from the weight of their ignited bodies, tend to fall rather than rise, and when extinguished are reduced to a kind of sooty material.

To the 16th 22. No negative, I think, can be subjoined to this instance. For in our experience every tangible body plainly grows hot from friction. So much so, that the ancients fancied that the heavenly bodies had no other means or power of making things hot than through friction with the air in their rapid and vehement rotation. But further inquiry is needed in this subject as to whether bodies projected by machines, such as cannon-balls from cannon, acquire any degree of heat from the percussion itself, so as to be found somewhat warm after they have fallen. On the other hand, air in motion tends to cool rather than heat things, as in the case of winds and bellows and blowing with pursed lips. Indeed, the motion of the air in this case is not fast enough to induce heat, and is the motion of a whole, not through particles, so it is not surprising that it does not generate heat.

To the 17th 23. This instance calls for more careful inquiry. For plants and other vegetable matter that are green and damp seem to have some heat hidden within them. But this heat is so slight that it cannot be felt in single pieces; but after they have been collected and shut up together, so that their spirit is not exhaled into the open air but reinforces itself, a very obvious heat then arises, and, in suitable material, sometimes a flame.

To the 18th 24. This instance also calls for more careful investigation. For quicklime when sprinkled with water seems to become hot, either because the heat formerly dispersed within it is concentrated, as I remarked just now about plants being shut up together, or from the stimulation and arousing of a fiery spirit by the water, leading to a certain conflict and antiperistasis.[155] Which of the two is the real cause will be more readily apparent if we mix in oil, instead of water, since oil serves just as well as water to concentrate the enclosed spirit, but not to stimulate it. We should also extend the experiment to include the ashes and calces of different substances,[156] and also by mixing them with other liquids.

To the 19th 25. To this instance is subjoined the negative of other metals that are softer and more pliable [than iron and tin]. For gold leaf, when dissolved into a liquor by aqua regia,[157] gives off no heat to the touch; nor does lead dissolved in aqua fortis, nor (as I recall) quicksilver either. Silver itself does, however, produce a little heat, and copper too, as far as I remember; tin more perceptibly, and most of all iron and steel,

---

[155]Bacon defines *antiperistasis* as a "rejection of a contrary nature" (Aphorism II, 27).

[156]A calx is the dry substance obtained by thoroughly roasting or 'calcining' a mineral or metal. In fact, it is usually the metal oxide; but this, of course, was not appreciated until well after Bacon's time.

[157]Aqua regia was so named for being the water that dissolves the royal metal, namely gold; it is a mixture of nitric and hydrochloric acids. Aqua fortis is nitric acid.

which not only arouse a vigorous heat in dissolution, but a violent boiling as well. The heat therefore seems to come about through conflict, as the strong solvents penetrate and dig into and tear asunder the parts of the substance, and they in turn resist it. But where the substances yield more readily, hardly any heat is roused.

To the 20th 26. No negative may be subjoined to the heat of animals, other than of insects (as I have said), on account of the smallness of their bodies. For in fish, compared with land animals, one observes a small degree of heat, rather than its absence. However, in vegetation and plants no degree of heat is perceptible to the touch, either in the fluids they exude or in their inner parts when freshly exposed. But in animals, a great diversity of heat is found, both in their parts (for there is one heat around the heart, another in the brain, another around their external parts) and also in their circumstances, for example, violent exercise and fevers.

To the 21st 27. It is hard to subjoin a negative to this instance. Indeed, the excrements of animals, when no longer fresh, clearly hold a potential heat, as is seen in the manuring of soil.

To the 22nd and 23rd 28. Liquids, whether they are called waters or oils, which are intensely acrid, have the effect of heat in tearing bodies apart, and after a little while consuming them. Yet to the touch they are not hot at first. But they operate in proportion to the porosity of the substance to which they are applied. For aqua regia dissolves gold, but silver hardly at all. On the other hand, aqua fortis dissolves silver, but gold hardly at all. Neither dissolves glass; and so on with others.

To the 24th 29. Have an experiment made of spirit of wine on wood, and also on butter or wax or pitch, to see whether it may to some extent liquefy them with its heat. For the 24th instance brings to our attention a power that imitates heat in producing incrustations. A similar experiment should therefore be done with respect to liquefactions. Also have an experiment made with a graduated or calendar glass, concave at the top on the outside.[158] Have some spirit of wine, well-

---

[158]Bacon is proposing a modification to the graduated glass described below under Instance 38 of the Table of Comparison, Aphorism II, 13.

rectified, poured into the concave part, and covered with a lid so as better to retain its heat; and mark whether its heat causes the water to descend.

To the 25th   30. Spices and herbs bitter to the palate are felt to be hot, and much more so if taken internally. It should therefore be noted on which other materials they produce the effects of heat. Sailors relate that when large masses of spices that have long been enclosed are suddenly opened up, those who first disturb them and take them out are at risk from fever and inflammation of the spirit. Likewise, an experiment could be made as to whether powders of such spices or herbs would not dry bacon and meat hung over them, as the smoke of a fire does.

To the 26th   31. There is a sharpness or piercing quality as much in cold things like vinegar and oil of vitriol as in things that are hot, such as oil of marjoram, and the like. They therefore cause pain in living creatures and also tear asunder and consume the parts of inanimate substances in the same way. To this instance again no negative is subjoined. And in living creatures no pain is found unless with a certain feeling of heat.

To the 27th   32. Many actions of hot and cold are common to both, though for different reasons. For even snowballs seem to burn boys' hands after a while, and frosts preserve meat from putrefaction no less than fire. And heat shrinks bodies, and so does cold. But these and similar instances may more suitably be referred to the inquiry into cold.

13

In the third place, we must make a *presentation to the understanding* of instances in which the nature under inquiry exists to a greater or lesser degree, either comparing an increase or a decrease in the same object, or comparing the same result in different objects. For since the form of a thing is the very thing itself, and a thing does not differ from its form in any way, otherwise than the apparent differs from the real, or the external from the internal, or as it relates to man and as it relates to the universe; it must then follow that no nature can be taken to be the true form, unless it always decreases when the nature itself decreases and, likewise, always increases when the nature itself increases. This table I call the *Table of Degrees* or the *Table of Comparison*.

Table of Degrees or Comparison in Heat

I will first mention those things that have no degree of heat at all to the touch, but seem to have only a certain, potential heat, or a disposition and readiness to be hot. After that I will pass on to substances that are hot in their actions or to the touch, and to their several strengths and degrees.

1 Among solid, tangible bodies we do not find any that are essentially and innately hot. For no stone of any kind, no metal, neither sulphur, nor any kind of rock or mineral, no wood or water or animal's carcass is found to be hot [naturally]. For the hot waters in hot springs seem to be heated by external agency, either by flame or subterranean fire, such as is spewed forth by Etna and many other mountains, or from a conflict of bodies, in the way heat is created in the dissolution of iron and tin [by acids]. There is, therefore, no [innate] degree of heat perceptible to human touch in inanimate objects, although they do differ in degree of cold, for wood is not so cold as metal. But this belongs to the *Table of Degrees in Cold*.

2 On the other hand, as far as potential heat and a tendency to catch fire is concerned, there are many inanimate substances strongly disposed that way, such as sulphur, naphtha and petroleum.

3 Substances that were once hot, like horse-dung from the animal, or lime or perhaps ashes or soot from fire, retain certain latent remnants of their former heat. Thus certain distillations and separations of bodies are made by burying them in horse-dung,[159] and heat is produced in [quick]lime when water is sprinkled on it, as I have already said [under Instance 24, Aphorism II, 12].

4 Among vegetable substances, there is no single plant, nor part of a plant, like its gum or pith, which is warm to the

---

[159]Early chemists used a variety of heats for distillation ranging from that of a sitting hen, dung, sunlight, and hot water, right up to the intense heat of a furnace. See R. J. Forbes, *A Short History of the Art of Distillation* (Leiden: E. J. Brill, 1948).

human touch. But nevertheless, as I mentioned above [under Instance 23 of Aphorism II, 12], green plants when shut up become heated; while to the internal touch, such as the palate or stomach, and also to the outer parts after a little while, as with plasters and ointments, some vegetable substances are found hot, others cold.

5   In the parts of animals after they become mortified or have been severed, nothing hot to the touch is found. Not even horse-dung retains its heat, unless it is enclosed and buried. Yet all dung seems to possess a potential heat, as is found in the manuring of fields. And in the same way, carcasses of animals have a similar latent and potential heat; so much so, that in cemeteries where burials are carried out daily, the earth accumulates a certain latent heat, which consumes a recently buried body much faster than uncontaminated earth does. And there is a story among orientals that a kind of cloth has been discovered, very fine and soft, made of the down of birds, which by an innate power dissolves and melts butter when lightly wrapped in it.

6   Substances which enrich the soil, such as dung of all kinds, chalk, sea-sand, salt[160] and the like, have some disposition to be hot.

7   All putrefaction contains in itself some traces of very slight heat, but not so much as to be felt by touch. For not even those substances, such as meat or cheese, that when putrefied turn into tiny creatures feel warm to the touch;[161] nor does rotten wood, which glows at night. Heat however sometimes shows its presence in rotting objects by strong and foul smells.

8   The first degree of heat therefore, of those things that feel

---

[160]Salt acts as a fertilizer for sugar beet, mangolds and certain market crops. In his *Sylva Sylvarum* (673), Bacon repeated what had been known since at least the time of Pliny that "some herbs like best being watered with salt water; as radish, beet, rue, pennyroyal".

[161]Bacon is here referring to the theory of spontaneous generation, which was endorsed by Aristotle and commonly held in Bacon's day. Francesco Redi (1621–1697), a physician and naturalist of Florence, first carried out controlled experiments which demonstrated that insects are not generated from decaying flesh, provided this is protected from intruding insects.

warm to human touch, seems to be the warmth of animals, which possesses a fairly wide range of degrees. Thus the lowest degree, as in insects, is hardly perceptible to the touch; but the highest scarcely reaches that of the sun's rays in the hottest countries and times of the year, nor is it too fierce to be borne by the hand. Yet it is said of Constantine,[162] and some others who had a rather a dry constitution and frame, that when seized by the most acute fevers, they became so hot that they appeared to burn slightly the hand that touched them.

9 Animals increase in heat by movement and exercise, wine, and feasting, copulation, burning fevers and pain.

10 Animals at the outset of intermittent fevers are seized by chill and shivering, and a little while later become very hot, as they also do from the first in burning and pestilential fevers.[163]

11 There should be further inquiry into the comparative heat in different kinds of animals, such as fish, quadrupeds, reptiles, birds; and also according to their species, as in the lion, the kite, and man. For according to common opinion, fish are the least hot internally, and birds the most, especially doves, hawks and ostriches.[164]

12 There should be further inquiry into the comparative degrees of heat in the various parts and limbs of the same animal. For milk, blood, sperm and eggs are found to have a slight degree of warmth, and are not so hot as the exterior flesh itself, in a moving or aroused animal. But no such inquiry has been made up to now as to the degree of heat in the brain, stomach, heart and other parts.

13 All animals are cold on the outside in winter and cold weather, but are thought to be much warmer within.

14 The heat of heavenly bodies, even in the hottest region and at the hottest times of the year and day, never reaches a sufficient degree to burn or scorch the driest wood or straw or

---

[162]Constantine II (AD 317–340), was Roman Emperor, son of Constantine the Great. This story is told by the fourth-century Greek historian, Ammianus Marcellinus, Book xxi, 15.

[163]"Burning fever" is a very high, or raging, fever; "pestilential fever" is typhus fever.

[164]Or perhaps, as Spedding thinks, sparrows, rather than ostriches.

even tinder, unless strengthened by burning-glasses. It is, however, able to draw steam from moist substances.

15 According to an astronomers' tradition, some stars rank above others in their heat. For instance among the planets, Mars is ranked hottest after the Sun, then Jupiter, then Venus; among those thought to be cold, are the moon, and then coldest of all is Saturn. Among the fixed stars on the other hand the hottest is thought to be Sirius, then Cor Leonis or Regulus, then Canicula and so on.

16 The sun gives more heat the closer it approaches to the perpendicular or zenith, which is to be believed of the other planets too, in proportion to their heat; Jupiter, for example, is hotter to us when in Cancer or Leo than when in Capricorn or Aquarius.

17 It is also to be believed that the sun itself and the other planets give out more heat when at their perigee, because of their closeness to the earth, than at their apogee. But if it should happen that in some region the sun is in perigee and at the same time near the perpendicular, it must necessarily give out more heat than if it were in a region where it is likewise in perigee but at a more oblique angle. So a comparison should be observed of the exaltation of the planets [i.e., the position from where they exert their greatest influence], according as it proceeds from perpendicularity and obliquity, in different regions.

18 The sun, too, and other planets likewise, are thought to give more heat when close to the major fixed stars; as when the sun stands in Leo, it is closer to Cor Leonis, Cauda Leonis, Spica Virginis, Sirius and Canicula, than when it is in Cancer, when however it stands nearer to the perpendicular.[165] And it must be supposed that those parts of the heavens shed the greater heat, albeit hardly perceptible, that are the more adorned with stars, especially with the larger ones.

---

[165]Sirius and Canicula are the large and small dog-stars, respectively; Spica, a first magnitude star in the constellation Virgo; Cor Leonis, also called alpha Leonis and Regulus, is a star of the first magnitude in the constellation of Leo; Cauda Leonis is a bright star, also called Denebola, which, as its name implies, lies in the tail of Leo.

19 In sum, then, the heat from the heavenly bodies is increased in three ways, namely, by their perpendicularity, their closeness to us, or perigee, and from the conjunction or juxtaposition of stars.

20 A very great difference is found between the heat of animals and also the rays of heavenly bodies (as they reach us) and that of even the gentlest flame, and all ignited solids, and of liquids as well, or of air itself when strongly heated by fire. For the flame of spirit of wine, which is especially rare and uncompressed, is still able to kindle straw or linen or paper, which the heat of animals will never do, nor that of the sun, unless by means of burning-glasses.

21 There are however many degrees of strength and weakness in the heat of a flame and ignited substances. But since no careful inquiry has been made of them, we must pass lightly over them. It does appear however that the flame of spirit of wine is the mildest of all, unless perhaps *ignis fatuus* or the flames or coruscations coming from the sweat of animals are milder. After this, I think, comes the flame of light and porous vegetable matter, like straw, rushes and dried leaves, which is not very different from that of hair or feathers. Next perhaps is the flame from wood, especially those woods that do not contain much resin or pitch; with this distinction, however, that the flame from small pieces of wood (such as are commonly bundled into faggots) is milder than that from the trunks and roots of trees. And this can be observed at any time in furnaces for smelting iron, in which a fire made from faggots and the branches of trees is not of much use. Next I think comes the flame from oil and tallow and wax and similar fatty substances, which has no great fierceness. But a very great heat is found in pitch and resin, and more still in sulphur and camphor, and naphtha and petroleum and saltpetre (after the crude matter has been extracted)[166] and in compounds of these like gunpowder, Greek fire (commonly called wildfire) and its

---

[166]Saltpetre arises naturally as a result of the decomposition of vegetable matter in an alkaline environment. Since it is found on and close to the surface of the soil, it needs to be separated from extraneous, or crude, matter.

different kinds, which have such a stubborn heat that they are not easily quenched with water.[167]

22 I think also that the flame that results from some base metals is very strong and fierce. But further inquiry should be made concerning all these.

23 It seems that a powerful lightning flame exceeds all those flames, to the extent that it sometimes even melts pure iron into droplets, which other flames cannot do.

24 There are also different degrees of heat in ignited substances, about which again no careful inquiry has been made. The weakest heat of all, I think, comes from tinder, such as we use to kindle a flame; and likewise from the touchwood or dried cord that are used for setting off cannon. After that comes ignited charcoal and coal and even ignited bricks and the like. But the fiercest heat of all ignited things comes, I think, from ignited metals, such as iron and copper, etc. But these also require further inquiry.

25 Some ignited substances are found to be much hotter than some flames. For instance, ignited iron is much hotter and more consuming than the flame of spirit of wine.

26 Furthermore, among things that are not ignited but are merely heated by fire, such as boiling water and the air enclosed in reverberatory furnaces, there are some that are hotter than even many flames and ignited substances.

27 Motion increases heat, as can be seen in bellows[168] and by blowing; so much so, that the harder metals are not melted or

---

[167]"Greek fire" or "wildfire" was a terrifying substance which ignited as soon as it was wetted and so could not be extinguished by water. It is said to have been discovered by the Byzantine Greeks and first used by them at the siege of Constantinople in AD 673 for setting fire to ships and fortifications. The composition of Greek fire was kept secret and is subject to conjecture; some suggested ingredients are saltpetre (unlikely), sulphur, petroleum and quicklime. Bacon himself says (in the *Sylva Sylvarum,* 783) that the principal ingredient of "wildfires" was bitumen. Porta (*Natural Magic,* book 12, ch. 2) gives the ingredients of Greek fire as willow charcoal, salt, spirit of wine, brimstone, pitch, the "yarn of the soft wool of Ethiopia" and camphor.

[168]Under Instance 22 of Aphorism II, 12, Bacon points out that the movement of air produced by bellows may also tend to cool. We are put in mind of the fable in which a satyr gave shelter to a traveller, until he

liquefied by a dying or dormant fire, unless it is roused by blowing.

28   Have an experiment made with burning-glasses, in which (as I remember) the following occurs: if the burning-glass is placed, for example, at the distance of a span from a combustible object, it does not kindle or burn it as much as if it had been placed at half a span's distance and gradually and slowly moved to the distance of a span. And yet the cone and focus of the rays are the same, but it is the motion itself that increases the operation of the heat.

29   Those fires that break out during a high wind are thought to make more progress against the wind than with it, doubtless because the flame recoils more violently when the wind slackens, than it advances when the wind drives it on.

30   A flame does not spring up, nor is generated, unless it is given a hollow space in which it can move and play, except in the explosive flames of gunpowder and similar substances, where the compression and confinement of the flame increase its fury.

31   An anvil struck by a hammer becomes quite hot, so much so that if it were made of thinner plate, I think it could redden like ignited iron, under repeated strong hammer-blows. But this should be tried by experiment.

32   But in ignited substances that are porous, so that the fire has room to move, if this movement is stopped by a strong compression, the fire is extinguished at once; as when tinder or the burning wick of a candle or lamp, or even glowing charcoal or coal, is squeezed together by means of a press or by trampling it under foot or the like, the action of the fire immediately ceases.

33   Approximation to a hot body increases heat, in proportion to how close it comes. This also happens with light; for the nearer an object is brought to a light the more visible it is.

34   The union of different heats increases heat, unless the bodies are mixed together. Thus a large fire and a small one in

---

noticed the traveller first blowing on his fingers to warm them, and then blowing on his broth to cool it. The satyr threw the traveller out for 'blowing hot and cold', which is said to be the origin of the phrase.

the same room augment each other's heat. But tepid water poured into boiling water cools it.

35 The length of time that a body is hot increases heat, because the heat continually passing through and emanating combines with the heat already there, and so multiplies it. Thus a fire does not heat a room so much in half an hour as the same fire would in a whole hour. But this is not the case with light, for a lamp or candle placed anywhere does not give any more light after a long lapse of time than immediately after it was lit.

36 Irritation by surrounding cold increases heat, as we see in fires during a severe frost. That happens, I think, not only from the confinement and contraction of the heat, which is a kind of union,[169] but also from exasperation; as when air or a stick is violently compressed or bent, it does not rebound to the exact point where it was before, but further in the opposite direction. A careful experiment should therefore be made with a stick or similar object put into a flame, to see whether it is not burnt faster at the sides of the flame than in the middle.

37 There are many degrees in the extent to which heat is taken up. And first of all it should be noted how a small, slight heat nevertheless alters and makes quite warm even substances that are the least susceptible to heat. Thus the mere warmth of the hand gives some heat to a little ball of lead or of any other metal held for a short time, so easily and generally is heat transmitted and aroused, the body concerned showing no change in appearance.

38 Of all the bodies that we know of, air both receives and gives out heat the most readily, and this is best seen in calendar glasses, which are made in the following fashion. Take a glass vessel with a hollow bulb and a long, narrow neck; turn it upside down and lower it, mouth downwards and bulb upwards, into another glass vessel where there should be water, so that the mouth of the inserted vessel touches the bottom of the receiving vessel; and let the neck of the inserted vessel lean a little against the mouth of the receiving one, so

---

[169]This is a reference to Instance 34, *above.*

that it can stand upright. This is most conveniently done by putting a little wax on the mouth of the receiving vessel, but not so as to stop up its mouth completely, lest the motion I am about to describe, which is very easy and delicate, be hindered by want of a supply of air.

Now the vessel to be lowered, before it is inserted into the other, should be heated at a fire in the upper part (that is in the bulb). When the vessel has been positioned in the manner described, and after enough time has elapsed for the added heat to be lost, the air (which will have expanded with the heat) will recede and contract to the extension or dimension which the surrounding or general air had at the time when the vessel was immersed, and will draw water upwards in a corresponding measure. A long narrow strip of paper should then be fixed to it, marked off with as many degrees as you like.[170] Now you will see the air contract through cold and expand through heat, according as the day grows warm or cold; and this will be apparent from the water rising when the air contracts, and falling or sinking when it expands. The sensitivity of the air to heat and cold is so subtle and exquisite as far to exceed the human tactile faculty, so much so, that any one ray of sunlight, or the warmth of a breath, much more the warmth of a hand placed over the top of the glass vessel, will at once make the water distinctly fall. And yet I think that animal spirits have a still more exquisite sense of hot and cold, except that it is impeded and dulled by the bulk of the body.

39   After air, I think the substances most sensitive to heat are those recently altered and compressed by freezing, such as snow and ice, for they begin to melt and liquefy under quite gentle warmth. After them comes perhaps quicksilver, and after that fatty substances such as oil, butter and the like; then wood, then water and lastly stones and metals, which do not

---

[170]The calendar glass, or weather glass, was first discussed in print in 1617 by the mystical writer Robert Fludd (1574–1673), though he claimed only to have recreated the device from a description in a 500-year-old manuscript. As is evident from Bacon's full description, the calendar glass, not being sealed, is subject to changes not only in ambient temperature but also in atmospheric pressure.

readily become warm, especially in their inner parts. They, on
the other hand, retain their heat for a very long time once they
have received it, so much so that an ignited brick or stone or
piece of iron plunged into a basin of cold water for about a
quarter of an hour will retain so much heat that it cannot be
touched.

40   The smaller the mass of a body, the faster it is warmed by
the approach of a hot object; which shows that all heat that we
know of is in some way in opposition to tangible matter.

41   So far as the human sense of touch is concerned, heat is a
variable and relative thing; so that tepid water feels hot, if
one's hand is cold, and cold, if one's hand is hot.

14

Anyone can see how poor we are in history from the
foregoing tables, where I sometimes not only include traditions
and stories (although always adding a note as to their doubtful
reliability and authority) instead of proved history and certain
instances, but am also often compelled to say "Have an
experiment done" or "Further inquiry is needed".

15

I call the work and business of these three tables the
Presentation of Instances to the Understanding. Once the
presentation has been made, *induction* itself should be set to
work. What we have to find, upon a presentation of each and
every instance, is a nature of such a kind that it is always
present or absent with the given nature, and always increases
and decreases with it, and is, as I have said above [in Aphorism
II, 4], a limitation of a more general nature. Now if the mind
tries from the very outset to do this affirmatively (as left to
itself it always tends to do), all sorts of fancies and guesses and
ill-defined notions and axioms that have daily to be corrected
will ensue, unless, like the schoolmen, we choose to fight for
what is false. But nevertheless these findings will doubtless be
better or worse according to the ability and strength of the
understanding making them. On the other hand, it belongs

only to God, the originator and creator of forms, or perhaps to the angels and supernatural intelligences to have immediate, affirmative knowledge of forms, from the moment of their contemplation. But this is certainly beyond man, to whom it is granted only to proceed first by negatives and finally reach an end in affirmatives after every kind of exclusion has been made.

16

We must therefore completely resolve and separate Nature, not by fire, certainly, but by the mind, which is a kind of divine fire. Therefore the first task of true induction (as far as discovering forms is concerned) is the *rejection* or *exclusion* of all the separate natures that are not found in any instance where the given nature is present, or are found in any instance where the given nature is absent, or are found to increase in any instance when the given nature decreases, or to decrease when the given nature increases. Then indeed, after the rejection and exclusion has been properly made, in the second place (at the bottom, as it were), there will remain, all volatile opinions vanishing into smoke, the affirmative form, solid, true and well-defined. Now this is quickly said, but it is only reached after many twists and turns. However, I will try not to overlook anything that will enable us to achieve this end.

17

But when I attribute such a prominent part to forms, I must give this warning over and over again, that what I say should not be applied to those forms to which men's studies and thoughts have up to now been accustomed.

For first, I am not for the moment speaking of compound forms, which are, as I have said,[171] conjunctions of simple natures occurring in the ordinary course of the world, things like a lion, an eagle, a rose, and gold. For the time to deal with

---

[171]In Aphorism II, 7.

these will be when we come to *latent processes* and *latent schematisms* and their discovery, as they are found in substances (as they are called) or concrete natures.[172]

And again, even as regards simple natures, what I have said should not be understood to refer to abstract forms and ideas that are either undefined or ill-defined in matter. For when I speak of forms I mean nothing but those laws and definitions of pure actuality, which govern and constitute any simple nature, such as heat, light, weight, in every kind of material and subject that is capable of receiving them. Therefore the form of heat or the form of light are the same things as the law of heat or the law of light. And, indeed, I never let myself be drawn away or retreat from things themselves and the operative part. So that when in the investigation of the form of heat, for example, I say, "reject rarity" or "rarity does not belong to the form of heat", it is the same as if I said, "It is possible to impose heat on a dense body" or, conversely, "It is possible to remove or keep heat out of a rare body."

But if anyone should think my forms also somewhat abstract, in that they mix and combine things that are heterogeneous (for the heat of heavenly bodies and of fire seem extremely heterogeneous; as do the fixed red in a rose and in similar objects, and the apparent red in a rainbow, or the rays from an opal or diamond; and also death from drowning, burning, a sword-wound, apoplexy or starvation: and yet they all severally agree in the nature of heat, redness and death), that man, I say, should know that his understanding has been held captive and detained by habit and the wholeness of things and by opinions. For there can be no doubt at all that those things, however heterogeneous and disparate, meet in the form or law that governs heat or redness or death; and that human power can never be set free from the ordinary course of Nature, and enlarged and exalted to new efficient causes and new ways of operating, except by revealing and discovering such forms. And yet, after I have spoken of this union of Nature, which is the most important point, I shall have

---

[172]In Aphorism II, 5, Bacon describes concrete natures as natures "conjoined in a structure".

something to say later, in their proper place, about the divisions and veins of Nature, both those that are ordinary and those that are more inward and true.[173]

18

But now I must give an example of the *exclusion* or *rejection* of natures, which have been found through the *tables of presentation* not to belong to the form of heat; with this observation, however, that not only does a particular table suffice for the rejection of any nature, but so too does any one of the particular instances contained in them. For it is obvious from what I have said that every contradictory instance overthrows a conjecture as to the form. Nevertheless, for the sake of clarity and to show more plainly the use of the tables, I sometimes give two or more exclusions.

An Example of *Exclusion,* or *Rejection of Natures* from the Form of Heat

1. On account of the sun's rays, *reject* an elemental nature.
2. On account of common fire, and especially subterranean fires (which are the most remote and most completely cut off from the rays of heavenly bodies), *reject* a celestial nature.[174]
3. On account of the warmth acquired by every kind of substance (namely minerals, vegetables, the external parts of animals, water, oil, air, and the

---

[173]Bacon deals with the union of Nature under the headings of Constitutive and Conforming Instances in Aphorisms II, 26 and 27; and with the divisions of Nature under Singular, Deviating and Boundary Instances, and Instances of Power.

[174]The term *elemental* refers to the four Aristotelian elements: earth, air, fire and water; and *celestial* to the unchangeable matter of the heavens. However, Bacon was opposed to the idea of a radical difference between sub- and superlunary matter and did not believe that ordinary matter was composed of the four elements. In the next aphorism, Bacon concedes that the notions of elemental and celestial are vague and ill-defined.

rest) by mere closeness to a fire or another hot body, *reject* all diversity or more subtle structure of bodies.

4. On account of ignited iron and ignited metals, which give warmth to other bodies, yet lose nothing of their weight or substance, *reject* the imparting or mixing of the substance of another hot body.

5. On account of boiling water and air, and even metals and other solids which have been heated, but not to ignition, or red heat, *reject* light or brightness.

6. On account of the rays of the moon and other stars, except the sun, again *reject* light and brightness.

7. On account of the comparison of ignited iron and the flame of spirit of wine, of which ignited iron has more heat and less light, while the flame of spirit of wine has more light and less heat, again *reject* light and brightness.

8. On account of ignited gold and other ignited metals, which are the densest in body, as a whole, *reject* rarity.

9. On account of air, which is usually found cold yet remains rare, again *reject* rarity.

10. On account of ignited iron, which does not expand in bulk but to the eye remains the same size, *reject* local or expansive motion of the body as a whole.

11. On account of the expansion of air in things like calendar glasses, where the air clearly has local and expansive motion, but receives no apparent increase of heat, again *reject* local and expansive motion of the body as a whole.

12. On account of the ease with which all bodies may be warmed to a moderate degree, without any destruction or perceptible alteration, *reject* a destructive nature, or the violent introduction of any new nature.

13. On account of the agreement and conformity of the similar effects produced by heat and cold, *reject* both expansive and contractive motion of the body as a whole.

14. On account of the heat arising from the friction of bodies, *reject* a principal nature, by which I mean that which is found positive in Nature, and is not caused by any antecedent nature.

There are other natures also. For I have not drawn up perfect tables, but examples only.

None of the natures mentioned above belongs to the form of heat. And man is freed from all of them in his operations on heat.

19

The foundations of true induction lie in the process of exclusion, which however is not completed until it arrives at an affirmative. Nor, however, is the exclusive part itself at all complete, and indeed it cannot possibly be so at first. For exclusion is obviously a rejection of simple natures, and if we do not yet have good and true notions of simple natures, how can exclusion be rectified? But some of the notions mentioned above, like those of the elemental nature, the celestial nature [in Instances 1 and 2 of Aphorism II, 18] and rarity, are vague and ill-defined. Since I am well aware and have not forgotten what a great task I am engaged on (namely, to make human understanding a match for things and Nature), I shall by no means rest content with the precepts I have so far put forward, but will proceed further, and devise and administer more powerful aids for the use of the understanding, which I shall now give. And surely in the interpretation of nature, the mind should in every way be so prepared and shaped that, while it keeps itself within appropriate degrees of certainty, it yet remembers (especially at the outset) that what is to come very much depends upon what has been done already.

20

But since truth will emerge more readily from error than from confusion, I consider it useful, once the three Tables of

First Presentation (such as I have given) have been assembled and weighed, for the understanding to be given leave to exert itself and attempt the task of the interpretation of nature in the affirmative way, using those instances in the tables, as well as any others it may come across elsewhere. And this kind of attempt I call the *Indulgence of the Understanding,* or the *Beginning of the Interpretation,* or the *First Vintage.*

First Vintage concerning the Form of Heat

It should be observed that the form of a thing exists, as is clear from what I have said, in each and all the instances in which the thing itself exists, otherwise it would not be the form; and therefore there simply cannot be a contradictory instance. Nevertheless, the form is found to be far more conspicuous and evident in some instances than in others, namely, in those in which the nature of the form is less constrained and obstructed and restricted by other natures. Instances of this kind I call *Shining* or *Revealing Instances.* That said, I now proceed to the First Vintage concerning the form of heat.

> *Throughout each and every instance [in the tables] the nature of which heat is a limitation appears to be motion. This is most plainly revealed in flame, which is always in motion, and in boiling or simmering liquids, which are also always in motion. And it is revealed also in the creating or increasing of heat through motion, as by bellows and winds, on which see Instance 29 in Table 3; and also in other kinds of motion, on which see Instances 28 and 31 in Table 3. It is revealed again in the extinction of fire and heat through any severe compression which reins in the motion and brings it to a halt, on which see Instances 30 and 32 in Table 3. It is also revealed by the fact that every body is destroyed, or at least markedly altered, by any strong, fierce fire or heat; from this, it is quite clear that heat causes tumult and agitation and violent motion in the internal parts of a body, which gradually tends to its breaking up.*

What I have said about motion (namely, that it is like a genus of which heat is a species) should not be taken to mean that heat generates motion or that motion generates heat (though these too are true in some cases) but that the very essence of heat, or the substantial self of heat, is motion and nothing else; but limited by the differences which I will add in a moment, after a few words of caution in order to avoid ambiguity.

Heat in regard to the sense is a relative thing; it relates to man, not to the universe, and is correctly set down as merely the effect of heat on the animal spirits. It is moreover variable in itself, since the same body can (depending on how the sense is prepared beforehand) give the sensation of both hot and cold, as is clear from Instance 41 in Table 3.

Nor indeed should the communication of heat, or its transitive nature [i.e., its capacity to operate beyond itself], whereby a body moved close to a hot body grows hot itself, be confused with the form of heat. For heat is one thing, heating another. Thus heat is induced by the motion of friction without any heat having been there before, so that heating is excluded from the form of heat. And even when heat is produced through the approach of a hot body, this does not happen because of the form of heat, but depends entirely on a higher and more general nature, namely on the nature of assimilation or self-multiplication, which requires a separate inquiry.[175]

Moreover, the notion of fire is a popular one, and of no value, being put together from the conjunction of heat and brightness in a particular body, as in an ordinary flame, and in bodies made red hot.

With all ambiguity out of the way, therefore, we come now at last to the true *differences* that limit motion and constitute it as the form of heat.

The *first difference* then is this, that heat is an expansive motion, through which a body strives to extend itself and assume a greater sphere or volume than it had previously occupied. This difference is best revealed in flame, where smoke or thick vapour manifestly swells and bursts into flame.

It is revealed too in all boiling liquid, which manifestly swells, rises, and bubbles, and vigorously continues the process of self-expansion until it turns into a body expanded to a

---

[175]Such an inquiry is outlined in Aphorism II, 48 (*11*).

much greater size than the liquid itself, namely into vapour or smoke or air.

It is revealed also in all wood and other combustible material, where there is sometimes sweating and always evaporation.

It is revealed also in the melting of metals, which, being the most compact bodies, do not readily swell and expand; and yet their spirit, once dilated in itself, and seized with a desire to expand further, clearly pushes and drives the coarser parts into a liquid state. And if the heat is greatly increased, it dissolves and converts much of them into a volatile state.

It is revealed also in iron or stones, which although they do not melt or run, nevertheless become soft. This happens also in sticks, which become flexible if heated a little in hot ashes.

But this motion is seen best of all in air, which under only slight heat expands steadily and visibly, as in Instance 38, Table 3.

It is revealed also in the opposite nature of cold. For cold contracts all bodies and makes them shrink; so much so, that during sharp frosts nails fall out of walls, brass vessels crack and heated glass when suddenly put into the cold shatters and breaks. In the same way, air shrinks when slightly cooled, as in Instance 38 in Table 3. But I shall speak of these effects at greater length in the inquiry into cold.

It is not surprising that heat and cold exhibit many actions in common (for which see Instance 32, Table 2), when we find two of the following differences (of which I shall speak shortly) that are appropriate to either nature, although in the difference I am now speaking of, their actions are diametrically opposite. For heat gives an expansive, enlarging motion, while cold gives a contracting and shrinking one.

The *second difference* is a modification of the first, namely, that heat is a motion that is expansive or towards the circumference [i.e., outward-tending]; with this qualification, however, that the body has at the same time a motion upwards. Indeed, there are certainly many mixed motions, for example in an arrow or dart, which revolves as it goes forward and goes forward as it revolves. And in the same way, the motion of heat is both expansive and upwards at the same time.

Now this difference is shown by putting a pair of tongs or a poker into a fire; because if it is put in upright, with the hand holding it at the top, it soon burns the hand; but it does so much more slowly if the hand is to one side, or below.

It is also to be seen in distillations by means of a descensory,[176] which men use for the more delicate flowers, whose scents readily vanish. For painstaking efforts have shown that by siting the fire not below but above, it would scorch them less. For not only flame but all heat tends to rise.

An experiment should also be made of this effect in the opposite nature of cold, namely to see whether cold does not contract a body downwards in the way heat expands a body upwards. Take therefore two iron rods, or two glass tubes, exactly alike, and heat them a little; then put a sponge full of cold water, or some snow, below the one and above the other. Now I think that there will be a more rapid chilling towards the extremity in the rod where the snow was placed above than in the one where the snow was placed below, contrary to what happens with heat.

The *third difference* is this, that heat is a motion that is not a uniformly expansive motion of the whole, but a motion that is expansive through the smaller particles of a body; and, at the same time is constrained, repelled and beaten back, so that the body takes on a vibrating motion, always trembling, straining and struggling, irritated by its rebuff; whence arises the fury of fire and heat.

This difference is best revealed in flame and boiling liquids, which are always trembling, swelling up in small parts and subsiding again.

It is revealed also in bodies that are of such a hard structure that when heated or ignited they do not swell or increase in size, like ignited iron, in which the heat is very fierce.

---

[176]A descensory is a kind of retort in which the heat is applied at the top and all round the vessel and the vapours are led off by a pipe through the bottom. Distillation is then said to be 'by descent'. Porta claimed to have invented this method of extracting oils from flowers, and he gave a detailed description of it in his *Natural Magic,* book 10, ch 9. Distillation by descent was by no means used only for delicate flowers—see *above,* footnote 136, p. 146.

It is revealed also in the fact that a fire on the hearth burns most fiercely in the coldest weather.

It is also revealed in the fact that when air in a calendar glass is expanded without impediment or repulsion, that is, smoothly and evenly, no heat is perceived. And also when winds burst out very violently from being closely confined, there is no very great heat perceptible; this must be because the motion is of the whole mass, with no vibrating motion in its particles. And to test this we should experiment to see whether a flame does not burn more fiercely at its edges than in the middle.

It is also revealed in the fact that all burning acts through minute pores of the body that is being burnt, so that the burning undermines and penetrates and pricks and stings, like an infinite number of needle-points. For the same reason we find that all strong solvents (if they are proportioned to the body on which they are acting) have the effect of fire, from their corrosive and piercing nature.

And this difference of which I now speak is shared by the nature of cold, in which the contractive motion is checked by an opposing tendency to expand, just as in heat the expansive motion is checked by an opposing tendency to contract.

Therefore, whether the parts of a body thrust inwards or outwards, the mode of action is the same; although the strength may be very different; for we have nowhere on the whole face of the earth anything that is extremely cold. See Instance 27, Table 1.[177]

The *fourth difference* is a modification of the last, namely, that the impelling or thrusting motion must be fairly rapid and not at all sluggish; it should also take place through minute particles; not, however, the very smallest, but ones that are just a little larger.

This difference is revealed in a comparison of the effects

---

[177]Bacon in fact refers to Table 9, which is presumably a mistake, since there are only 3 tables in this work. Instance 27 of Table 1 is meant to show the similar burning effect of cold and heat, thus illustrating the similar actions of heat and cold, of which Bacon speaks here.

The point concerning the extremity of cold is expanded upon in Aphorism II, 50 (3).

exerted by fire with those of time or age. For age or time dries, consumes, undermines and reduces things to ashes no less than fire; indeed, it does so much more subtly. But because such motion is extremely slow, and acts on exceedingly small particles, no heat is perceived.

It is revealed also in a comparison of iron and gold. For gold is dissolved without any heat being produced, whereas iron is dissolved with a vehement production of heat, although it takes about the same length of time. The reason is that in gold the entry of the separating solvent is mild and subtly insinuating, and the particles of gold yield easily; whereas in iron the entry is rough and provokes a struggle, the particles of iron being more stubborn.[178]

It is revealed also to a certain extent in some gangrenes and mortifications,[179] which do not arouse any great heat or pain because of the subtle nature of putrefaction.

Let this then be the *First Vintage, or Beginning of the Interpretation* of the form of heat, made through the *Indulgence of the Understanding.*

According to this First Vintage, the form or true definition of heat (of heat that relates to the universe, and is not simply relative to the sense) is, in a few words, this: *Heat is an expansive motion, checked, and exerting itself through the smaller parts of bodies.* But the expansion is modified, in that *while it expands towards the circumference, it yet has some tendency to go upwards.* And this exertion through the parts is also qualified in that *it is not sluggish at all, but hurried and somewhat violent.*

Viewed with reference to the operative part, it is the same thing, and the description is this: *if in any natural body you can arouse a dilating or expanding motion, and so check this motion and turn it back on itself, so that the dilation does not proceed evenly, but prevails in one part and is rebuffed in another, then without doubt you will generate heat:* this is

---

[178]The reference here is to Instances 19 of Table 1, and 25 of Table 2.

[179]Mortification in this context is the death of a part of the body while the rest is still living. Bacon is alluding to Instance 5 of the Table of Degrees.

without taking into account whether the body concerned is elementary (as they call it) or imbued by the heavens,[180] whether luminous or dark, whether rare or dense, locally expanded or contained within the bounds of its original dimensions, whether on the brink of dissolution or remaining in the same state; whether animal, vegetable or mineral, water, oil or air or any other substance whatever that is susceptible of the aforesaid motion. Now heat in regard to the sense is the same thing; only it must be considered with reference to the sense. But now let us proceed to further aids.

21

After the Tables of First Presentation and the Rejection, or Exclusion, and the First Vintage prepared in accordance with them, I now proceed to the other aids for the understanding in the interpretation of Nature and true and perfect induction. In proposing these, where tables are needed, I will proceed using those of hot and cold: where, however, only a few examples are required, I will use any others; in this way the inquiry will not become confused, and at the same time, my teaching will be less narrowly confined.

First of all, I propose to speak of the *Prerogatives of Instances.* Secondly, of the *Supports of Induction;* thirdly, of the *Rectification of Induction;* fourthly, of *Varying the Investigation According to the Nature of the Subject;* fifthly, of *Prerogatives of Natures* as they relate to investigation, or of what should be investigated first and what later; sixthly, of the *Limits of Investigation,* or a synopsis of all natures in the universe; seventhly, of *Application to Practice,* or of things in their relation to man; eighthly, of *Preparations for Investigation;*[181] and lastly, of the *Ascending and Descending Scale of Axioms.*

---

[180]This is a reference to the first two examples of the "rejection of natures from the form of heat" in the previous aphorism.

[181]Some part of what Bacon intended to be included under this head is evidently to be found in his *Preparation towards a Natural and Experimental History,* which is printed below, after *Novum Organum.*

22

Among prerogatives of instances, I will put first *Solitary Instances*.[182] They are those that show the nature in question in subjects having nothing else in common with other subjects, apart from that nature itself; or, on the other hand, those that do not show the nature in question in subjects similar in all respects to other subjects, apart from not having that nature;[183] for, clearly, such instances shorten the way and accelerate and strengthen the exclusion, so that a few of them are as good as many.

If, for example, we are inquiring into the nature of colour, Solitary Instances are prisms, crystalline gems that show colours not only in themselves but externally on a wall, also dewdrops, etc. For they have nothing in common with the colours fixed in flowers, coloured gems, metals, wood, etc., apart from the colour itself; from which we easily gather that colour is just a modification of the appearance of the light that is sent in and received; in the former kind [of object], through the different degrees of incidence; in the latter, through the various structures and schematisms of the body. These instances then are Solitary in regard to similarity.

Again, in the same investigation, the distinct veins of white and black in marble, and the variegations of colour in flowers of the same species, are Solitary Instances. For the white and black in marble, and the white and purple spots in the flower of the clove pink, agree in almost everything apart from their colour, and we easily gather from this that colour has little to do with the intrinsic natures of a body, but lies merely in the coarser and as it were mechanical arrangement

---

[182]The remainder of *Novum Organum* is taken up with prerogatives of instances, of which there are twenty-seven classes. In Aphorism II, 52, Bacon says that the first twenty are concerned with "the informative part", Instances 1 to 15 serving the intellect and 16–20, the sense; while Instances 21–27 concern the "operative part".

The phrase *prærogativas instantiarum* (prerogatives *of* instances) is generally translated "prerogative instances", which is plausible in the context, but strictly incorrect.

[183]These two are what later in this aphorism Bacon calls instances solitary in regard to similarity and difference, respectively.

of its parts.[184] These instances are Solitary in regard to difference. But both kinds are what I call Solitary, or Feral,[185] to borrow a term from the astronomers.

23

Among prerogatives of instances, I will put in second place *Migratory Instances*. These are those in which the nature in question migrates towards generation, when previously it did not exist, or on the other hand, migrates towards destruction, when it had existed previously. Thus in either transition, such instances are always paired, or rather there is a single instance in motion or transit carried on until it reaches its opposite. And such instances not only hasten and strengthen exclusion, they also drive the affirmative or the form itself into a narrow space. For the form of a thing must of necessity be something that in the course of such a migration is imparted or, on the other hand, is removed and destroyed. And, although every exclusion promotes the affirmative, yet it does so more directly when it occurs in the same subject than in different ones. Moreover, the form, as is clear from all I have said, by showing itself in one instance leads to all. And the simpler the migration, the more the instance should be valued. Moreover, Migratory Instances are of very great use for the operative part, because in suggesting a form linked with causes which either bring it into being (efficient causes) or make it pass out of existence (privative causes) they provide a clear plan for practice in some cases; and from this there is an easy passage to cases that lie nearby. And yet in these instances, there is a certain danger calling for caution, namely that they may drag

---

[184]The variegated *caryophillus*—the clove-scented pink, or gillyflower —was a familiar flower in Bacon's time. Compare

> The fairest flowers o' the season
> Are our carnations and streak'd gillyvors
> Which some call nature's bastards.
> *The Winter's Tale*

[185]*Feral* was an astronomical term used in the seventeenth century to mean "wild", in a sense analogous to that in the phrase 'wild card'.

the form too much towards the efficient, and fill or at least touch the understanding with a false opinion as to the form, as a result of looking at the efficient. For the efficient is always held to be no more than the vehicle that carries the form. The process of exclusion, however, if rightly applied, provides a simple remedy for that danger.

I must now give an example of a Migratory Instance. Suppose the nature in question is whiteness, where an instance migrating towards generation is unbroken glass and powdered glass, and likewise, still water and water shaken into froth. For unbroken glass and still water are transparent, not white, whereas powdered glass and water in a froth are white, not transparent. The question therefore is what happened to the glass and the water in that migration. Clearly the form of whiteness is conveyed and introduced through the crushing of the glass and the agitation of the water. But nothing is found to have been added other than the minute division of the parts of glass and water and the insertion of air. Yet it brings no small progress towards discovering the form of whiteness to know that two bodies, transparent in themselves, but to a greater and lesser degree[186] (viz., air and water, or air and glass), when mixed together throughout in minute portions produce whiteness, through the unequal refraction of the rays of light.

I must point out, however, that this matter also provides an example of the danger and caution that I mentioned. For here it might easily occur to an understanding misled by efficient causes of this kind to believe that air is always required for the form of whiteness, or that whiteness is only generated by transparent bodies; both are entirely false, and refuted by numerous exclusions. Rather it will become apparent that, apart from air and the like, bodies that are absolutely uniform in their optical portions give transparency; those that are uneven but through a simple structure give whiteness; those that are uneven but through an ordered, composite structure give the other colours, except black; while those that are uneven through a composite but totally disordered and

---

[186]Most likely Bacon means two bodies, both transparent, but one more so than the other.

confused structure give blackness.[187] Here then I have given an example of an instance migrating towards generation in the nature of whiteness that we are investigating. On the other hand, an instance migrating to destruction in the same nature of whiteness is provided by froth or snow when dissolved. For water sheds whiteness and dons transparency after it becomes whole and no longer contains air.

And we must not by any means overlook the fact that Migratory Instances ought to include not only those that migrate to generation and privation, but also those that migrate to either increase or decrease, since these also help us discover the form, as is very clear from the above definition of form and the table of degrees. Thus paper, which when dry is white, but when wetted (the air being excluded and water absorbed) is less white and verges more towards the transparent, is comparable to the instances mentioned above.

24

Among prerogatives of instances, I will put in third place *Revealing Instances,* which I mentioned in the First Vintage on heat, which I also call *Shining* or *Liberated and Predominant Instances.* They are those that reveal the nature in question naked and standing on its own, in its exaltation, or to the highest degree of its power, that is to say, emancipated and freed from impediments, or at least dominating them by its own strength and forcing them into submission. For since every body contains many forms of natures, linked and in a concrete state, they all beat back, suppress, break and bind one another, so that each individual form is obscured. But in some subjects, the nature in question is found to exceed the others in

---

[187]In his incomplete work, *Valerius Terminus,* composed in English but not published until after his death, Bacon expounded the same theory in the following words: "absolute equality produceth transparence, inequality in simple order or proportion produceth whiteness, inequality in compound or respective [relative] order or proportion produceth all other colours, and absolute or orderless inequality produceth blackness". This theory of colour is expounded, though even more briefly, in Bacon's *De Augmentis Scientiarum,* III, iv.

its vigour, either from the absence of any impediment or by the predominance of its power. And instances of this kind are the most revealing of the form. But at the same time, we must be careful how we use them, and keep in check the impetuosity of the understanding. For whatever reveals the form, and seems to push and thrust it before the understanding, should be viewed with suspicion, and recourse had to rigorous and careful exclusion.

For example, say we are inquiring into the nature of heat. A Revealing Instance of the motion of expansion, which, as said above, is the principal part of the form of heat, is a calendar glass of air. For a flame, although it clearly displays expansion, yet because of its instantaneous extinction does not reveal the progress of the expansion.[188] On the other hand, boiling water, because it passes so readily into steam and air, does not reveal so well the expansion of water in its own body. And again, very hot iron and similar substances are so far from revealing the progress [of expansion], that, on the contrary, through the restraint and weakening of the spirit in their compact and coarse parts (which subdue and rein in expansion), the expansion itself is entirely imperceptible to the sense. But a calendar glass reveals clearly an expansion in air that is plain to see, progressing, enduring and not transient.

Or to take another example, say we are inquiring into the nature of weight. A Revealing Instance of weight is quicksilver. It is by far the heaviest of all substances except gold, which is not much heavier.[189] But quicksilver is a better indicator of the form of weight than gold, because gold is solid and consistent, qualities that seem related to density, while quicksilver is liquid and teeming with spirit, and yet is heavier by many degrees than diamond and other substances deemed to

---

[188]This progress is evidently the same as the upward and outward motion mentioned as part of the second difference in the form of heat. See under "First Vintage concerning the Form of Heat", Aphorism II, 20, *above*. The supposed instantaneous extinction of flame is discussed more fully under example 10 of Aphorism II, 36, *below*.

[189]According to Bacon's own measurements, the densities of gold, mercury and lead, the three densest substances he found, are in the proportions 1 : 0.97 : 0.60. *(History of Dense and Rare)* The corresponding modern values are 1 : 0.60 : 0.72.

be the most solid. From this it is obvious that the form of heaviness or weight lies chiefly and simply in quantity of matter and not in a close-knit structure.

25

Among prerogatives of instances, I will put in fourth place *Clandestine* or *Twilight Instances,* as I also call them. They are, as it were, the opposite of Revealing Instances, since they show the nature in question at its weakest, in its rudiments, its swaddling clothes you might say, tentative, as if making its first effort, but hidden and subdued beneath a contrary nature. For all that, instances of this kind are of great importance in the discovery of forms; for just as Revealing Instances are good guides to differences, so Clandestine ones are the best guides to kinds, that is, to those general natures of which the natures in question are but limiting cases.

For example, say we are inquiring into the nature of consistency or self-determination [i.e., the ability of a body to maintain its shape], the opposite of which is liquid or fluid. Clandestine Instances of this are those which exhibit some weak and slight degree of consistency in a fluid; such as a bubble of water, which is like a thin film that is consistent and of determinate shape, made out of the substance of the water. Of a similar kind are the drops of rainwater from the eaves of a house, which, if more water follows, lengthen into a very thin thread, so that the water may retain its continuity. But if there is not enough water to follow, the water falls in round drops, this being the shape that best keeps the water from losing its continuity. However, the moment the thread of water ceases and begins to fall in drops, the water itself leaps back upwards to avoid discontinuity. Again in the case of molten metals, which when poured are liquid but more cohesive, the liquid drops often retreat upwards and so remain attached. A rather similar instance is that of the toy looking-glasses, which children often make out of spittle on rushes, where a consistent film of water can also be seen. This shows itself better in that other children's sport, when they take water, made rather more cohesive with soap, and blow into it through a hollow reed, and so make the water into a sort of castle of bubbles,

which through the introduction of air acquires such consistency that it allows itself to be thrown some distance without
losing its continuity. But this effect is seen best of all in froth
and in snow, which take on such consistency that they can
almost be cut, when really they are only made of air and water,
both fluids. All these things clearly intimate that liquid and
consistent are merely vulgar notions, and relative to the sense,
and that the truth is that all bodies have an inherent tendency
to escape and evade discontinuity; but that this tendency is
weak and faint in homogeneous bodies, like liquids, while in
bodies with heterogeneous parts, it is more lively and strong;
the reason being that the approach of heterogeneous matter
binds bodies together, while the stealthy entry of homogeneous matter loosens and relaxes them.

Similarly, for example, let the nature in question be
attraction or the coition of bodies. The outstanding Revealing
Instance concerning this form is the loadstone. And the
contrary nature to attracting is non-attracting, which may
exist in a similar substance. Iron, for example, does not attract
iron, just as lead does not attract lead, nor wood wood, nor
water water. Now a Clandestine Instance is a loadstone armed
with iron, or rather the iron in an armed loadstone.[190] For it is a
fact of Nature that an armed loadstone some distance away
does not attract iron any more strongly than an unarmed
loadstone. But if the iron is moved towards it so that it touches
the iron in the armed loadstone, then the latter can bear a
much greater weight of iron than can a simple unarmed
loadstone, because of the similarity of the substance of iron
against iron. This operation was entirely Clandestine and
hidden in the iron, before the loadstone was brought to touch
it, so clearly the form of coition must be something which in a
loadstone is lively and strong, but in iron is weak and hidden.
In the same way, it has been noticed that small wooden arrows
without iron points, when shot from large engines of war,
penetrate deeper into wood (like the sides of ships) than the

---

[190]Gilbert showed that the power of a loadstone is greatly increased
when it is armed, that is, provided with iron caps over its poles. Thus he
demonstrated that an armed loadstone can hold suspended from it a far
greater weight than the same one unarmed.

same arrows tipped with iron, because of the similarity of
substance of wood against wood, although previously this lay
hidden within it. And in the same way, although air plainly
does not attract air nor water, water in whole bodies, nevertheless a bubble placed near another bubble more easily dissolves
than if that second bubble were not there, because of the
tendency to coition of water with water, and air with air. And
Clandestine Instances of this kind (which are of the most
excellent usefulness, as I have said) present themselves most
conspicuously in the small and subtle portions of bodies. This
is because the greater masses of things follow more universal
and general forms, as will be described in their appropriate
place.[191]

26

Among prerogatives of instances, I will put in fifth place
what I call *Constitutive* or *Group Instances*. These are those
that constitute one species of the nature in question, as it were,
a lesser form. For since genuine forms (which are always
interchangeable with the natures in question) lie hidden deep
within and are hard to find, the subject itself and the infirmity
of human understanding require that we should not neglect,
but rather study more carefully, those partial forms that
assemble together certain *Groups* of instances (but by no
means all) into a common notion. For whatever unifies Nature,
however imperfectly, paves the way to the discovery of forms.
Therefore, instances that advance this purpose possess a
power that is not to be despised, and enjoy some prerogative.

There is great need for caution here, however, lest the
human understanding, having discovered many of those partial forms and from them constructed partitions or divisions of
the nature in question, should rest quite content in them, and
make no effort to discover legitimately the great form, but take
it for granted that the nature is from its very roots, as it were,

---

[191]These greater masses, of which fire, air, water and earth are Bacon's main examples, are distinguished by their simple homogeneous
structure. They are briefly discussed below in Aphorism 4 of the *Description of a Natural and Experimental History*.

manifold and divided, and shrink from and reject any further union of Nature, as a thing of unnecessary subtlety, and verging on mere abstraction.[192]

For example, let the nature in question be memory, or what stimulates and assists memory. Constitutive Instances are: order or distribution, which clearly helps the memory; also places in artificial memory, which can either be places in the literal sense, as a door, corner, window and things like that, or can be familiar and well-known people, or can be anything you like (provided they are arranged in a certain order), such as animals and plants, and also words, letters, characteristic marks, historical personages, etc., although some of these are more suitable and convenient than others. Places in this sense are striking aids to memory, and raise it far above its natural powers. Also songs and poems are remembered and learned by heart more easily than prose. And that *Group* of three instances, namely order, artificial memory of places, and verses, constitutes a single species of aid to memory, which can well be called a *Cutting Off of Infinity*. For when we try to remember and call something to mind, if we have no notion of it already, no picture of what we are looking for, surely we seek and strive and wander around hither and thither as if in an infinite space. But if we have some definite prenotion, infinity is at once cut off and the range of the memory narrows to what is nearby.[193] Now in the three instances I have just mentioned, the prenotion is clear and definite. In the first, that is, there has to be something that fits the context; in the second, there has to be an image which has some relation or agreement with those specified places; in the third, there must be words that fit the verse; and in those ways, infinity is cut off. Other instances provide a second species, namely, that whatever leads the intellectual conception into contact with the sense (which is indeed the principal

---

[192]The role of forms in expressing the unity of Nature is also described in Aphorism II, 3.

[193]*Prenotion* is Bacon's own term, corresponding to "preconception", which is the more common term now: "Prenotion dischargeth the indefinite seeking of that we would remember and directeth us to seek in a narrow compass" (*Advancement of Learning;* see also *De Augmentis,* V, v).

method used in artificial memory) helps the memory. Other instances provide this third species, namely those things which make an impression in a strong feeling, arousing, say, fear, admiration, shame or delight, all help the memory. Other instances provide a fourth species, namely those things that are chiefly impressed on a mind when it is clear and not occupied with other things either before or after, like those learned in childhood or what we think about before falling asleep, and also things that happen for the first time: all these stay longer in the memory. Other instances again give us this fifth species, namely, that a multitude of attendant circumstances or handles [i.e., points to get hold of] help the memory, as with writing with disconnected parts, and reading or reciting aloud. Other instances give this sixth and last species, namely, that things we are expecting and that arouse our interest are remembered better than those that simply fly past. So if you read something twenty times you will not commit it to memory so easily as if you were to read it ten times, trying in between to recall it, and looking in the book whenever your memory fails you. There are therefore six lesser forms one might say which assist the memory: *1.* the cutting off of infinity; *2.* the leading of the intellectual to the sensible; *3.* an impression in a strong feeling; *4.* an impression in a disengaged mind; *5.* a multitude of handles; *6.* a prior expectation.

Or take another example, and suppose the nature in question to be taste or tasting. The following instances are Constitutive: those who naturally lack a sense of smell cannot distinguish by taste food that is rancid or has gone bad, or is flavoured with garlic or roses or the like. Again, those whose nostrils happen to be blocked by an onset of catarrh cannot distinguish or perceive anything bad or rancid or sprinkled with rose-water. Again, if anyone thus affected with catarrh blows his nose violently when he has something fetid or sweet-scented in his mouth or on his palate, he will at that moment receive a clear perception of rancidness or perfume. These instances give and constitute the species, or part rather, of taste; so that the sense of taste is in part simply an internal smell, passing and descending from the upper passages of the nose into the mouth and palate. On the other hand, salt, sweet, bitter, acid, tart and sour, and tastes of that kind are all felt, I say, by those with no sense of smell, or whose sense is blocked, no less than by anyone else: so clearly the sense of taste is a sort of composite, made up of an internal sense of smell and a certain delicate tactile sense, of which this is not the place to speak.

Likewise, for example, let the nature in question be the communication of quality without any mixing of substance. The instance of light will give or constitute a simple species of communication; heat and the loadstone another. For the communication of light is instantaneous, and vanishes as soon as the original light is removed. But heat and magnetic force, after they have been transmitted to or rather aroused in another body, adhere and remain for some time after that which first caused them has been removed.

To sum up, the prerogative of Constitutive Instances is very great, in that they frequently help to create both definitions (especially particular ones)[194] and divisions or partitions of natures; on which Plato aptly said: "he who knows well how to define and divide should be deemed a god."[195]

27

Among prerogatives of instances, I will put in sixth place *Conforming* or *Proportionate Instances,* which I also call *Parallels,* or *Physical Similarities.* They are those that show similarities and connections of things, not in lesser forms (as Constitutive Instances do) but simply in the concrete. So they are like the very first and lowest steps towards the union of Nature. They do not establish any axiom right at the start, but they merely point out and record a certain agreement among bodies. But although they are of no great help in the discovery of forms, they nevertheless are very useful in showing the structure of the parts of the universe, performing you might say an anatomy of its members; and from that they lead us now

---

[194]Bacon is referring here to the partial *(formae particulares)* or lesser forms which he discussed at the beginning of this aphorism.

[195]This is a paraphrase of a passage in Plato's *Phaedrus,* 266b.

and then to lofty and noble axioms, especially those which concern the configuration of the world, rather than simple forms and natures.

For example, the following are Conforming Instances: a looking-glass and the eye; likewise the structure of the ear, and places that return an echo. From this conformity, apart from the observation of the similarity itself, which is helpful in many ways, it is a simple matter to put together and form this axiom, namely, that our organs of sense and objects that create reflections to the senses, are of a similar nature. Furthermore, upon this hint, the understanding rises to a more exalted and noble axiom, namely, that there is no difference between the consents or sympathies of bodies endowed with sensation and those of inanimate bodies lacking sensation, except that in the former there is an animal spirit added to the body that is thus disposed, which in the latter is absent. So that there could be as many senses in living creatures as there are sympathies in inanimate bodies, if there were perforations in the animate body allowing the animal spirit to make its way into a member rightly disposed, as into a suitable organ. And again, there are, no doubt, as many motions in an inanimate body, where there is no animal spirit, as there are senses in living creatures; in fact, there must be many more motions in inanimate bodies than there are senses in animate, because of the small number of organs of sense. A good example of this is shown in pain. For since there are many kinds of pain in living creatures, all of different character (as for example, there is one pain of burning, another of intense cold, others of pricking, squeezing, stretching), it is most certain that all these, as far as the motion is concerned, occur in inanimate bodies; as in wood or stone, when they are burnt, or frozen or pricked or cut or bent or beaten, and so on, although there is no feeling in them, because of the absence of any animal spirit.

Other Conforming Instances, strange perhaps to say, are the roots and branches of plants. For all vegetation swells and pushes out its parts into the space around it, both upwards and downwards. And there is no difference between roots and branches other than that the root is buried in the soil and the branches are exposed to the air and sun. For if you take a tender and living branch of a tree and bend it down onto a clod of earth, even though it does not adhere to the ground itself, it will at once put out not a branch, but a root. And vice versa, if earth is placed on top of it, and the plant is so obstructed by a stone or other hard substance that it is prevented from putting out shoots upwards, it will send out branches downward into the air.

Other Conforming Instances are the gums of trees and most rock-gems.[196] For both are no more than juices that have filtered and exuded, the former from trees and the latter from rocks; whence comes that clarity and splendour in each, a result of the fine and delicate filtering. This is also the reason why the fur of animals is not so beautiful and brightly coloured as many birds' plumage, since the juices are not filtered so finely through skin as through quills.

Other Conforming Instances are the scrotum in male animals and the womb in females: inasmuch as that remarkable structure by which the sexes differ (at least in land animals) appears simply to follow from one being external and the other internal; that is to say, the greater heat in the male pushes the genitalia to the outside, while in females the heat is too faint to enable it to do this, with the result that they are contained within.

Other Conforming Instances are the fins of fish and the feet of quadrupeds, or the feet and wings of birds, to which Aristotle added the four folds in the motion of snakes,[197] so that in the structure of the universe the motions of living creatures generally seem to be achieved by combinations of four limbs or four bending movements.

Again, teeth in land animals and beaks in birds are Conforming Instances, from which it is clear that in all perfect animals some hard substance finds its way to the mouth.

---

[196]In another exposition of this point, in the *Sylva Sylvarum,* 4, Bacon talks of rock-rubies, which are a species of garnet or amethyst, and of "Cornish diamond", which is rock-crystal.

[197]Aristotle, in his *History of Animals,* 490a27–32, argues that "all animals which can move about do so with four or more motion-points, the blooded ones with four only, for example, man, who uses two hands and two feet, and birds, which use two wings and two feet; whereas quadrupeds use four feet and fishes four fins. Animals which have two fins, or none (e.g., snakes), use four motion-points nevertheless: we find there are four bends in their bodies, or two bends in addition to their fins."

Again, it is not far-fetched to see a similarity and conformity between a man and an inverted plant. For the root of the nerves and faculties of animals is the head, while the seminal parts are the lowest, not counting the extremities of the legs and arms, whereas in a plant, the root (which corresponds to the head) is regularly sited at the lowest point, while the seeds are in the highest.

In sum, the lesson of this is one that I would repeat often, that men's diligence in investigating and compiling natural history should change entirely from now on, and be turned in the opposite direction from that which it now faces. For up to now men have taken great pains with excessive curiosity to note the variety of things, and give elaborate explanations of the differentiae of animals, plants and minerals, things which are often more sports of Nature than of serious use to the sciences. To be sure, such things serve to give pleasure and sometimes even practical advantage, but they contribute little or nothing to any search deep into Nature. For this reason, our labour must be entirely redirected to investigating and noting the similarities and analogies of things, both in whole things and in their parts. For it is they that unify Nature and are the origin and foundations of the sciences.

But there is here a strict and serious caution to be observed, that we should only accept as Conforming and Proportionate Instances those that mark out physical similarities, as I said at the beginning; that is, necessary and essential ones, grounded in Nature, not contingent and apparent, far less superstitious or curious similarities, such as are everywhere paraded by writers on natural magic (the most frivolous people, hardly worth naming in such serious business as I am now engaged on); in their great vanity and foolishness, describing and sometimes even inventing empty resemblances and sympathies.

But leaving these aside, the very configuration of the world shows in its larger parts some Conforming Instances which should not be neglected, like Africa and the region of Peru with the continent stretching down to the Strait of Magellan. Both regions have similar isthmuses and promontories, which can hardly have come about by chance. Or take the New and the Old World, and the fact that both are broad and spread out towards the north, but narrow and pointed towards the south.

Other very noteworthy Conforming Instances are the intense cold areas in what is called the middle region of the air,[198] and the very fierce fires that are often found erupting from underground. Both are ultimates and extremes; that is, the extreme of the nature of cold lies towards the surrounding heavens, that of heat towards the bowels of the earth, by reason of antiperistasis, or rejection of a contrary nature.

Finally, it is worth noticing the Conformity of Instances in the axioms of the sciences; like the rhetorical device called deceived expectation, which conforms to the musical device of a plagal cadence.[199] In the same way the mathematical postulate that 'if two things are equal to a third, they are equal to each other' conforms to the structure of the syllogism in logic, which unites propositions agreeing in a middle term.[200] In short, a certain keenness in searching for and hunting out conformities and physical similarities is often very useful.

28

Among prerogatives of instances, I will put in seventh place *Singular Instances,* which I also call *Irregular* or *Heteroclitic,* to borrow a word from the grammarians. They are those that show bodies in the concrete, which seem to be outlandish and broken off in Nature, and to have very little in common with other things of the same kind. For while Conforming Instances resemble other things, Singular Instances are like themselves. They have the same use as Clandestine Instances, viz., to raise up and unify Nature in order to discover kinds or

---

[198]The middle region of the air corresponds roughly to the tops of mountains, as is evident from Bacon's remarks under Instance 2, Table 2, *above.*

[199]There is a corresponding passage in the *Advancement of Learning,* II, *Works* III, pp. 348–49: "Is not the trope of music, to avoid or slide from the close or cadence, common with the trope of rhetoric, or figure of speech, of deceiving expectation?" An example from Cicero (*De Oratore,* II, 70) of this rhetorical device is "What does this gentleman lack—except cash and character?" Another would be Lady Bracknell's remark in Oscar Wilde's play *The Importance of Being Earnest:* "To lose one parent . . . may be regarded as a misfortune; to lose both looks like carelessness".

[200]Concerning the syllogism, see footnote 2, in the *Plan of the Work, above.*

general natures, to be afterwards limited by true differences.[201]
For we should not cease our investigation until properties and
qualities found in things of this kind, which could be deemed
miracles of Nature, are reduced and comprehended under
some form or certain law; so that every irregularity or singu-
larity will be found to depend on some general form, and to be a
miracle only in some precise differences and unusual degree
and combination and not in the species itself; whereas current
thinking does not go beyond holding such things to be secrets
and mighty works of Nature, as if they were uncaused and
exceptions to general rules.

Examples of Singular Instances are the sun and moon,
among the stars; the loadstone, among stones; quicksilver,
among metals; the elephant, among quadrupeds; the erotic
sense, among kinds of touch; and the scent in hounds, among
kinds of smell. Also the letter S is held by grammarians to be
Singular, on account of its combining readily with consonants,
sometimes with two, sometimes three, which no other letter
does. Instances of this kind can be very useful, because they
whet and enliven investigation, and correct the intellect misled by habit and things of common occurrence.

29

Among prerogatives of instances, I will put in eighth place
Deviating Instances; that is, errors of Nature, sports and
monsters, where Nature deviates and turns from her ordinary
course. Errors of Nature differ from Singular Instances in that
Singular Instances are prodigies of species, while errors are
those of individuals. Their uses however are more or less the
same; they correct the understanding in regard to ordinary
things, and reveal general forms. This too calls for ceaseless
investigation until the cause of such a deviation is discovered.
This cause, however, does not, strictly speaking, rise to any
form, but only to the *latent process* [leading] towards a form.
For whoever knows the ways of Nature will more easily notice

---

[201]Clandestine Instances are discussed in Aphorism II, 25.

her deviations; and, on the other hand, whoever knows her deviations will more accurately describe her ways.

They differ also from Singular Instances in that they provide better pointers to practice and the operative part. For it would be very difficult to create new species, but less so to vary known species and thereby produce many rare and extraordinary effects. On the other hand, the transition from miracles of Nature to miracles of art is quite easy. For once Nature has been detected in her variation, and the reason for that variation becomes clear, it will not be difficult to lead her back by art to the place where she chanced to go astray. And not only in that case, but in others as well. For errors on one side show and open up the way to errors and deviations on all sides. There is no need for examples of this, there are so many of them. For we should compile a collection or special natural history of all monsters and prodigious births of Nature, of everything in fact that is novel, rare and unusual in Nature. But to inspire confidence, this should be done with the most rigorous discrimination. Cases that depend in any way on religion, like Livy's prodigies,[202] are to be treated with the greatest suspicion, no less than those found among the writers on natural magic, and on alchemy, and men of that kind, who are infatuated with fables. Such a compilation should be derived from serious and reliable history and trustworthy reports.

30

Among prerogatives of instances, I will put in ninth place *Boundary Instances,* which I also call *Participles.*[203] These are

---

[202]This refers to Livy's *Book of Prodigies after the 505th Year of Rome,* which has come down to us only in fragmentary form. The book records such prodigious events as a mule giving birth to a colt, another being born with three feet, it raining blood, etc.

[203]A participle is a person or thing that partakes of the nature of two or more different classes. Thus in grammar, a participle is a word that partakes of a verb and an adjective.

those that show species of bodies which appear to be composed of two species, or to be rudiments or intermediate stages between one species and another. These instances can well be numbered among the Singular or Heteroclitic instances, for they are rare and extraordinary in the whole scheme of things. Nevertheless their importance entitles them to special treatment, for they point very clearly to the composition and structure of things, and suggest the causes of the number and quality of ordinary species in the universe, and lead the understanding on from what is to what is possible.

Examples of these are moss, which is between putrescence and a plant;[204] some comets, which are between stars and fiery meteors; flying fish, which are between birds and fish; bats, which are between birds and quadrupeds; and also the ape, "the lowliest beast, yet so like us";[205] and biform offspring of animals, hybrids from diverse species; and so on.

31

Among prerogatives of instances, I will put in tenth place *Instances of Power,* or of the *Fasces* (to borrow a word from the insignia of empire), which I also call *Instances of the Ingenuity* or *Hand of Man.* These are the most outstanding and perfect works, the very ultimate in any particular art. For since it is my chief concern that Nature should serve the affairs and convenience of man, it is entirely fitting that the works already in his power (like provinces already occupied and subdued) should be noted and enumerated, especially those that are the most complete and perfect, since if we start from them, we shall have an easier and nearer journey to new and hitherto

---

[204]Bacon elsewhere says that "Moss is a kind of mould of earth and trees. But it may be better sorted [i.e., classified] as a rudiment of germination, to which we refer it." And he explains moulds as "inceptions of putrefactions; as the moulds of oranges and lemons; which moulds afterwards turn into worms, or more odious putrefactions; and therefore (commonly) prove to be of ill odour" (*Sylva Sylvarum,* 339 and 340).

[205]This is quoted from Ennius by Cicero, *The Nature of the Gods,* I, 35.

undiscovered works. For anyone who after close study of them strives keenly and hard will assuredly advance them a little further, or redirect them to some adjacent area, or even apply and adapt them to a still nobler use.

Nor is this all. For just as rare and unusual works of Nature arouse and inspire the understanding to search for and discover forms able to embrace them, so also do outstanding and admirable works of mechanical art; indeed, much more so, because the way that such miracles of art are accomplished and constructed is usually plain to see, while the way in which the marvels of Nature come about is often more hidden from sight. But much caution is called for in those matters, lest they weigh down the understanding and, as it were, pin it to the ground.

For the danger is that such works of mechanical art, which represent the very pinnacles and summits of man's labour, might so astonish the understanding as to leave it spellbound at them, so that it cannot accustom itself to anything else, but assumes that nothing like them can be done except in the same way as they were, only taking more trouble and making more elaborate preparation.

On the contrary, it is certain that the ways and means of achieving the results and works that have been discovered and observed up to now have mostly been poor things indeed, and that all greater power depends on and in turn is derived from the sources of forms, not one of which has so far been discovered.

So, as I have said elsewhere,[206] a man could give much thought to engines of war and battering rams such as the ancients possessed, but even if he went about it as hard as he could and spent a lifetime on it, he would never light on the discovery of cannon working by gunpowder; nor for that matter, would anyone giving all his attention and thought to the manufacture of woollens and vegetable fibres have ever in that way discovered the nature of the silkworm and silk.

Hence all the more noteworthy discoveries already made have, you will notice, been brought to light not by any small

---

[206]In Aphorism I, 109.

clarifications and extensions of arts, but wholly by chance. And nothing can forestall or anticipate chance (which usually works its effects over long ages of time), except the discovery of forms.

There is no need to furnish particular examples of such instances, since there are so many of them. What we have to do is simply to seek out and examine closely all the mechanical arts, and also the liberal arts (to the extent that they relate to works) and from them compile a collection or special history of all the masterpieces and mighty and complete works in each art, together with the methods of their production or operation.

And I would not restrict the diligence with which such a collection should be made, and confine it to those things only that are held to be the master-works and mysteries of any art, and which excite our wonder. For wonder is the child of rarity, and if things are rare, even though of a kind arising from quite common natures, they will nevertheless arouse wonder.

On the other hand, things that really are to be wondered at because they contain some difference in species, compared with other species, attract slight notice if they are met with every day. And the Singularities of art should be noted no less than those of Nature, which I have already mentioned [in Aphorism II, 28]; and just as I have counted among the Singularities of Nature the sun and moon, the loadstone and the like, which in fact are very common, but in their nature almost unique, so we should do the same for the Singularities of art.

Paper, for example, is a Singular Instance of art, and a common enough thing. But if you consider the matter carefully, you will realize that artificial materials are either simply woven by means of upright and transverse threads, as silk, wool or linen cloth and the like, or else are solidified out of thickened juices, as for example brick, earthenware, glass, enamel, and porcelain, which are glossy if well united, but if not, although they are certainly hardened, have no gloss. Yet all such substances made of thickened juices are brittle, not cohesive or tough at all. Paper, on the other hand, is a tough material and can be cut and torn, so that it imitates and almost rivals any animal hide or membrane or the leaf of any plant and such works of Nature. For it is neither brittle, like glass, nor woven, like cloth; it has fibres, certainly, but not separate threads, being in every way similar to natural materials, so that among artifical materials almost nothing is found like it, and it is obviously Singular. And certainly we prefer in artificial materials those that most closely copy Nature, or, on the other hand, those that powerfully overrule and overturn her.

Moreover among Instances of the Ingenuity and Hand of Man, we must not look down on juggling and conjuring tricks, for some of them, although made for light-hearted and humorous purposes, can nonetheless give us valuable information.[207]

Finally, we should not leave out altogether superstition, or magic (in the common sense of the word). For although such matters are to a great extent buried beneath a huge mass of lies and fables, nevertheless we should briefly look into them, in case there may happen to be underlying and hidden in any of them some operation of Nature, as in fascination, fortification of the imagination, sympathy of things at a distance, and the transmission of impressions from one spirit [i.e., mind] to another, no less than from body to body, and things of that kind.[208]

---

[207]Bacon relates how he saw "a kind of juggler, that had a pair of cards, and would tell a man what card he thought". He considers the possibility that the juggler did not really have any knowledge of the man's thought, but had the power by some ingenious trick to suggest the thought to him (*Sylva Sylvarum,* 946).

[208]These various putative phenomena are discussed in Bacon's *Sylva Sylvarum,* 939 ff., together with experiments by which they might be tested. Fascination is a power of thought over other minds or physical bodies, for instance, causing a request to be granted by "constantly and strongly believing" that this will happen; the power of suggestion which the juggler referred to in the last footnote may have had would, if real, also be a case of fascination, as too, the 'evil eye'. Fortification of the imagination is the strengthening of thoughts or beliefs or memories, for instance, by ritual incantations. Bacon is sceptical of most of these supposed phenomena, but regards them as nevertheless worth testing. However, the idea that the mind could operate on physical bodies enjoys "so little credit", Bacon says, that he does not regard their testing as a matter of urgency.

32

It is clear from what I said earlier that those five kinds of instances last mentioned (viz., Conforming, Singular, Deviating, and Boundary Instances and Instances of Power) should not be saved up until some certain nature is to be looked into (as the other instances, which I set out in the first place, and also most of those that follow should); but the very first thing to do is to make a collection of them, a special history as it were, because they sort out whatever comes into the understanding and cure the perverse habit of the understanding itself, which is unavoidably imbued and coloured and in the end perverted and distorted by the incursions of everyday and customary things.

These instances therefore should be used as a preliminary step, to rectify and purge the understanding. For whatever draws the understanding away from things to which it is accustomed levels and smooths its floor for the reception of the dry, pure light of true notions.[209]

Instances of this kind also pave and prepare the way for the operative part, as I shall describe in its proper place, when I come to discuss *Application to Practice*.

33

Among prerogatives of instances, I will put in eleventh place *Instances of Companionship* and of *Hostility,* which I also call *Instances of Fixed Propositions.* These are instances that show some body or material object which is always accompanied by the nature in question, as if by an inseparable companion; or, on the other hand, which the nature in question always shuns and is excluded from companionship, like an enemy and foe. For from instances of this kind are formed certain and universal propositions, either affirmative or negative, in which the subject will be such a material body, and the predicate the nature itself that is in question. For particular

---

[209]For the meaning of 'dry light', see footnote 28, p. 59.

propositions are in no case *fixed;* those, that is, in which the nature in question is found in a certain material body to be variable and inconstant—either approaching or being acquired or, on the other hand, receding or being removed. For this reason, particular propositions have no superior prerogative, except only in the case of Migration, which I have already spoken of.[210] Nevertheless, even those particular propositions are very helpful if brought together and compared with universal propositions, as will be discussed in their proper place. Not that we require precise or absolute affirmation or negation even in those universal propositions. It is enough for our purpose, even if they allow some unique or rare exception.

Now the use of Instances of Companionship is to circumscribe the affirmative of the form. For just as in Migratory Instances the Affirmative of the form is narrowed to the point where the form of a thing must necessarily be something that is introduced or destroyed, so too the affirmative of the form is also narrowed in Instances of Companionship, in such a way that the form of a thing must necessarily be something that enters such a material body unobserved, or else on the contrary shrinks from it. Thus a good knowledge of the constitution or schematism[211] of such a body will do much to bring to light the form of the nature in question.

For example, let the nature in question be heat. An Instance of Companionship is a flame. For in water, air, stone, metal and numerous other substances, heat is not constant, and may come and go; but all flame is hot, so that heat always follows when flame is created. But we find no Hostile Instance of heat in our experience. To be sure, our senses know nothing of the bowels of the earth; but of the bodies that are known to us there is absolutely no material substance not susceptible to heat.

And again, suppose the nature in question is consistency.[212] A Hostile Instance is air; for metal can flow and also be

---

[210]Migratory Instances were discussed in Aphorism II, 23.

[211]The notion of a body's schematism is discussed in footnote 113, p. 133.

[212]Bacon defined "consistency" in Aphorism II, 25, as the ability of a body to keep its shape, as opposed to liquidity or fluidity.

consistent, and similarly glass; even water can be consistent, when it freezes; but it is impossible that air should ever become consistent or throw off its fluidity.

But in considering these Instances of Fixed Propositions, there are two pieces of advice useful for my purpose. First, that if there is clearly no universal affirmative or negative present, that fact should itself be carefully recorded, as something that is non-existent; as I have done in the case of heat, where a universal negative (as far as entities that we know of are concerned) is not present in the nature of things. Likewise, if the nature in question is eternal duration or incorruptibility, there is no universal affirmative here among us, nor can eternal duration or incorruptibility be predicated of any body below the heavens or above the earth's interior. My other piece of advice is that universal propositions, whether affirmative or negative, about any material thing, should at the same time be subjoined to those material things that seem to come closest to that which is not; as in heat, the gentlest and coolest flames; and in incorruptibility, gold, which comes nearest to it. For all those things point to the boundaries in Nature between that which exists and that which does not, and they make for the circumscribing of forms, to prevent them from slipping and straying beyond the conditions of matter.

34

Among prerogatives of instances, I will put in twelfth place those same *Subjoined Instances* which I mentioned in the preceding aphorism, which I also call *Instances of Extremity* or *Limit*. For instances of this kind are useful not only when subjoined to fixed propositions, but also by themselves and by virtue of their own nature. For they show clearly the real divisions of Nature and the measures of things, and *the extent,* in any case, that Nature may act or be acted upon, and then the transitions of Nature to something else. Examples of this are gold in weight; iron in hardness; the whale in animal size; the dog in scent; the combustion of gunpowder in rapid expansion; and others of that kind. And we should record the least and lowest instances no less than the highest, like spirit of wine in weight; silk in softness; minute skin worms in animal size;[213] etc.

35

Among prerogatives of instances, I will put in thirteenth place *Instances of Alliance* or *Union.* These are ones that mix together and unite natures thought to be heterogeneous, and are noted and labelled as such in the accepted classifications.

Instances of Alliance show that operations and effects that are attributed to one particular, heterogeneous nature as peculiar to it, are found also in others, so that this supposed heterogeneity is proved to be not real or essential, but only a modification of a general nature. They are therefore most useful in raising the understanding and carrying it forward from differences to kinds, and in dispelling the phantoms and false images of things, which in material substances come before us in disguise.

1 Suppose for example that the nature in question is *heat.* There seems to be a very common and authoritative division of heat into three kinds, namely the heat of heavenly bodies, that of animals and that of fire; and those heats (especially one of them compared with the other two) seem to be of their very essence and species, or specific nature, distinct from each other and heterogeneous; since the heat of the heavenly bodies and that of animals gives life and cherishes, whereas the heat of fire breaks down and destroys. An Instance of Alliance, therefore, is that common enough practice of bringing a vine branch into a house where a fire is constantly burning, as a result of which the grapes ripen as much as a whole month sooner than out of doors; so that fruit can be ripened by fire even if it is hanging on the tree, when that seems to be the proper work of the sun alone. From this beginning, therefore, the understanding, having repudiated the [supposed] essential heterogeneity, can easily bestir itself to find out what the

---

[213]It is not clear what kind of creature these skin worms were. They are referred to again in Aphorism II, 43.

differences really are between the heat of the sun and that of
fire, which cause their operations to be so dissimilar, however
much they themselves may partake of a common nature.

These differences will be found to be four in number:
firstly, that the heat of the sun compared with that of fire is far
more mild and gentle; secondly, that it is of a much moister
quality, at least as it is brought to us through the air; thirdly
(and this is the main difference), that it is very variable, now
approaching and full, now receding and low; a fact most
conducive to the generation of bodies. For Aristotle was right
when he said that the principal cause of both the generation
and decay which occur here among us on the face of the earth
was the oblique path of the sun through the zodiac; from which
the sun's heat, partly though the alternations of day and night,
partly through the successions of summer and winter, comes
to us as extraordinarily variable.[214] And yet this great man
straightway goes on to spoil and pervert what he has correctly
discovered. For sitting in judgement on nature, if you please
(as is his habit), he magisterially assigns the cause of generation to the approach of the sun, and the cause of decay to its
retreat; whereas both events, the approach and the retreat of
the sun, not respectively, but as it were, equally, together
furnish the cause of generation and decay alike; since the
variability of heat assists both the generation and decay of
things; while a steady heat merely conserves them. There is
also a fourth difference between the heat of the sun and that of
fire, and one of great importance, namely, that the sun carries
out its operations subtly, over long spaces of time, whereas the
operations of fire, driven on by the impatience of man, are
brought to their end after shorter periods. But if one were to go
carefully about it, and temper and reduce the heat of fire to a
more moderate and gentle degree (as can easily be done in
many ways) and then sprinkle over and mix in some moisture,
and most of all if one were to imitate the variation of the sun's
heat, and finally were to bear patiently a space of time (not
indeed as long as to be proportionate to the works of the sun,
but longer than men usually bring to the works of fire), then, I

---

[214]See Aristotle's *Meteorology,* I 9 and I 14 and IV 1.

say, one will easily dismiss that difference in quality of heat, and will put to the test, or rival, or in some cases outdo the works of the sun, through the heat of fire.

A similar Instance of Alliance is the revival of butterflies inert and almost dead with cold, by warming them gently before a fire; so you can easily see that fire is no more denied the power of giving life to animals than of ripening plants. Also that famous invention of Fracastoro, of the well-heated pan [cupping-glass], with which doctors cover the heads of apoplectics for whom all hope has been abandoned, obviously expands the animal spirits oppressed and all but extinguished by the humours and obstructions of the brain, and rouses them to motion in the same way that fire works on water or air, and in consequence brings them to life.[215] Also eggs are sometimes hatched by the warmth of a fire, which closely imitates animal heat. There are many examples of this kind, so that no one can doubt that the heat of fire can be modified in many subjects to resemble the heat of heavenly bodies and of animals.

2 In the same way, suppose the natures in question are *motion and rest*. There appears to be an accepted division, springing from the heart of philosophy, that natural bodies either rotate, or move straight ahead, or remain at rest. For either there is motion without limit, or rest at a limit, or movement towards a limit. But that endless motion of rotation seems to belong only to heavenly bodies; the state of rest or stillness seems to belong to the globe of the earth; and other bodies (which are called heavy or light, being, that is, outside the places where they naturally belong) are carried in straight lines towards masses or collections of similar bodies, the light upwards, towards the circumference of the heaven, the heavy downwards, towards the earth. And all this sounds very fine.

But an Instance of Alliance is any of the lower comets,[216] which, though far below the heaven, nevertheless rotate. And Aristotle's fiction of a comet's being tied to or following some

---

[215]Girolamo Fracastoro (1483–1553) was a celebrated Italian physician and poet. He himself died of apoplexy, a stroke, that is, near Verona.

[216]Bacon mentions higher and lower comets on several occasions, though he does not say what he understands by the distinction.

particular star has long ago been exploded, not only because
the reasoning for it is improbable, but because of our manifest
experience of the erratic and irregular motion of comets
through different parts of the sky.

Again, another Instance of Alliance on this subject is the
motion of air, which within the tropics, where the circles of
rotation are larger, seems itself to rotate from east to west.

And the flow and ebb of the sea would be yet another
instance, if it were found that the waters themselves were
carried along, albeit slowly and feebly, in a rotating motion
from east to west, though in such a way that they were driven
back twice a day. Therefore, if such is the case, it is clear that
rotatory motion is not confined to heavenly bodies, but is also
shared by air and water.

And that property of light bodies, namely that they are
carried upwards, is also somewhat shaky. And a water bubble
can be taken as an Instance of Alliance on this point. For if air
is under water, it rises rapidly to the surface, through that
motion of percussion (as Democritus calls it) whereby descending water strikes and raises the air upwards; not however
through any effort or striving of the air itself. And when it has
come to the surface of the water, the air is then prevented from
any further ascent by a slight resistance that it meets in the
water, which does not immediately allow itself to be parted
from it: so that the air has but little inclination to rise.

3 In the same way, suppose that *weight* is the nature in
question. It is a thoroughly accepted distinction that dense and
solid things are carried towards the centre of the earth, while
rare and light things rise towards the circumference of the
heaven, as if to their proper places. But as for this idea of
places, although such concepts flourish in the schools, it is
evidently silly and childish to think that a place can have any
power. Therefore philosophers are talking nonsense when they
say that if there were a hole bored right through the earth,
heavy bodies dropped down it would come to a stop when they
reached the centre. For it certainly would be a very powerful
and efficacious kind of nothing, or mathematical point, that
would either draw other things to it, or, again, that other
things would seek. For a body is only acted on by another body.
In reality, that tendency to rise or fall either lies in the

schematism of the moving body, or in a sympathy or consent with another body. But if a dense and solid body were to be found that nevertheless was not carried down to the earth, that aforesaid distinction would collapse. And if Gilbert's opinion is to be believed, that the magnetic power of the earth to draw heavy things to it does not extend beyond the sphere of its influence (which always acts up to a certain distance and no further) and if this opinion were to be verified by some instance, that would at last be an Instance of Alliance on this subject. But there has not been any certain and clear instance of this at the present time. What seems to come nearest to this are waterspouts, which are often seen in voyages over the Atlantic towards either of the Indies. For so great is the volume and mass of water suddenly poured down by these waterspouts that they seem to have been collections of water accumulated some time before, and to have remained hanging in these places, and later from some violent cause to have been thrown and driven down, rather than to have fallen by the natural motion of gravity. So that it may be conjectured that a dense, compact bodily mass at a great distance from the earth might stay hanging there as if it were an earth itself, and not fall unless it were thrust down. But I cannot say anything with certainty about this. Meanwhile in this and many other cases, it will easily be seen how poor we are in natural history, when instead of reliable accounts of instances I am sometimes forced to quote mere suppositions for examples.

4   In the same way, suppose the nature in question to be the *power of reasoning*. There seems to be a real division between human reasoning and the cleverness of animals. But yet there are some instances of actions performed by animals, from which it seems that they too can reason almost syllogistically; as in the old story of the raven which at a time of great drought, being half-dead with thirst, saw some water in the hollow trunk of a tree; and since the hole was too narrow for it to enter, it continued to drop in numerous pebbles, with the result that the water rose until it could drink: and this afterwards passed into proverb.[217]

---

[217]This story appears in Pliny, *Natural History*, X, 60.

5 In the same way, suppose the nature in question to be *visibility*. There seems to be a real and undoubted distinction between light, which is the source of visibility and provides the primary power of sight; and colour, which is secondarily [i.e., derivatively] visible, and cannot be perceived without light, so that it seems to be just an image or modification of light. But on both counts in this matter we seem to have Instances of Alliance, namely snow en masse, and a sulphur flame, in one of which there seems to be colour primarily giving out light, in the other light verging on colour.[218]

36

Among prerogatives of instances, I will put in fourteenth place *Crucial Instances,* taking the word from the crux or signpost erected at a fork in the road, which points to the different ways. I also call them *Decisive* and *Judicial Instances* and in some cases *Oracular* and *Commanding Instances.* They operate as follows. When in the investigation of any nature the understanding stands evenly balanced, unable to decide to which of two or sometimes more natures the cause of the nature in question should be ascribed (on account of the frequent and ordinary concurrence of many natures), Crucial Instances show the union of one of those natures with the nature in question to be constant and unbreakable, but that of the other variable and separable. The inquiry then is over, and the former nature is accepted as the cause, the latter dismissed and denied. Such instances, then, are most illuminating and authoritative, so that the course of interpretation sometimes ends in them and is accomplished through them. Sometimes we come across these Crucial Instances among those we have already observed, but most of them are new, and are intentionally looked for and applied, and are finally brought to light by unremitting and zealous diligence.

---

[218]Liquid sulphur burns with a characteristic deep blue flame. Bacon seems to be suggesting that the sulphur flame is colour without light (in Aphorism II, 36 [7], a dull, bluish flame, presumably of sulphur, is described as one of the darker flames).

1 Suppose for example that the nature in question is the *flow and ebb of the sea,* which is repeated twice a day, each flow and ebb taking six hours, subject to some small difference coinciding with the motion of the moon. The fork in the road concerning this nature is as follows.

This motion must of necessity come about either by an advance and retreat of the waters, like water that is rocked in a basin, which leaves one side of the basin as it washes against the other, or by a rising and sinking of the waters from the deep, like water boiling up and then subsiding. The question is to which of the two causes the flow and ebb should be ascribed. Now if the first assertion is accepted, whenever the tide comes in at one side of the sea it must necessarily at the same time go out somewhere on the other. So the question comes down to this. Now Acosta[219] and a few others have observed after careful research that the tides come in at the same time on the coast of Florida and on the opposite coast of Spain and Africa, and go out at the same time also, and do not go out on the shores of Spain and Africa when they are coming in on those of Florida. And yet, if one considers the matter more carefully, this does not prove the case for the rising motion and disprove that of the advancing. For it is possible for there to be an advancing motion of the waters which would still flood into opposite shores of the same sea bed at the same time; if, that is, those waters were impelled and driven together from elsewhere, as happens in rivers, which flow and ebb at the same hours on either bank, where however the motion is certainly one of advancing, namely of waters entering river estuaries from the sea. It is therefore possible that waters coming in a vast mass from the East Indian Ocean are driven and pushed in the same way into the sea bed of the Atlantic, and for that reason flood each side of it at the same time. The question is, therefore, whether there is another sea bed through which the waters could diminish and ebb at the same

---

[219]José de Acosta was the Spanish author of a celebrated treatise entitled *A Natural and Moral History of the Indies,* first published in Spanish in 1590 and translated into a number of other languages, including Latin, soon after.

times. And here we have the South Sea [i.e., the Pacific Ocean] which is certainly as wide as the Atlantic, in fact wider and larger, which could answer this purpose.

We have therefore at last reached a Crucial Instance in this subject, namely this. If it can be found with certainty that the tide is at the flood on the opposite shores of the Atlantic in Florida and Spain, when at the same time it is also in flood on the shores of Peru and the far side of China, then for sure, by this Decisive Instance, we must reject the assertion that the flow and ebb of the sea, which is the nature we are looking into, comes about through an advancing motion, since there is no sea or place left where it could at the same time be retreating or ebbing. And the easiest way to find this out would be to ask the inhabitants of Panama and Lima (where the two oceans, the Atlantic and Southern, are separated by a narrow isthmus[220]) whether or not the flow and ebb of the sea on the opposite sides of the isthmus comes at the same time. Now this decision or judgement seems certain, on the supposition that the earth stands motionless. But if the earth rotates, it could perhaps be that in consequence of the different speeds of rotation of the earth and the waters of the sea, the waters are pressed violently upwards into a bulge, which would be the inflowing tide; and when they relaxed, unable to be piled up any further, and came down, that would be the ebb. But that must be the subject of a separate investigation. And yet even on that supposition we are left with the equally firm fact that there must be an ebbing going on somewhere at the time when there is a flow elsewhere.

2   In the same way, suppose the nature in question to be the latter motion of the two I have supposed, namely *the rising and subsequent sinking motion of the sea,* if it falls out, after a careful examination, that we reject the other motion—the advancing one—I discussed. Then indeed the road branches into three with regard to this nature. It must be that this motion, by which the tides in their flows and ebbs rise up and then fall back, without any addition of other waters rolling in,

---

[220]Bacon's geography is somewhat awry here; as every map of the time shows, Lima is a long way from the Panama Isthmus.

comes about in one of these three ways. Either a mass of water issues from the interior of the earth and withdraws back there again; or there is not any greater volume of water, but the same waters (without any increase in quantity) become extended and rarefied so that they occupy a larger space and dimension, and then contract again; or there is no additional greater mass, nor wider extension, but the same waters (the same in mass and in density or rarity), through some magnetic force drawing and raising them from above, and by consent, rise and then fall back. And so, if this is accepted, let inquiry be reduced to this last kind of motion (passing over the two before-mentioned), and let the question be whether any such rising may occur, either by consent or magnetic force. Now in the first place it is obvious that all the waters, as they lie in the trench or hollow of the sea, cannot possibly be raised at the same time, because there would not be anything to take their place at the bottom, so that if there were in the waters any such strong desire to rise, that would be subdued and restrained by the cohesion of things, or (as is commonly said) to avoid a vacuum. All that remains then is that the waters are raised in one part, and are thereby diminished and fall back in another. And also it necessarily follows that this magnetic force, since it cannot operate upon the whole, will operate with the greatest intensity over the middle, in such a way that it raises the waters in the middle, and they, being raised, by moving thither, abandon and leave the sides.

Thus at length we come to a Crucial Instance on this subject. It is this: if we find that in the ebb of the sea, the surface of the waters is more curved and rounded, by reason of the waters rising in the middle of the sea and withdrawing at the sides, that is, the coasts, and that in flood tides the same surface is more level and even, as the waters return to their former position, then assuredly through this Decisive Instance this rising by magnetic force can be accepted, otherwise judgement must certainly be passed against it. Now this is not a difficult thing to discover using mariners' sounding-lines in straits; [to discover] that is to say, whether during ebb tides the sea is not higher or deeper towards the middle than during flood tides. It is worth noting, however, that if this were so, it would entail that the waters (contrary to common belief) rise during ebb tides, and sink only during flood tides, so as to clothe and cover the shores.

3   In the same way, let the nature in question be the *spontaneous motion of rotation* and, in particular, whether the diurnal motion, whereby the sun and stars to our eyes rise and set, is a real motion of rotation in the heavenly bodies, or an apparent motion in them, and a real motion in the earth. There can be a Crucial Instance on this point, as follows: if there is found to be any motion in the ocean from east to west, however sluggish and weak; if the same motion, but a little more lively, is found in the air, particularly within the tropics, where it would be more perceptible on account of the larger circles; if the same motion were found in the lower comets, now made active and strong; if the same motion were found in the planets, but so ordered and graduated as to be slower, the nearer the planet is to the earth, and faster the further away, and, finally, fastest of all in the starry heaven; then the diurnal motion must certainly be accepted as being real in the heavens, and terrestrial motion must be denied; because it will be obvious that motion from east to west is entirely cosmic, and resulting from the consents of the universe, which is most rapid in the highest regions of the heavens and gradually falls away, finally ceasing and vanishing at that which is immobile, namely the earth.

4   In the same way, let the nature in question be that *other motion of rotation* which astronomers are always talking of, opposing and contrary to the diurnal motion, that is to say, from west to east, which the ancient astronomers attributed to the planets, and also to the starry heaven, but Copernicus and his followers to the earth as well. And we should investigate and see whether there is any such motion in the nature of things, or whether it is rather a thing made up and conjectured for the advantage and convenience of calculations, and for that attractive idea of explaining celestial motions by means of perfect circles. For this motion of the heavens is by no means proved to be true and real, either by the failure of a planet to return in its diurnal motion to the same point of the starry heaven, or through the zodiac having different poles than the earth; which two phenomena have given birth to our idea of this motion. For the first phenomenon is well explained by

outrunning and leaving behind,[221] and the second, by spiral lines; so that the variability of return and the declination towards the tropics could be modifications of that one diurnal motion, rather than motions in the opposite direction or around different poles. And it is most certain, if I may play the plain man for a moment, and dismiss the inventions of the astronomers and schoolmen, who make a practice of over-ruling the senses, often without reason, and favouring things that are more obscure, that this motion is such as appears to the sense, as I have described; a model of which I once had built with iron wires, as in a machine.

Now a Crucial Instance on this subject would be as follows: if in any trustworthy history there were found to have been any comet, whether higher or lower, that has not revolved in manifest harmony (even if very irregularly) with the diurnal motion, but has rather rotated counter to the motion of the heavens, then certainly we should judge that, to this extent, there could be some such motion in Nature. But if nothing of this kind is found, it must be regarded as questionable, and we must have recourse to other Crucial Instances on this subject. 5   In the same way, let the nature in question be *weight or heaviness*. Here the road branches into two, thus. It must be that heavy and weighty objects either tend by their own nature towards the centre of the earth, through their own schema-tism; or they are attracted and dragged by the bodily mass of the earth itself, as if by an assembly of bodies of like nature, and are borne towards it by consent. But if the latter of these is the cause, it follows that the nearer heavy things approach the earth, the harder and faster they are carried towards it; the further from it they are, the weaker and slower (as with magnetic attraction); and that this would happen within a certain distance, so that if they were removed to such a distance that the earth's power could not act on them, they would remain hanging there, as does the earth itself, and would not fall at all.

The following therefore could be a Crucial Instance on this

---

[221]That is, by the fixed stars outrunning the planets and leaving them behind.

subject. Take a clock of the sort that works by leaden weights, and another that works by compression of an iron spring. They should be properly tested, so that neither is faster or slower than the other. Then have the clock working by weights placed at the top of some very high church and the other kept below, and let careful note be taken whether the clock placed on high goes more slowly than usual, on account of the diminished power of its weights. A similar experiment should be made in the depths of mines sunk deep below the earth, to see whether a clock of the same kind does not move faster than usual, through the increased power of its weights. If the power of the weights is found to be diminished when the clock is high up and increased when it is underground, then we may take it that attraction by the bodily mass of the earth is the cause of weight.

6 In the same way, let the nature in question be the *polarity of an iron needle when it has been touched by a loadstone*.[222] With regard to this nature, the road will branch into two, thus. Of necessity, the touch of the loadstone either imparts from itself to the iron a tendency to turn to the north and south; or it merely arouses and prepares the iron, and the motion itself is imparted by the presence of the earth, as Gilbert thinks, and strives with such great efforts to prove. This therefore is the direction in which point the facts which he has with discerning labours collected. One of these is that an iron nail which has remained for a long time in a position pointing to north and south, acquires polarity in that long lapse of time without having been touched by a loadstone; as if the earth itself, which because of its distance acts only weakly (for the surface or outer crust of the earth is, as he would have it, without magnetic power), has made up for the touch of the loadstone through the long period, and stimulated the iron, and then, when it [the earth] has done so, has brought it [the iron nail] into conformity with itself and polarized it. Another is that if white-hot iron is laid when cooling in a north-south position, it too acquires polarity without the touch of a loadstone; as if the

---

[222]Touching was the action of magnetizing a steel bar or needle by contact with one or more magnets; different methods were known as single, double and separate touch.

parts of the iron, set in motion by the heating and afterwards recovering themselves, were, in that very moment of their cooling, more susceptible and sensitive, so to speak, to the power emanating from the earth than at other times, and thus became stimulated. But these things, although well observed, yet do not wholly prove what he asserts.

Now a Crucial Instance concerning this question would be as follows; take a small loadstone globe,[223] and mark its poles; place the poles facing east and west, not north and south, and let them remain so; then place on it an untouched iron needle, and let it remain in that position for six or seven days. Now while the needle remains over the loadstone, it will, without doubt, leave the poles of the earth and turn towards the poles of the loadstone, and will therefore, so long as it stays in that position, turn towards the earth's east and west. But if this needle, on being removed from the loadstone and placed on a pivot, is found to point at once to north and south, or even to return gradually in that direction, then the presence of the earth must be accepted as the cause; but if it either turns as before towards east and west or if it loses its polarity, that cause must be regarded as doubtful, and further investigation made.

7 In the same way, suppose that the nature in question is the *bodily substance of the moon:* whether it is rare, flame-like or airy, as most early philosophers supposed, or solid and dense, as Gilbert holds, with many of the moderns and some of the ancients. The reasons for the latter opinion are chiefly based on the fact that the moon reflects the rays of the sun, and that no reflection of light seems to take place except from solid objects.

Therefore, Crucial Instances concerning this question, if indeed there are any, could be those that demonstrate reflection from a rare body, such as a flame, provided it is dense enough. Certainly one cause of twilight, among others, is the reflection of the sun's rays by the upper part of the air. Moreover, we sometimes see that the sun's rays are reflected

---

[223]Such magnetic globes, or 'terrellas' (little earths), were used by Gilbert to illustrate and test the notion that the earth as a whole was a magnet.

on fine evenings by the fringes of dewy clouds with no less
brilliance, rather with even greater and more glorious light,
than is returned by the body of the moon; and it is not certain
that those clouds have coalesced into a dense body of water. We
also see dark air behind windows at night reflect the light of a
candle, just as a dense body would. We should also try an
experiment of letting the rays of the sun pass through an
aperture onto a somewhat dull, bluish flame.[224] For indeed the
unobstructed rays of the sun falling on darker flames appear to
deaden them, so that they take on the appearance more of
white smoke than of flame. These things then occur to me at
the present time as being in the nature of Crucial Instances
concerning this matter, and better ones perhaps can be found.
But it must always be observed that reflection from a flame
cannot be expected except from one of some depth, for otherwise it borders on transparency. But this we can set down as
certain, that light falling on a uniform body is always either
received and transmitted or it rebounds.

8   In the same way, suppose the nature in question to be the
motion through the air of missiles, such as darts, arrows and
[musket] balls. The schoolmen, as usual, explain this motion
extremely carelessly, thinking it enough to give it the name of
violent motion, to distinguish it from what they call natural
motion; and they satisfy themselves in the matter of the initial
striking or impulse by the principle 'that two bodies cannot
exist in one place, or else penetration of dimensions would
occur', and do not concern themselves with the continued
progress of the motion. Now with regard to this nature the
road branches in two, thus: either this motion comes about
from the air carrying the projected body and gathering itself
behind it, in the way rivers do with a boat, or the winds do with
chaff; or from the parts of the body itself not enduring the
pressure, but moving forwards in succession to relax it. Now
the first of these is accepted by Fracastoro,[225] and almost all
those who have investigated this motion with any subtlety, nor
is there any doubt that air does play some part in this matter.

---

[224]Bacon perhaps had the deep blue sulphur flame in mind.

[225]In his work *On the Sympathies and Antipathies of Things.*

But the other motion is undoubtedly the true one, as is confirmed by numberless experiments.. But the following, among others, could be a Crucial Instance concerning this question: that an iron sheet, or a fairly stiff iron wire, or even a reed or a quill sliced down the middle, after being pressed into a curve between finger and thumb, springs up. For it is obvious that this cannot be ascribed to the air collecting behind the body, because the source of the motion is in the middle of the sheet or reed, not in the extremities.

9 In the same way, suppose the nature in question to be that rapid and powerful motion of the *expansion of gunpowder into flame*, by which such great masses of material are thrown down, and such great weights propelled, as we see in large mines and in mortars. Now with regard to this nature the road branches in two, thus. Either this motion is aroused by the simple urge of the body to expand when it has been set on fire; or by this, combined with the urge of the crude spirit, which rapidly flies from the fire, and bursts violently from the surrounding heat, as if from a prison. Now the schoolmen and common opinion consider only that former urge. For men think themselves fine philosophers if they assert that by some necessity arising from the form of the element [of fire], the flame is given a greater space to occupy than that body filled when it was in powder form, and that this motion followed from it. They fail to notice, however, that although this is true, given that a flame is generated, the generation of the flame can nevertheless be hindered by a mass sufficiently great to suppress and stifle it; thus the question may not be reduced to that necessity of which they speak. For they rightly believe that if a flame is generated, expansion must of necessity take place, and from that the propulsion or removal of the body obstructing it will follow. But that necessity is entirely avoided if that solid mass suppresses the flame before it is generated. And we see that flame, especially when it is first generated, is soft and gentle, and requires space in which to test itself and move about. Such great violence therefore cannot be attributed to flame by itself. But the fact is that the generation of these windy flames, these fiery winds, as it were, comes about from the conflict of two bodies which are of quite opposite natures, the one highly inflammable, which flourishes in sulphur, and the other abhorring flame, such as the crude spirit in saltpetre; so that a strange conflict occurs, the sulphur bursting into flame with all its strength (for the third body, that is, willow charcoal, is only there to hold the other two together in a body),[226] while the spirit of the saltpetre erupts with all its strength and at the same time expands (for this is what happens when air, and all crude substances, and water are swollen by heat), and through that flight and eruption it meanwhile fans the flame of the sulphur from all sides, as if by invisible bellows.

Now there could be two kinds of Crucial Instances on this question. The first concerns those bodies which are most inflammable, such as sulphur, camphor, naphtha and the like, as well as mixtures of them, which catch fire faster and more readily than gunpowder, provided they are not hindered, from which it appears that their tendency to catch fire does not of itself produce that stupendous effect. The second concerns those bodies that fly from and abhor flame, as do all salts. For we see that, if they are thrown into a fire, their watery spirit erupts with a loud crack before the flame takes hold; which also happens, in a milder way, in the stiffer kinds of leaves, where the watery part bursts out before the oily part catches fire. But the effect is most clearly seen in quicksilver, which is aptly called 'mineral water'.[227] For this, without catching fire, almost matches the force of gunpowder by mere eruption and expansion; and quicksilver is also said to multiply the force of gunpowder if mixed with it.

10 In the same way, suppose the nature in question is the *transitory nature of flame, and its instantaneous extinction.* For the nature of flame as we know it seems not to have any fixed consistency, but to be generated, as it were, each moment, and immediately extinguished. For in flames that we see continue and endure, it is obvious that that duration is not of the same individual flame, but is made through a succession of new

---

[226]Bacon is discussing in turn the three constituents of gunpowder: sulphur, saltpetre and charcoal.

[227]Paracelsus sometimes called quicksilver "a mineral water of metals", for instance, in his *Book About Minerals.*

flame, consecutively generated, without the flame remaining numerically identical. This can easily be seen from the fact that if the food or fuel of the flame is withdrawn, the flame goes out at once. Now with regard to this nature the road branches in two, thus: either that momentary nature arises from the cessation of the cause that first generated it, as happens with light, sound, and so-called violent motions; or because the flame, though of its own nature capable of remaining here before us, is put out and destroyed by the force of opposing natures surrounding it.

There could therefore be the following Crucial Instance regarding this question: in larger fires we see how high the flames ascend; for the wider the base of the flame, the higher its peak. Thus extinction seems to have its beginning around the sides, where the flame is compressed and harassed by the air. But the middle of the flame, which air does not reach but which the rest of the flame surrounds, stays numerically identical, nor is it extinguished until it is gradually narrowed by the air surrounding it at the sides. Therefore all flame is pyramid-shaped, wider at its base where its fuel is, but sharper at its tip (where the air is hostile and there is no supply of fuel). Smoke, however, which is narrower at its base, expands as it rises, and becomes like an inverted pyramid. This is because air absorbs smoke and compresses flame (for no one should dream that a lighted flame is air, since they are bodies of entirely different kinds).

Now there could be a Crucial Instance more precisely suited to this question, if it were perhaps possible to exhibit the phenomenon through two-colour flames. Take therefore a little metal stand, and fix in it a small lighted wax candle; place the stand in a bowl, and pour round it a moderate quantity of spirit of wine, which should not reach the lips of the stand; then light the spirit of wine. Now the spirit of wine will show a more bluish flame, but the light of the candle a more yellow one. Observe therefore whether the candle flame (which it is easy to distinguish from the flame of the spirit of wine, for flames do not, like liquids, immediately mingle together) remains pyramidal or tends rather towards a spherical shape, since there appears to be nothing to destroy or compress it. And if this does occur, it must be set down as certain that flame stays numerically identical as long as it is enclosed within another flame and does not feel the hostile force of the air.

Now let this be all I have to say about Crucial Instances. I have dwelt on them at some length in order that men may little by little learn and become accustomed to make judgements about nature by means of Crucial Instances and light-bearing experiments, and not by probable reasonings.

37

Among prerogatives of instances, I will put in fifteenth place *Instances of Divorce,* which point to separations of those natures that occur for the most part [together].[228] They differ however from the Instances subjoined to Instances of Companionship, because the latter point to separations of some nature from some concrete thing with which it is habitually associated, while these indicate separations of some one nature from another. They differ also from Crucial Instances in that they determine nothing, but merely give notice that one nature can be separated from another. Their use is to reveal false forms and to dispel slight conjectures arising from whatever is met with by the way, thus they add leaden weights as ballast, as it were, to the understanding.

Suppose, for example, that the natures in question are those four natures that Telesio would have to be comrades in arms, as it were, sharing the same quarters; namely heat, brightness, rarity and mobility, or readiness to move. Now very many Instances of Divorce are found among these. Air, for example, is rare and readily mobile, but is neither hot nor bright; the moon is bright, but is without heat; boiling water is

---

[228]We have followed Fowler's translation here, since it fits in well with the rest of Bacon's discussion of Instances of Divorce. However, the word 'together' has no direct counterpart in the Latin. The Ellis translation is "separations of natures of most familiar occurrence", which is hard to make sense of. The same Latin phrase *quae ut plurimum occurrunt* is used at the beginning of Aphorism I, 25, where, however, the Ellis translation does seem the more appropriate.

hot, but not bright; the motion of an iron needle on a pivot is
quick and nimble, and yet occurs in a body that is cold, dense
and opaque; and many others of that kind.

In the same way, suppose that the natures in question are
the corporeal nature and natural action. For natural action
seems only to be found subsisting in some body. Yet there may
possibly be some Instance of Divorce bearing on this matter,
namely, magnetic action, whereby iron is drawn towards a
loadstone, and heavy bodies towards the globe of the earth.
Still other cases of operation at a distance might be added. For
such action takes place both in time, through moments, not
instants of time, and in space, through steps and over distances. There is therefore some moment of time and some
spatial interval, in which that power or action hangs suspended in the medium between those two bodies that produce
the motion. The question therefore comes down to this: whether the bodies that are the ends of the motion dispose or alter
the intervening medium, so that by a succession of actual
contacts the power glides from one terminal body towards the
other, and subsists meanwhile in the intervening medium, or
whether none of these exists, beyond the bodies, the power and
the spaces. Now in the cases of optical rays and sounds and
heat and some other actions at a distance, it is probable that
the intervening matter is disposed and altered; the more so,
because such an action requires a medium that is qualified to
convey it. But that magnetic or attractive power admits media
which are, so to speak, neutral, and it is not hindered by any
kind of medium. And if that power or action has nothing to do
with the intervening matter, it follows that there is a natural
power or action subsisting at some time and in some place
without a body; since it subsists neither in the bodies at the
ends nor in the intervening media, which means that magnetic
action may be an Instance of Divorce regarding the corporeal
nature and natural action; to which we can add as a corollary,
and an advantage not to be overlooked, namely, that even to a
philosopher going by his senses this could be taken as proof
that there are entities and substances existing apart and
incorporeal. For if a natural power and action emanating from
a body can subsist for a certain time and in a certain place
entirely without a body, then that is close to saying that it can

also emanate of its own accord from an incorporeal substance. For it seems that a corporeal nature is required no less for sustaining and conveying natural action than it is for calling it forth or generating it.

38

There now follow five classes of instances to which I give the one general name of *Instances of the Lamp,* or of *First Information.* These are those that aid our senses. For since all interpretation of Nature begins with the senses and it is from the perceptions of the senses that a straight, reliable and well-built way leads to perceptions of the understanding, which are true notions and axioms, it must of necessity be that the more plentiful and accurate are the representations or offerings of the senses themselves, the more everything will go forward easily and successfully.

Of these five Instances of the Lamp, then, the first strengthen, enlarge and rectify the immediate actions of the senses; the second bring what cannot be perceived down to that which can; the third indicate continuing processes or series of those things and motions which are mostly unobserved except in their exit or periods;[229] the fourth provide some substitute to the sense when it utterly forsakes us; and the fifth rouse the attention and notice of the sense, and at the same time limit the subtlety of things. I will now speak of each of these separately [in Aphorisms II, 39 to 43, *below*].

39

Among prerogatives of instances, I will put in sixteenth place *Instances of the Door* or *Gate,* and I call by that name those that help the immediate actions of the senses. Now

---

[229]When Bacon develops this point in Aphorism II, 41, he says: "men study Nature only in a desultory and intermittent way (*per periodos*), and when bodies are finished and completed, not while she is still operating."

among the senses, vision clearly holds the first place for providing information, so it is chiefly for this sense that we should seek out aids. And these aids appear to be three in number: they enable the sense to perceive things that are not seen, or are a long way off, or to perceive them more precisely and distinctly.

Apart from spectacles and the like, which are useful only to correct or ease the weakness of poor sight, and so do nothing to enlarge our information, aids of the first kind are those recently invented optic glasses [microscopes],[230] which show the latent and invisible fine details of bodies, and their hidden schematisms and motions, by greatly increasing the size of the inspected object. By their means, we can perceive and marvel at the precise shape and features of the body in a flea, a fly, or a grub, and also colours and motions never seen before. In fact they say that a straight line drawn by a pen or pencil is perceived through a glass of this kind to be quite irregular and crooked; because of course no motion of the hand, even if aided by a ruler, nor any imprint of ink or colour is truly regular, although those irregularities are so minute as to be invisible without the aid of such glasses. And men have added a kind of superstitious gloss in the matter, as happens with novel and strange things, to the effect that glasses like this add lustre to the works of Nature, but discredit those of mechanical art. The truth however is simply that natural structures are much more subtle than artificial ones. For that microscope is only useful for looking at very small things, and if Democritus had seen such an instrument, he would perhaps have jumped for joy, and thought that a method had been found for seeing the atom (which he declared to be completely invisible). But the inadequacy of these glasses, except for fine details (and not even for those, if they are in a somewhat larger body), impairs the usefulness of the invention. For if it could be extended to larger bodies, or to the fine details of larger bodies, so that the

---

[230]The first, rudimentary compound microscope, consisting of a convex lens together with a concave lens as eyepiece, is said to have been invented by two Middleburg lens-grinders, Johann and Zacharias Janssen, around 1590.

structure of a linen cloth could be as clearly seen as if it were a net, and [if] in this way the hidden minutiae and irregularities of gems, liquors, urine, blood, wounds and many other things could be seen, [then] without doubt many great advantages could be gained from this invention.

Aids of the second kind are those other optic glasses [telescopes] invented by Galileo's remarkable efforts. With their help, we can open up and maintain a closer commerce with the heavenly bodies, as if by boats or ships. For from these we know that the galaxy is a group or cluster of small stars, entirely separate and distinct, a fact which was only suspected by the ancients. They also seem to demonstrate that the spaces of the planetary orbs, as they are called, are not entirely void of other stars, but that the heaven begins to be marked by stars before the stellar heaven itself is reached, although with stars too small to be seen without these glasses. With them we can see those small stars circling in dance round the planet Jupiter (from which it is possible to conclude that there are several centres in the motions of the stars). With them the different areas of light and dark on the moon can be more distinctly perceived and located, so that a kind of lunar geography could be created. With these we can see the spots in the sun, and things of that kind; all certainly noble discoveries, so far as we can safely trust demonstrations of this kind, which I regard with suspicion, chiefly for this reason; that the experiment stops with these few discoveries, and that many others, equally worthy of investigation, have not been made by the same means.[231]

Aids of the third kind are those rods used for land-measurement, astrolabes, and the like, which do not enlarge the sense of sight, but rectify and guide it. And although there may be other instances that assist the other senses in their

---

[231]Bacon's position seems equivocal here, at once applauding Galileo's discoveries of the satellites of Jupiter, the details of the lunar surface, etc., yet mistrusting telescopic demonstrations. Spedding suggested that Bacon doubted the reliability of the telescope, because he had expected many more discoveries to have followed thick and fast, whereas this had not happened.

immediate and direct actions, if they nevertheless add nothing to the information we already have, they do not concern our present purpose, so I will make no mention of them.

40

Among prerogatives of instances, I will put in seventeenth place *Summoning Instances,* borrowing a word from the law courts; because they summon objects to appear which have not appeared before. I also call them *Evoking Instances.* They are those which deduce what cannot be perceived to that which can.[232]

An object escapes our sense either (1) because of the distance at which it stands; or (2) because the sense is intercepted by intervening bodies; or (3) because the object is incapable of making an impression on the sense; or (4) because there is not enough of the object to strike the sense; or (5) because there is not time enough for the sense to be activated; or (6) because the impact of the object is such that the sense cannot bear it; or (7) because another object has filled and occupied the sense beforehand, leaving no room for a new motion. These factors apply chiefly to the sight, and next to that, to the sense of touch. For these two senses give information over a wide area, and about all kinds of object, while the other three senses give hardly any information except by direct contact and concerning their own objects.

1   In the first kind, an object that is imperceptible by reason of its distance can only be deduced to what is perceptible by the addition or substitution of another thing which can arouse and strike the sense from a greater distance, as in the communication of news by means of beacons, bells and such things.

2   In the second kind, the deduction is made when things that are within and are hidden by intervening bodies and cannot readily be opened to view are conveyed to the sense by things

---

[232]That is to say, they make manifest things that are themselves not perceptible, by means of others that are. Bacon uses "deduce" (*deduco*) in the sense of "convey" or "bring down".

that lie on the surface, or make their way there from within, as
the condition of human bodies is conveyed to the sense through
the pulse, or urine and such like.

3, 4 Deductions of the third and fourth kinds apply to a great
many things, and should be looked for everywhere in the
investigation of Nature. For example, it is clear that air and
spirit, and similar things that are rare and subtle throughout,
can neither be seen nor touched, so that deductions are an
absolute necessity in investigating bodies of this kind.

(i) Suppose then that the nature in question is the *action
and motion of the spirit that is enclosed in tangible bodies*. For
every tangible body that we know of contains an invisible and
intangible spirit which it envelops and clothes, as it were.
From this springs that powerful threefold source and remarkable process of the spirit in a tangible body. For once the spirit
in a tangible substance has been released, it shrinks and
desiccates bodies; if detained, it softens and liquefies them. If
not entirely released nor entirely detained, it imbues things
with specific attributes, creates limbs, reproduces, excretes,
gives an organic structure and such like. And all these
processes are deduced [brought down] to what can be perceived
by the senses through effects that are plain to see.

For in every tangible, inanimate body, the spirit enclosed
in it at first multiplies itself and, as it were, feeds upon those
tangible parts that are most suitable and prepared for this
purpose, and digests and compounds them and turns them
into spirit, and then they escape together. And this compounding and multiplication of the spirit, is conveyed to the sense
through a diminution of weight. For in all desiccation there is
some loss of bulk, not only of the spirit that existed in it
beforehand, but of the body that was formerly tangible and has
newly been transformed; for spirit has no weight. Now the
discharge or release of the spirit is conveyed to the sense in the
rust of metals and other putrefactions of that kind that show
themselves before they come to the rudiments of life; for they
belong to the third kind of process. For in bodies that are more
compact, the spirit does not find pores or channels through
which it can escape, and is therefore compelled to push and
drive those same tangible parts before it, so that they all leave
at the same time. And that is how rust and similar things
occur. On the other hand, the contraction of the tangible parts

after some of the spirit has been released (from which that desiccation follows) is conveyed to the sense not only by the increased hardness of the object, but much more by the fissures, shrinkings, wrinklings and foldings of bodies that follow from it. For the parts of wood split and shrink, skins become wrinkled; moreover, if there is any sudden discharge of the spirit through the heat of a fire, they so hasten to contract that they fold and curl up.

On the other hand, when the spirit is detained and yet is expanded and aroused by heat or things analogous to heat (as occurs in more solid or tenacious bodies), then indeed bodies are softened, as white-hot iron, become fluid, as metals do, or liquefy, as gums, wax and the like. These contrary operations of heat, therefore (namely hardening some things, liquefying others),[233] are easily reconciled, because in the former cases the spirit is released, in the latter it is agitated and detained. Of these, the latter is the natural action of heat and spirit together, while the former is the action merely of the tangible parts, on the occasion of the release of the spirit.

But when the spirit is neither wholly detained nor wholly released, but merely tentatively explores within its confines, and meets tangible parts that are obedient and ready to follow it, so that they follow at once wherever the spirit leads, then there results the formation into an organic body and the making of limbs and the rest of the vital functions, both in vegetation and in animals. And these are chiefly conveyed to the sense through careful observations of the first beginnings and rudiments and attempts of life in the minute creatures born out of putrefaction, as in ants' eggs, maggots, flies and frogs after heavy rain,[234] and so on. For the production of life,

---

[233]In his work *A History of Dense and Rare,* Bacon quotes Virgil (*Eclogues,* VIII, 80) in this connection: "As this clay grows hard and that wax grows soft, in one and the same fire . . ."

[234]The idea that it could rain frogs was a widespread superstition, affirmed, for example, by Porta in the second book of his *Natural Magic:* "Frogs are wonderfully generated of rotten dust and rain; for a summer shower lighting upon the putrified sands of the shore, and dust of highways, engenders frogs. . . . The generation of them is so easy, and sudden, that some write it hath rained frogs; as if they were engendered in the air".

moreover, a mild degree of heat and a yielding substance are necessary, so that the spirit neither bursts forth in haste, nor becomes constrained by the stubbornness of the parts, but rather is able to fold and fashion the parts as if they were wax.

Again, that most noble difference of spirit, with applications in many fields (namely, of spirit cut off, spirit simply branching, and spirit simultaneously branching and cellular; of which the first is the spirit of all inanimate bodies, the second of vegetable bodies, and the third, of animals), is placed, as it were, before our eyes by many deductive instances.

In the same way, it is clear that the more subtle structures and schematisms of things (although visible or tangible over the whole body) can neither be seen nor touched, so that information about these also comes by deduction. But the principal and most fundamental difference of schematism is taken from the abundance or scarcity of matter that occupies the same space or dimension.[235] For all other schematisms (which are related to dissimilarities of the parts contained in the same body, and to their arrangements and dispositions), compared with the former, are secondary.

(ii) Suppose therefore that the nature in question is the *relative expansion or contraction of matter in bodies,* that is to say, how much matter fills how much space in each case. For there is nothing truer in Nature than that two-fold proposition, that "nothing is made from nothing, nor can anything be reduced to nothing"; but the actual quantity of matter, its sum total, remains constant, being neither increased nor diminished. Nor is it less true that 'of that quantity of matter, more or less is contained in the same spaces or dimensions, according to the diversity of bodies'; thus in water more, in air less. So that if anyone were to assert that a certain volume of water could be converted into an equal volume of air, it is as if he were to say that something could be reduced to nothing; while, on the other hand, if one were to assert that a certain volume of air could be converted into the same volume of water, that

---

[235]That is, a body's density is the chief feature of its schematism, or constitution. Indeed, in Bacon's lists of schematisms, density is generally placed first.

would be the same as saying that something could be made out of nothing. And from this abundance and scarcity of matter our notions of dense and rare, variously and indiscriminately used as they are, are properly derived. And there is a third statement that should be made that is also sufficiently certain, namely that the greater or lesser amount of matter in this or that body, of which I am speaking, can, by comparison, be reduced to calculation and to exact or near-exact proportions. So one could rightly say that a given amount of gold contains such an aggregation of matter, that for spirit of wine to make up an equal quantity of matter, twenty-one times the space occupied by the gold would be needed.

Now the aggregation of matter and its ratios are brought down to what can be perceived by means of weight. For weight corresponds to the abundance of matter, in respect of the parts of a tangible thing; whereas spirit, and the quantity of matter that it contains, cannot be calculated by weight, for it lightens weight rather than making it heavier. But I have compiled a fairly accurate table in this matter, in which I have included the weights and volumes of each of the metals, the principal stones, woods, liquors, oils and very many other bodies, both natural and artificial; a thing that is useful in many ways, as much for light of information as for a model in practice, and which reveals many wholly unexpected facts. Not the least of these is that it shows that all the variety that exists in tangible bodies known to us (by which I mean bodies fairly compact, not spongy and hollow and mostly full of air) does not exceed the ratio of 21 to one; so limited, in fact, is Nature, or at least that part of it with which we are most concerned.[236]

I have also taken care to try whether I could perhaps find the ratios of intangible or airy bodies to tangible bodies. I went

---

[236]Bacon's table, which is based on his own experiments, appears in his *History of Dense and Rare;* it lists the weights of a given volume of a variety of substances, and hence their relative densities. These weights range from 20 pennyweights for gold to 22 grains for spirit of wine and down to 15 grains for fir wood. Bacon remarks that spirit of wine is the least dense of fairly compact bodies. A pennyweight is equivalent to 20 grains, giving only just over 18 to one as the ratio of densities of gold and spirit of wine.

about it in the following way. I took a glass phial which could hold perhaps one ounce, using a small vessel, so as to require less heat to produce evaporation. I filled this phial almost to the neck with spirit of wine, choosing spirit of wine because I had noted from the earlier table [mentioned above] that this was the rarest of tangible bodies (which are tolerably compact and not hollow), containing the least amount of matter for its volume. Then I took precise note of the weight of the liquid with the phial itself. After that I took a bladder of about two pints capacity, and as far as possible squeezed all the air out of it, so that the two sides of the bladder touched each other. I had previously rubbed the bladder gently with oil to make it more secure, its pores, if there were any, being stopped up by the oil. Then I inserted the mouth of the phial into the mouth of the bladder and tied the latter firmly round the neck of the phial, waxing the thread a little to bind more tightly and make a better seal. Then finally I put the phial on hot coals in a brazier. In a little time, the vapour, or breath, of the spirit of wine, dilated with the heat and turned into an airy substance, gradually inflated the bladder and swelled the whole thing in every direction, like a sail. As soon as this occurred I quickly took the phial from the fire and placed it on a carpet lest it should crack from the cold; I at once made an opening in the top of the bladder, lest with the cessation of heat the vapour should turn liquid again and spoil my calculations. I then removed the bladder and again measured the weight of the spirit of wine remaining. From that I calculated how much had been consumed into vapour or airy material; and then, comparing the room or space that this body had occupied as spirit of wine in the phial, with the space it occupied after it had evaporated into the bladder, I computed the ratios. And from them it was quite clear that this body, when converted and changed in this way, had gained an expansion of a hundredfold over what it was before.

(iii) In the same way, suppose the nature in question is *heat* or *cold*, in degrees that are so slight as to be imperceptible by the sense. These are conveyed to the sense by means of a calendar glass, such I described earlier [in Aphorism II, 13, under Instance 38]. For the heat and cold are not themselves felt by touch, but the heat expands the air and the cold contracts it. And again that expansion and contraction of the air are not perceived by sight, but the air when expanded depresses the water, and causes it to rise when it contracts. And only then, and in no other way, is the imperceptible brought to our sight.

(iv) In the same way, suppose the nature in question is the *mixture of bodies,* that is, what aqueous substance they contain, what oily, what spirit, ash, and salts, etc; also, to take a particular example, what milk contains of butter, curds, whey, etc. These mixtures, so far as tangible substances are concerned, are brought to the sense by expert, artificial separations. And the nature of the spirit in them, although not perceived immediately, is nevertheless comprehended through the various motions and endeavours of the tangible bodies in the very action and process of their separation; and also through the acrid and corrosive powers, and the divers colours, smells and tastes of the same bodies after separation. And in this department men have certainly worked very hard with distillations and artificial methods of separation, but with little more success than in other experiments that have been performed hitherto; in simply groping along on unlit paths, with more industry than intelligence; and (worst of all) without imitating or vying with Nature, but by destroying through violent heat or excessive forces all the more subtle schematism, in which the hidden powers and sympathies of things mostly lie. Nor do they remember or observe, in the course of such separations, that fact to which I have drawn attention elsewhere, that when bodies are subjected to violent treatment, either by fire or by other means, they take on very many qualities from the fire itself or from the bodies used in effecting the separations, that were not there before in the compound; from which extraordinary fallacies have arisen. For of course none of the vapour which is driven from water by fire existed previously as vapour or air in the body of the water, but is, for the most part, made through the expansion of water by the heat of the fire.

So, in general, all the elaborate tests of bodies, whether [those bodies are] natural or artificial, by means of which the genuine are distinguished from the adulterated, the better from the baser, should be referred to this: for they deduce what is not perceptible to that which is. They should therefore be collected from all quarters as carefully as possible.

5   With regard to the fifth way in which things are concealed, it is obvious that the action of the sense is conducted in motion, and motion is conducted in time. If therefore the motion of any body is either too slow or too fast to be proportionate to the time in which the action of the sense is conducted, the object is not perceived at all; as in the motion of the hand of a clock, or conversely in the motion of a musketball. But motion that is not perceived on account of its slowness is easily and commonly brought down to the sense through aggregates of motion; but that which is unperceived because of its quickness we do not usually measure accurately; yet nevertheless the investigation of Nature requires in some cases that this be done.

6   The sixth kind, when the sense is impeded by the brilliance of an object, can be brought from the imperceptible to the perceptible either by removing the object further from the sense, or by weakening the object by interposing some medium, such as will weaken the object, but not reduce it to nothing; or by admitting and receiving the object reflected, where direct impact would be too strong, as that of the sun in a bowl of water.

7   The seventh kind of concealment, when the sense is so burdened by one object that it has no room for the admission of another, is almost entirely confined to smells and the sense of smell, and does not have much bearing on the subject in hand. This therefore is all I have to say about deducing, or conveying, the imperceptible to the perceptible.

Sometimes however this deduction leads, not to the human sense, but to that of some other creature, whose sense in certain cases excels that of a man; as of some smells, to the sense of a dog; of light, which exists, in a hidden way, in air that is not illuminated from without, to the sense of a cat, an owl, and animals of that kind, that can see at night. For as Telesio rightly observed, there is some natural light in air itself, albeit faint and weak, and for the most part useless to the eyes of men and very many animals; because those animals to whose sense light of that kind is suited do see at night; and it is hard to believe they do this without any light, or by means of internal light.

It should be noted of course that I am only dealing here

with how the senses forsake us,[237] and the remedies for them. For the deceptions of the senses should be referred to the particular inquiries concerning the sense and the objects of sense, with the exception of that great deception of the senses, namely that they draw the lines of Nature by reference to man, and not by reference to the universe; which is only corrected by reason and a universal philosophy.

41

Among prerogatives of instances, I will put in eighteenth place *Instances of the Road,* which I also call *Itinerant* and *Articulated Instances.* They are those that indicate the motions of Nature as they gradually proceed. Now this kind of instances escapes observation rather than the sense; for men are extraordinarily careless in this matter, and study Nature only in a desultory and intermittent way, and when bodies are finished and completed, not while she is still operating. But if anyone wants to examine and study the skill and industry of some craftsman, he will desire to see not so much the raw materials of the craft, and then the finished works, but rather to be present while the craftsman is at work and proceeding with his task. And the same should be done with regard to Nature. If, for example, one were inquiring into the growth of plants, one should investigate it from the very sowing of the seed (which can easily be done by every day or so taking out one of the seeds that have lain in the earth two, three and four days, and so on, and carefully examining them), and see how and when the seed begins to swell and become as if filled with spirit; then how it bursts its shell and puts out fibres, at the same time rising upwards a little, unless the ground is too unyielding; how also it puts out fibres, some downwards as roots, some upwards as little stalks, sometimes creeping sideways, if it should find the ground open and suitable there; and many things of that kind. And one should do the same for

---

[237]These are cases where the senses, unaided, are insufficient to detect some phenomenon; Bacon distinguishes them from cases where the senses actively deceive.

the hatching of eggs, where it will be easy to observe the process of imparting life and organization, and what, and which parts, are formed from the yolk, and what from the white of the egg, and so on. And the same procedure should be applied to animals arising from putrefaction, for it would be most inhumane to examine these matters in land-animals that are perfect[238] by cutting the foetus from the womb, except perhaps in cases of abortion and animals killed in the hunt, and so forth. So one should always keep a kind of nightwatch over Nature, since she offers herself better to view at night than by day. For studies of this kind can be thought of as nocturnal, on account of the smallness and lasting nature of our lantern.

And the same should be tried for inanimate things, as I have done myself in investigating the expansion of liquids by fire. For there is one mode of opening in water, another in wine, another in vinegar, another in verjuice;[239] a very different one in milk and oil, and so on.[240] This was easy to observe by boiling them over a gentle fire in a glass vessel, where

---

[238]A perfect animal is one that is not born by spontaneous generation. Land-animals are terrestrial in their habits, as distinct from aquatic animals.

[239]Verjuice is an acid liquor derived from unripe grapes, crab-apples, etc.

[240]Bacon describes how these different liquids 'open' when subjected to heat in his *History of Dense and Rare*. Thus on the opening of water, he wrote: "On the first heat it emits a small and rarefied vapour, without any perceptible change in the body. If the heat be continued, the water does not rise in its whole body, nor even in small bubbles as in froth, but it ascends in larger and rarer bubbles, and resolves itself into a copious vapour. This vapour, if it be not obstructed or driven back, mixes with the air, being at first visible, then disappearing and losing itself to view." The opening of oil: "On the first heat certain little drops or grains diffused through the body of the oil rise up with a kind of crackling noise. Meanwhile no bubbles play on the surface (as in water), nor does the whole body swell, nor does any exhalation almost escape. But after some time the whole rises and dilates with a manifest expansion to about twice the size, and a very thick and copious exhalation issues forth. This exhalation, unless it catches fire in the meantime, mixes at last with the air, as vapour of water does. Oil however requires a greater heat than water to make it boil, and is much longer in beginning to boil".

everything could be seen clearly. These matters, however, I touch on only briefly, since I shall discuss them at greater length and in more detail when I come to the discovery of the *latent process* of things, so it should always be borne in mind that I am not here dealing with the things themselves, but only quoting examples.

42

Among prerogatives of instances, I will put in nineteenth place *Supplementary* or *Substitutive Instances,* which I also call *Instances of Refuge.* These are those that supply information when the sense entirely forsakes us, and so we resort to them when proper instances are not to be had. There are two kinds of substitution, either by *Degrees,* or by *Analogy.* For example, no medium is found which, when interposed, inhibits completely the action of a loadstone in imparting motion to iron; neither gold, nor silver, nor stone, nor glass, wood, water, oil, cloth or fibrous bodies, air, flame, etc. And yet by precise testing, it might be possible to find some medium that would weaken the loadstone's power more than another, comparatively and to a certain degree; thus it may be that a loadstone would not attract iron through as great a thickness of gold as through the same distance of air; or through so much ignited silver as through cold, and in the same way with similar materials. For I have not myself made experiments in these cases, but it suffices to mention them in place of examples. Likewise we know of no body which does not become hot when brought near fire, but air does so far more quickly than stone. Now that is Substitution made by Degrees.

Substitution by Analogy is no doubt useful, but less certain, and for that reason should be used judiciously. It comes about when the non-sensible is conveyed to the sense, not by perceptible operations of the non-sensible body itself [as with Instances of the Gate], but by studying some related body that is sensible. For example, in the investigation of the mixture of spirits, which are invisible bodies, there seems to be some relationship between those bodies and their fuel or nourishment. For the fuel of flame seems to be oil and fatty substances; of air, water and aqueous substances. For flames multiply themselves over the vapour of oil, and air over the vapour of water. We must look therefore at the mixture of water and oil, which is manifest to the sense, since a mixture of air and any kind of flame escapes the sense. Now oil and water, combined and shaken together, make a very imperfect mixture; but in plants and blood and the parts of animals, they are subtly and delicately mingled. Some similar effect could therefore arise with a mixture of flame and air in spirituous bodies, which although not forming a good mixture when simply stirred together, nonetheless do seem to be mixed in the spirits of plants and animals; especially since every animate spirit feeds on both kinds of moist substances, the aqueous and the fatty, as its proper food.

Likewise, if inquiry is made, not into the more perfect mixtures of spirituous substances, but merely into their combination; that is, whether they readily become incorporated into one another or whether there are, for example, some winds and exhalations or other spirituous things which do not mix with common air, but merely hang and float in it, in globules and drops, and are broken up into smaller parts by the air rather than being received and incorporated therein; this cannot be perceived by the sense in common air and other spirituous things, because of the subtlety of their substances. Yet a kind of image of this effect, and the extent to which it may occur, can be conceived in the liquids of quicksilver, oil and water; and also in air, and its breaking up, when it is dispersed through water and rises in tiny bubbles; and also in thicker kinds of smoke; and finally, in dust when it is stirred up and hangs in the air; in all of which no incorporation takes place. Now the image or representation in this subject that I have just mentioned is not a bad one, provided careful inquiry has first been made as to whether there can be such heterogeneity between spirituous things as exists between liquids. For, then, these images by Analogy may be conveniently substituted.

Now on the subject of these Supplementary Instances, although I said that information was to be drawn from them in default of instances proper, as a place of Refuge, I still would have it understood that they are also very useful even when there are proper instances to hand, namely to corroborate the information when taken together with them. But I will discuss these in more detail when I come in due course to speak of the Supports of Induction.[241]

43

Among prerogatives of instances, I will put in twentieth place *Dissecting Instances,* which I also call *Awakening Instances,* but for a different reason. I call them Awakening, because they awaken the understanding; Dissecting, because they dissect Nature; for which reason I also sometimes call them *Instances of Democritus.* They are those that gently remind the understanding of the wonderful and exquisite subtlety of Nature, so as to stir and rouse it to attend to and observe and inquire into it, as it ought. For example, that a little drop of ink may be spread over so many letters or lines; that silver, gilded only on the surface, can be drawn out into such a length of gilded wire; that a minute worm, such as is found in the skin,[242] should have in itself both spirit and a varied arrangement of its parts; that a little saffron colours even a whole cask of water; that a little civet or spice scents a much larger volume of air; that such a great cloud of smoke can be produced from a very little incense; that such precise differences in sounds, as spoken words, are carried through the air in every direction, and though considerably weakened, penetrate the openings and pores even of wood and water, and are echoed back as well, and that so distinctly and quickly; that light and colour permeate the solid bodies of glass and water so nimbly and over such a wide area, with such a great and exquisite variety of images, and are also refracted and reflected; that a loadstone exerts its force through bodies of every kind, even the most compact. But what is more astonishing still, is that in all these, the action of one in a neutral

---

[241]As Bacon tells us in Aphorism II, 21, 'Supports of Induction' is the title of one of the projected sections of *Novum Organum;* however, he gives little indication of what its contents would have been.

[242]These mysterious worms are also mentioned at the end of Aphorism II, 34. Perhaps they are the same as the grubs which Bacon says in Aphorism II, 39, have been examined under the microscope.

medium such as air does not greatly impede that of another;
that is to say, at one and the same time so many images of
visible things are carried through the spaces of the air, and so
many impressions of spoken words, so many distinct scents,
like that of the violet and the rose, and also heat and cold and
magnetic powers; all of them, as I say, are carried through at
the same time, without impeding each other, as if all of them
had their own separate ways and paths, not one striking or
running into another.

It is useful however to append to these Dissecting Instances others that I call *Limits of Dissection;* thus taking the
examples given above, while one action does not disturb or
hinder another of a different kind, it does nevertheless dominate and smother another of the same kind, as sunlight
smothers the light of a glow-worm, the report of a cannon the
sound of a voice, a strong odour a more delicate one, intense
heat a milder one, and a sheet of iron placed between a
loadstone and another piece of iron the operation of the
loadstone. But it will be more fitting to mention these also
among Supports of Induction.

44

Now this is all I have to say about instances that help the
sense, the chief use of which is in the Informative Part. For
information begins with the sense, but the whole business
ends in works; and just as the former is the beginning, so the
latter is the conclusion of the matter. I will proceed therefore
to the instances that are of especial use for the Operative Part.
They are of two kinds, and seven in number, and I call them all
by the general term of *Practical Instances.* In the Operative
Part there are two defects and two kinds of dignities of
instances.[243] For operation either fails us or overtasks us.
Operation fails us (especially after a diligent investigation of
natures) chiefly because the forces and actions of bodies have

---

[243]Dignities [i.e., ranks] of instances and prerogatives of instances are
the same in Bacon's terminology, as is evident from the rest of this
Aphorism, and from the start of Aphorism II, 52.

been badly determined and measured. Now the forces and actions of bodies are circumscribed and measured either by spatial intervals, or by moments of time, or by concentration of quantity, or by predominance of power; and unless these four are accurately and carefully weighed, the sciences concerned will be elegant speculations perhaps but of no practical use. The four instances which apply here I put into one group and call *Mathematical Instances* and *Instances of Measurement*. [They are discussed respectively in Aphorisms II, 45–48.]

Now operation overtasks us either because it involves useless matters, or because of the multiplicity of instruments, or because of the quantity of materials and substances that may happen to be required for any particular task. Those instances ought therefore to be held in high regard that either guide the operative part to objects of most benefit to mankind; or that are sparing in their need for instruments, or quantities of materials or equipment. The three instances that meet these requirements I put in one group and call *Propitious* or *Benevolent Instances*. [These are discussed respectively in Aphorisms II, 49–51.] These seven instances I will therefore discuss separately, and with them I will close that part of my subject that deals with prerogatives or dignities of instances.

45

Among prerogatives of instances, I will put in twenty-first place *Instances of the Measuring Rod* or *Ruler,* which I also call *Instances of Range* or *Non Ultra.* For the powers and motions of things act and take effect over spaces that are not indefinite or fortuitous, but definite and certain, so that it is of the greatest advantage to practice in the investigation of particular natures that these [spaces] are borne in mind and noted, not only to prevent it from failing, but also to increase and enlarge its effect. For we are sometimes able to extend powers, and, as it were, to diminish distances, as with telescopes.

Now most powers operate and take effect only by manifest contact, as happens in the collision of two bodies, where one does not move the other, unless it touches it. Also medicines that are applied externally, like ointments and plasters, only exercise their powers by touching the body. Finally the objects of the senses of touch and taste do not affect the sense, unless they are in contact with those organs.

There are also other powers that act at a distance, though only a very short one, a few of which have been observed up to now, although there are more of them than men suspect; as when—to take everyday examples—amber or jet attracts chaff, bubbles on approaching other bubbles dissolve them, some purgative medicines draw down humours from above, and things of that kind. But that magnetic force through which iron and a loadstone, or two loadstones reciprocally, come together acts within a certain sphere of influence, though a small one. If, on the other hand, there is some magnetic force emanating from the earth itself (from a little below the surface, that is) that acts upon an iron needle, to the extent of its polarity, then that operation must occur at a great distance.

Again, if there is any magnetic force operating by consent between the globe of the earth and heavy objects, or between the globe of the moon and the waters of the sea, (which seems very likely in view of the semi-monthly spring and neap tides), or between the starry heaven and the planets, through which the latter are summoned and drawn to their apogees, then all these forces operate at very great distances indeed. There are also found certain cases of flame bursting out or starting in some materials at very great distances, as is reported to occur in Babylonian naphtha.[244] There are cases too of heat, and cold as well, stealing over wide distances, so much so that cold is distinctly felt from afar by the inhabitants of the lands around Canada, from the large masses of ice that are broken off and float through the northern seas, and are carried by the Atlantic towards those shores. Scents also (although in their case, there seems always to be something emitted from the body) have an effect at a remarkable distance, as often happens to those sailing along the coast of Florida, and some

---

[244]Pliny, in his *Natural History*, cix, 235, gives an account of Babyloni-an naphtha: "Naphtha is of a similar nature [to petroleum]—this is the name of a substance that flows out like bitumen in the neighbourhood of Babylon and the parts of Parthia near Astacus. Naphtha has a close affinity with fire, which leaps to it at once when it sees it in any direc-tion".

parts of Spain, where there are whole groves of lemon and orange trees and scented plants of that kind, or shrubs of rosemary, marjoram and the like. Lastly, rays of light and the impressions of sound, of course, operate at enormous distances.

But whether the distances at which all these powers act is great or small, it is certain they are finite and known to Nature, so that there is a certain *Non Ultra,* or limit, which depends either on the size or quantity of the bodies, or the vigour or weakness of the powers, or on the favorable or hindering passage afforded by the media, which should all be computed and noted. Moreover the measurements of so-called violent motions—of missiles, cannon-balls, wheels and the like—should be noted, since these, clearly, also have their definite limits.

Some motions and powers are also found that are contrary to those which operate by contact and not at a distance; namely, those that operate at a distance and not on contact; and some again, that operate only weakly at a lesser distance, but more strongly at a greater. Vision, for example, does not work well by contact, but requires a medium and a distance. Although I remember hearing from a trustworthy person who had undergone an operation on his eyes to cure cataracts, which involved inserting a kind of small silver needle under the first tunic of the eye,[245] to remove the film of the cataract and push it into the corner of the eye that he saw quite clearly the needle moving across the pupil itself.[246] Though this may

---

[245]The first tunic of the eye is the eyeball's external covering, comprising the hard opaque sclerotic and the transparent cornea.

[246]Bacon relates the same story in his *Sylva Sylvarum,* 272: "I have heard of a person very credible (who himself was cured of a cataract in one of his eyes), that while the silver needle did work upon the sight of his eye to remove the film of the cataract, he never saw any thing more clear or perfect than that white needle: which (no doubt) was because the needle was lesser than the pupil of the eye, and so took not the light from it." Bacon gives the impression that he thought a cataract was an opaque film, rather than a clouding of the lens of the eye. The operation described is known as couching, in which the opaque crystalline lens is depressed with a needle, until it lies below the axis of vision. But the focussing needed for the patient to have seen the needle hardly seems possible under the conditions of the operation.

be true it is, however, evident that larger bodies are only well or distinctly seen when the eye is at the apex of a cone, with the rays of the object converging at some distance. Moreover, in old people, the eye can see an object better that is a little distance away, rather than closer to it. In missiles also, it is certain that their impact [on striking an object] is not so strong from a very short distance, as it is from a little further away. Therefore these and similar things in the measurements of motions with regard to distances should be observed.

There is also another kind of local measurement of motions which should not be omitted. This concerns motions that are not progressive, but spherical; that is, the expansion of bodies into a larger sphere, or contraction into a smaller. For the measurements of those motions should be investigated, as to how much compression or expansion bodies will readily and freely tolerate (according to their respective natures), and at which point they begin to resist, until at last they will absolutely bear it *No Further* (Non Ultra); as when an inflated bladder is squeezed, it bears a certain pressure of the air, but if more is applied, the air does not endure it, and the bladder bursts.

Now I have tested this more precisely with a rather subtle experiment. For I took a small metal bell, one fairly light and thin, such as we use for holding salt, and plunged it into a basin of water, so that it took down with it the air contained inside to the bottom of the basin, where I had previously placed a small ball, over which the bell was to be placed. By these means, I found that if the ball was very small (in proportion to the cavity of the bell), the air withdrew into a smaller space, and was only squeezed together, not squeezed out. But if it was of a larger size than the air would freely allow, then the air, unable to bear the greater pressure, raised the bell on one side and rose up in bubbles.

And in order to test how much expansion, as well as compression, air may tolerate, I devised the following. I took a glass egg, with a small hole in one end of it. By sucking hard, I extracted air through the hole, and at once stopped up the hole with my finger, immersed the egg in water, and then took my finger away. The air, strained by the pull of the suction and dilated beyond its natural size, and thus struggling to withdraw and contract (so that it would have drawn in air with a hiss, had not the egg been immersed in the water), drew in as much water as was necessary to enable the air to recover its old sphere or volume.

And it is certain that rarer bodies, such as air, allow a certain noticeable contraction, as I have said; but that tangible bodies, such as water, do so only with much more difficulty and to a smaller extent. Just how much it allows, I investigated by the following experiment.

I had a hollow, lead globe made, to hold about two pints of wine and with sides thick enough to bear considerable force. I filled this with water through a hole made in it, and when the globe was full, I stopped up the hole with molten lead, so that the globe became entirely solid. Then I flattened the globe by heavy hammer blows on two opposite sides, as a result of which the water must have contracted into a smaller space, since a sphere is the figure with the greatest capacity [for a given surface area]. Then, when the hammering could do no more, the water only contracting with some difficulty, I made use of a mill or press, until finally the water, unable to bear this further pressure, exuded from the solid lead like a fine dew. After that I calculated by how much space it had shrunk through that compression, and so understood that this was the compression that the water allowed (though only when subjected to great force).

But more solid, dry or more compact bodies like stones and pieces of wood, and metals also, stand very much less, in fact, an almost imperceptible compression or extension. They release themselves either by breaking up, or by moving forward or by other efforts, as is apparent in the bending in wood or metal, in the movements of clocks by the coil of their spring, in missiles, in hammerings and numberless other motions. And in the investigation of Nature, all those things, together with their measurements, should be noted and explored, either in their certitude,[247] or through estimates, or by comparison, as the case will admit.

---

[247]The phrase "in their certitude" refers to precise measurements, as opposed to estimates and relative values.

46

Among prerogatives of instances, I will put in twenty-second place *Instances of the Running-Track,* which I also call *Instances of Water,* taking the word from the water-clocks of the ancients, into which water was poured in place of sand. These measure Nature through moments of time, just as *Instances of the Measuring Rod* measure it through spatial intervals. For every motion, or natural action, is performed in time; some more quickly, some more slowly, but howsoever, in definite periods of time, known to Nature. Even those actions that appear to be performed instantaneously, and in the twinkling of an eye, as we say, are found to take a greater or lesser time.

Thus, in the first place, we see that the heavenly bodies return at measured intervals of time, and so too the flow and ebb of the sea. Also, the movement of heavy bodies towards the earth, and of light bodies towards the surrounding heavens, takes place over definite periods of time, depending upon the body that is moved, and the medium through which it moves. The sailing of ships, the motions of animals, the throwing of missiles, all take place likewise through moments of time that can be measured, at least in total. And as regards heat, we see that boys in winter-time bathe their hands in flame,[248] yet are not burned; and jugglers, by deft and balanced movements, turn vessels full of water or wine upside down and back up again, without spilling any liquid; and many other things of this kind. So also compressions and expansions and eruptions of bodies take place, some more quickly, some more slowly, depending on the nature of the body and the motion, but in definite moments of time. Moreover, in the simultaneous firing of several guns, which are sometimes heard at a distance of thirty miles, the sound is perceived earlier by those close to where it was made than by those far off. And in vision (whose action is the fastest of all) it is also clear that definite intervals of time are required for it to act, which is proved by those

---

[248]Perhaps playing snapdragon, a Christmas game familiar in Bacon's time and mentioned in *Love's Labour's Lost,* in which the players try to snatch raisins out of a dish of burning brandy or other spirit and to eat them while they are alight.

objects that are not seen because of the speed of their motion, as in the flight of a ball fired from a musket; for the ball flies past more quickly than the impression of its appearance can be conveyed to the sight.

Now this, and other things like it, has led me from time to time to a very strange doubt, namely, whether the face of a clear and starlit sky is seen at the same moment that it actually exists, or rather a short time later; and whether there might not be (as far as the appearance of the heavens is concerned) a true time and an apparent time,[249] just as there is true position and apparent position, which is observed by astronomers in parallaxes. For it seemed incredible to me that the images or rays of the heavenly bodies could be conveyed to our sight through such immense distances in an instant; it seemed they must rather come down to us in some measurable space of time. But that doubt (as to whether there is some large interval between real and apparent time) later quite vanished, when I considered the infinite loss and diminution of quantity, that the appearance must suffer between the true body of a star and the image of it that we see, which is caused by the distance; remembering at the same time at what a great distance (at least sixty miles) bodies that are merely white are seen by us here in an instant; and since there is no doubt that the light of the heavenly bodies very much exceeds not only a bright white colour, but also the light of any known flame in the vigour of its radiation. Again, that enormous velocity in the body itself, which is seen in its diurnal motion (which has so astonished even serious men that they prefer to believe in terrestrial motion) renders more believable that motion of the emission of rays from them, though astonishing, as I said, for its speed. But what persuades me most of all is that if some perceptible interval of time were interposed between the true and the apparent, then the images would often be intercepted and confused by clouds arising during that time, and by similar disturbances of the medium. That is all I have to say about simple measurements of time.

---

[249]That is, the time when a star appears to be in some position and when it is actually there.

But we should not only seek the absolute measure of motions and actions but much more, the comparative, for this is extremely useful and of wide application. Indeed, we see that the flash of a gun is perceived sooner than the report is heard, even though the ball must necessarily strike the air before the flame behind it can emerge, which happens because of the faster motion of light than of sound. We also see that visible images are received by the sight more quickly than they are lost, so that the strings of violins, when plucked by the finger, appear doubled or tripled, because a new image is received before the previous one is lost. And this is also the reason why spinning rings look like globes, and a burning torch, carried quickly along at night, appears to have a tail. And it was upon this foundation of an inequality of the velocities of motions that Galileo erected his explanation for the flow and ebb of the sea; namely, the earth rotating faster and the waters more slowly, so that the waters pile themselves up and then in turn sink again, as is shown in a vessel of water that is moved quickly. But he devised this on an assumption that cannot be conceded (namely that the earth moves), and he was also badly informed about the six-hourly movement of the ocean.[250]

Now an example of the thing I am discussing, namely the comparative measures of motions—and not only of the fact itself, but of its outstanding usefulness (of which I spoke just now)—can be seen in underground mines, in which gunpowder has been placed, where immense masses of earth, buildings, and the like are overturned and thrown high up by a very small quantity of gunpowder. And the reason for this is certainly that the expansive, driving motion of the powder is

----

[250]Bacon reports Galileo's theory of the tides with excessive brevity. In that theory, the tides are caused by the different accelerations of different parts of the earth due to its diurnal motion and its revolution around the sun. Those parts that are spinning on the earth's axis in the same direction as the earth is revolving around the sun are accelerated in the direction of the earth's revolution; while those parts spinning in the opposite direction and against the earth's revolution, are decelerated. These changes of velocity are then communicated to the waters of the seas, thereby producing the movements of the tides.

very much quicker than the motion of gravity, which is responsible for any resistance; so much so, that the first motion is finished before the opposing motion has begun, so that at first there is no resistance at all. Thus it is that in all missiles too, it is not so much a strong blow but a sharp and quick one that carries through most powerfully. Nor could the small quantity of animal spirit in animals, particularly in such vast bodies as whales and elephants, bend and guide such a great bodily mass, except by the velocity of motion of the spirit, and the sluggishness of the bodily mass in exerting its resistance.

This effect, indeed, is one of the principal foundations of the experiments in magic, of which I shall speak shortly [in Aphorism II, 51], namely, where a small mass of matter overcomes and brings under control one much larger: this could occur, I say, if the one, by the velocity of its motion, could be given a start, before the other exerted itself.

Finally, this matter of *First* and *Subsequent* should be marked in every natural action. Thus in making an infusion of rhubarb, the purgative power is drawn out first, the binding power afterwards;[251] and I have found something similar also on steeping violets in vinegar, when, first of all, the sweet delicate scent of the flower is extracted, and then the more earthy part of the flower, which spoils the scent. For this reason, if violets are steeped for a whole day, a very feeble scent is obtained, but if they are steeped for only a quarter of an hour, then taken out and (because the scented spirit in violets is small) more fresh violets are added for a quarter of an hour, as many as six times, then the infusion is in the end so enriched that, although there have been violets in it for no more than an hour and a half (however often renewed), the most pleasing scent, as good as that of a violet itself, remains for a whole year. It should be noted, however, that the scent does not assume its full strength until a month after the infusion is made. Indeed, in the distillation of aromatic herbs crushed in spirit of wine, it appears that there first arises an

---

[251]In his *Sylva Sylvarum,* 19, Bacon observes that "Rhubarb hath manifestly in it parts of contrary operations: parts that purge, and parts that bind the body: and the first lie looser, and the latter lie deeper."

aqueous and useless phlegm,[252] then a liquid containing more of the spirit of wine, and then lastly a liquid containing more of the aroma. And there are many facts of this kind worth noting in distillations, but let these suffice as examples.

47

Among prerogatives of instances, I will put in twenty-third place *Instances of Quantity,* which I also call *Doses of Nature,* borrowing the term from medicine. These are those that measure powers by the *quantities* of bodies, and show how much the *quantity of the body* contributes to the *extent of the power.* Now in the first place, there are certain powers that are found only in a cosmical quantity, that is, in such a quantity as agrees with the shape and structure of the world. For instance, the earth stands still; its parts fall. The water in the oceans flow and ebb; in rivers hardly at all, except for the incoming tide. In the second place, almost all particular powers act according to how large or small the body concerned is. Large bodies of water do not readily become foul, small ones do so quickly. New wine and beer mature and become drinkable much faster in small flasks than in large casks. If a herb is put into a large amount of liquid, infusion takes place more than absorption, and if in a smaller amount, then absorption takes place more than infusion. Thus a bath has one effect on the human body, a light sprinkling another. Also, small dews never fall through the air, but are dissipated and incorporated into the air. And in breathing on gem-stones, we see the small trace of moisture disappear at once, like a cloudlet dispersed by the wind. Also, a piece of a loadstone does not attract such a weight of iron as the whole loadstone. There are, on the other hand, some powers in which smallness of quantity has more effect, as in cases of penetration—a sharp stylus pierces more quickly than a blunt one, a pointed diamond cuts glass, etc.

But I must not spend time here on indefinite matters, but

---

[252]Phlegm was the name of a watery, odourless, tasteless product of distillation.

go on to investigate what *proportion* the quantity of a body bears to the measure of its power. For it would be easy to believe that powers are in proportion to quantity, and that if a leaden bullet of one ounce falls in such-and-such a time, then a bullet of two ounces ought to fall twice as fast, which is quite wrong.[253] Nor do the same proportions hold good in every kind of power, in fact, they are very different. These measurements therefore should be sought from the things themselves, not from what seems to be the truth, or from conjectures.

To sum up, then, in all investigation of Nature, the *quantity* of body required to produce a particular effect, the dose as it were, should be noted, with frequent reminders against *Too Much* and *Too Little*.

48

Among prerogatives of instances, I will put in twenty-fourth place *Wrestling Instances,* which I also call *Instances of Predominance.*[254] These indicate the mutual predominance and yielding of powers, and which of these is the stronger and prevails, and which the weaker and succumbs. For the motions and exertions of bodies are compounded, further compounded, and folded together, no less than bodies themselves. I will therefore first propound the principal kinds of motions or active powers, so that there can be a clearer comparison between their strengths, and thereby a demonstration and designation of *Wrestling and Predominant Instances.*

1 Let the first motion be that of *Resistance of Matter,* which exists in every single portion of it, and through which it refuses to be entirely annihilated; so much so that no fire, no weight or pressure, no violence, no lapse of time can reduce even the

---

[253]In the *De Augmentis,* V, ii, Bacon illustrates this point with the story of a woman in Aesop's fable "who expected that with a double measure of barley her hen would lay two eggs a day; whereas the hen grew fat and laid none".

[254]Bacon has already used the term *Predominant* for a quite different type of instance in Aphorism II, 24, presumably through an oversight.

smallest portion of matter to nothing; on the contrary, it will always be something, and occupy some space, and, in whatever hard straits it is placed, free itself, either by changing shape or position, or will, if this may not be, subsist as it is; and the point will never come when it is either nothing, or nowhere. The schoolmen (who almost always denominate and define things by their effects and inabilities rather than by their interior causes) denote this motion either by the axiom that 'two bodies cannot be in a single place', or they call it the motion that 'forbids interpenetration of dimensions'. And there is no point in giving examples of this motion, for it exists in every body.

2 Let the second motion be that which I call the *Motion of Connection*, by which bodies do not allow themselves at any point to be separated from contact with another body, as if they were delighting in their mutual connection and contact. The schoolmen call this the motion that 'denies a vacuum', as when water is drawn up by suction, or through pipes; the flesh through cupping-glasses; or when water stays in perforated jugs without running out, unless the mouth of the jug is opened in order to admit air; and countless things of that kind.

3 Let the third motion be that which I call the *Motion of Liberation,* whereby bodies strive to liberate themselves from abnormal pressure or tension, and to recover themselves into the dimension appropriate to their body.

There are numberless examples of this motion: as regards liberation from pressure, the motion of water in swimming; of air in flying; of water in rowing; of air in the undulations of winds; of the spring in clocks. And the motion of compressed air is shown very neatly in children's toy guns, when they hollow out a piece of alder[255] or similar wood and plug it at both ends with some sappy root, or like material; then, using a makeshift piston, they ram the root, or whatever the plug is, towards the other opening, whereupon the root at that opening

---

[255]This may well be an error in an original translation from the English to Latin, for alder is too hard a wood for this purpose. The young branches of the elder tree, on the other hand, are full of pith, and were popular for making pea-shooters, whistles and also pop-guns, these being known as elder-guns (they are mentioned in Shakespeare's *Henry V).*

is shot out with a report; and that before it is touched either by the root, or plug at this end, or by the stick.

And as regards liberation from tension, this motion is shown in air remaining in glass eggs after some has been sucked out, in musical strings, in hide, and in cloth, which spring back after being stretched, unless the tensions grow too strong from being prolonged, and so on. This motion the Schoolmen refer to under the name of motion arising from the 'form of the element'; a thoughtless enough name, since this motion not only applies to air, water or fire, but to every different kind of solid substance, like wood, iron, lead, cloth, parchment, and so on, in which each body has its own natural size and shape, from which it cannot easily be pulled to any appreciable extent. But because this Motion of Liberation is the most obvious of all, and applies to innumerable things, it would be wise to distinguish it well and clearly. For some very carelessly confuse this motion with those twin motions of Resistance and Connection; that is, they confuse liberation from pressure with the Motion of Resistance, and liberation from tension with the Motion of Connection; just as if bodies, which have been compressed, yield or expand, in order that no 'penetration of dimensions' should ensue; and likewise bodies which have been placed under tension spring back and contract, in order that a 'vacuum' should not result. Whereas if compressed air tried to gather itself into the density of water, or wood into the density of stone, there would be no need for penetration of dimensions; and yet there could be a far greater compression of them than they do in fact sustain. In the same way, if water tried to expand to the rarity of air, or stone to the rarity of wood, there would be no need for a vacuum, yet there could be a far greater extension of them than they ever do in fact sustain. The matter therefore comes down to penetration of dimensions and a vacuum only in the extreme limits of compression and rarefaction; whereas these motions stop far short of those limits, and are just the desires of bodies to preserve themselves in their own consistencies (or, if they [the schoolmen] prefer, in their own forms), and only depart suddenly from them [i.e., their consistencies] if they are altered by gentle means and by consent.

But it is far more necessary (because much hangs on it) that men should realize that violent motion (which I call

'Mechanical', and Democritus, who in explaining his primary motions must be ranked below even mediocre philosophers, called Motion of 'Percussion') is nothing other than Motion of Liberation, that is to say, a motion from compression to relaxation. For neither in a simple forward push, nor in flight through the air, does any movement away or change of place occur before the parts of a body are abnormally acted upon and compressed by the impelling body. Then indeed, with one part pushing the next, the whole is moved; and not only forwards, but also rotating at the same time, the parts seeking in that way also to liberate themselves, or to bear the pressure more uniformly. So much then for this kind of motion.

4   Let the fourth motion be that to which I have given the name of the *Motion of Matter,* which is in some way the converse of the Motion of Liberation I have just spoken of. For in the Motion of Liberation, the bodies concerned fear, reject and shun a new dimension or sphere or expansion or contraction (which are all names for the same thing), and strive with all their strength to spring back and recover their old consistency. In this Motion of Matter, on the other hand, bodies seek a new sphere or dimension, and aspire to it readily and quickly and, sometimes (as in the case of gunpowder), with extremely powerful effort. Now the instruments of this motion, not the only ones certainly, but the most powerful, or at least the most common, are heat and cold. For example, if air is dilated by tension (as by suction from glass eggs), it labours with great desire to restore itself. But if heat is applied, it longs on the contrary to expand, and desires a new sphere and goes into it readily, as if into a new form (as they say); and after some little expansion, it has no care to return, unless invited to do so by the application of cold—which is not a return so much as a fresh transformation. Similarly, water also, if confined by compression, resists and wishes to become what it was before, namely larger.[256] But if intense and continued cold should intervene, it changes itself freely and of its own accord to the density of ice; and if the cold persists for some time, and is not

---

[256]Bacon's own experiment on this point is recounted in Aphorism II, 45.

interrupted by periods of warmth (as happens in caves and caverns some way underground), it turns into crystal or similar material, and never recovers its former state.[257]

5   Let the Fifth Motion be the Motion of *Continuity*. I mean by that not simple and primary continuity with another body (for that is the Motion of Connection), but self-continuity in a particular body. For it is most certain that all bodies dread to have their continuity destroyed; some dread it more, some less, but all to some extent. Thus, just as in hard bodies, like steel or glass, the reluctance to lose continuity is very sturdy and strong, so too in liquids, where a motion of this kind seems to cease or at least to become quite feeble, it is still not lacking altogether; it does exist there, as it were, in the smallest degree, and betrays itself in many experiments; as in bubbles, in the roundness of water-drops, in the thin threads of water dripping from roofs, and in the stickiness of glutinous bodies, and so on.[258] But that feeling [of dread] shows itself most of all if one attempts to destroy the continuity of smaller fragments. Thus, after a certain amount of crushing has taken place, a pestle has no further effect in mortars; water does not penetrate into very small cracks; and indeed air itself, notwithstanding the subtlety of its own body, does not penetrate the pores of slightly more solid vessels all at once, but only after insinuating itself over a long period.

6   Let the sixth motion be that which I call *Motion for Gain,* or *Motion of Want*. This is one by which bodies, when they are among quite heterogeneous and, as it were, hostile bodies, and chance upon the opportunity of escaping and joining others that are more akin (although these latter may be such as have no close affinity with them), immediately embrace them, preferring them as if more to their liking; and they seem to consider this a gain, as if they stood in want of such bodies. Gold, for example, or any other metal in leaf form, does not like being surrounded by air, so that if it meets any dense, tangible body, such as a finger, a piece of paper, etc., it immediately

---

[257]The crystals that occur in caves, in Bacon's example, are stalactites and stalagmites, as is indicated in a parallel passage in Bacon's *History of Dense and Rare, Works,* V, p. 389.

[258]This topic is discussed also in Aphorism II, 25.

sticks to it and is not easily detached. Also paper, or cloth and things of that kind, are uncomfortable with the air which is lodged and mixed in their pores, so that they freely drink in water or other liquid, and drive out the air. Also sugar or a sponge dipped in water or wine, although a part of them may project well above the wine or water, nevertheless gradually and by degrees draw up the water or wine.

From this we derive a very good rule for the opening and resolving of bodies. Leaving aside corrosives and strong solvents that open a way for themselves, if a body can be found that is proportioned to and more in harmony and friendship with any other solid body than with that with which it is (as if by necessity) mingled, it immediately opens and relaxes itself and takes this second body into itself, shutting out or removing the first one. Nor does this Motion for Gain operate or take effect only by contact. Thus the electric effect (about which Gilbert and others after him have told such great stories) is simply an appetite of a body aroused by gentle rubbing, an appetite which does not easily tolerate air, but prefers another tangible body, if one may be found nearby.

7   Let the seventh motion be the one I call the *Motion of Greater Congregation,* by which bodies are carried towards masses of a like nature to themselves: heavy things to the globe of the earth, light things to the surrounding heaven. To this the schoolmen have given the name 'natural motion', on the superficial grounds that either there was nothing to be seen outside them which could produce such motion (and therefore they thought it must be innate and inherent in them), or perhaps because it never ceases. But this is not surprising, for heaven and earth are always with us, while on the other hand, the causes and origins of most other motions are sometimes absent, sometimes present. And because this motion does not cease but occurs directly the others cease, they believe it to be perpetual and peculiar to itself, and the others to be due to some external agency. This motion, however, is in fact quite weak and faint, and (except in a very large body) gives way to and is overcome by other motions, for as long as they are operating. And though this motion has so filled the thoughts of men that it has almost blotted out all the others, nevertheless men know little about it, but are involved in many errors about it.

8 Let the eighth motion be the *Motion of Lesser Congregation,* whereby the homogeneous parts in any body separate
themselves from the heterogeneous, and congregate together;
whereby also whole bodies, from the similarity of their substance, embrace and cherish each other, and are sometimes
drawn together and congregate to quite a distance; as when
the cream in milk after a time floats at the top, and in wine the
dregs and lees sink to the bottom. And these effects take place
not only because of the motion of gravity or of levity,[259] whereby
some parts rise towards the top and others move towards the
bottom, but much more from the desire of homogeneous things
to come together and become united. And this motion is
different from the Motion of Want, in two respects. One, that in
the Motion of Want, the greater stimulus is that of a malign
and contrary nature, while in this motion (provided there are
no hindrances to shackle it), the parts are united through
friendship, even though there may be no alien nature to arouse
strife. The other difference is that the union is closer, and is, as
it were, more selective. For in the former, so long as any hostile
body is avoided, even bodies that are not closely akin come
together; whereas in the latter, substances unite that are
bound together entirely by a real similarity, and flow as it were
into one. And this motion exists in all compound bodies, and
would be easy to see in particular cases, if it were not bound
and reined in by other appetites and compulsions of bodies,
which disturb that coming together.

Now this motion is generally bound in one of three ways: (i)
by the torpor of a body, (ii) by the restraint of a dominating
body, and (iii) by an external motion.

(i) As regards the torpor of bodies, it is certain that there is
in tangible bodies a certain laziness, to a greater or lesser
degree, and a fear of being moved from their place, so that,
unless they are roused, they prefer to remain content as they
are rather than escape to something better. But this torpor is
shaken off with the help of three things: either (*a*) by heat or
(*b*) by the superior power of some kindred body or (*c*) by a lively

---

[259]These motions of gravity and levity, that is the tendencies of some
bodies to fall and others to rise, are referred to, in passing, in Aphorism
II, 46, and also Aphorisms II, 35 and 36 (*5*).

and powerful motion. (a) Now take first the help given by heat, as a result of which heat has been declared to be 'that which separates the heterogeneous and congregates the homogeneous'. This definition of the Peripatetics was deservedly laughed at by Gilbert, who said that it was just like defining a man as a thing that sows wheat and plants vines; for it was a definition through effects alone, and only particular ones at that.[260] But that definition is still more reprehensible, because even those effects (such as they are) are not the result of any property of heat, but are merely accidental (for cold does the same, as I shall describe later), indeed the truth is that they result from the desire to come together, heat doing no more than dispelling the torpor that formerly kept the desire in check. (b) As for the help given by the power of a kindred body, this is admirably displayed in an armed loadstone, which arouses in iron the power of holding iron through similarity of substance, the torpor of the iron being dispelled by the power of the loadstone. (c) And as for the help given by motion, that is shown clearly in wooden arrows, tipped also with wood, which penetrate deeper into other wooden objects than if they were armed with iron, as a result of the similarity of substance, the torpor of the wood being shaken off by the rapid motion. I have also described these two experiments in the aphorism [II, 25] dealing with Clandestine Instances.

(ii) Now the restraint imposed on the Motion of Lesser Congregation by a dominant body can be seen in the resolution of blood and of urine by cold. For as long as those bodies are filled with active spirit (which like a lord of the whole, regulates and holds in check their several parts, of whatever kind they are), the homogeneous parts do not come together, because of the restraint placed on them; but after that spirit has evaporated, or been choked by cold, the parts, freed from the restraint, then come together in accordance with their natural desire. And so it happens, that all bodies that contain a fierce spirit (such as salts), on account of the permanent and

---

[260]William Gilbert's censure appears in his *De Mundo nostro sublunari Philosophia nova*, which was posthumously published in 1651, but a manuscript copy of which was possessed by Bacon.

lasting restraint of the dominating and imperious spirit, remain stable and are not resolved [into their parts].

(iii) Now the restraint imposed on the motion of Lesser Congregation that comes about through an external motion is best seen in the shaking of bodies in order to prevent putrefaction. For all putrefaction is based on the congregation of homogeneous parts; from which comes the gradual corruption of the old form, as they call it, and the generation of the new. For putrefaction, which paves the way for the generation of a new form, is preceded by the dissolution of the old, which is itself a coming together to homogeneity. Now this, if it is not impeded, is simple dissolution; but if it meets various obstacles, putrefactions follow that are the rudiments of a new generation. But if (and this is the point I am now making) there is frequent shaking by an external motion, this congregative motion (which is delicate and gentle and needs peace from outside annoyance) is disturbed and ceases, as we see in numberless cases; as when the daily stirring or flowing of water prevents it from becoming foul; winds keep away pestilence in the air; grain in granaries stays sound if turned and shaken; in short, all things shaken from without do not readily putrefy within.

It remains for me not to omit that uniting of the parts of bodies from which hardening and drying chiefly derive. For after the spirit, or moisture turned into spirit, has escaped from any more porous body, such as wood, bone and parchment, the denser parts contract and unite with increased effort, whence follow hardening and drying, which I think comes about, not so much from the Motion of Connection in avoidance of a vacuum, as through this motion of friendship and union.

Now as regards drawing together at a distance, that is very infrequent, and yet it does exist in more things than those in which it is noticed. There are illustrations of it when one bubble dissolves another, when medicines through similarity of substance draw out humours; when one string moves another in unison in different stringed instruments; and effects of this kind. I suspect that this motion is also active in the spirits of animals, though quite unrecognized; but it is certainly prominent in the loadstone and magnetized iron.

Now when speaking of the motions of the loadstone, they should be distinguished clearly from each other. For there are four powers or operations in a loadstone, which should be kept separate and not confused, although men's wonder and astonishment have mixed them together. One is the attraction of loadstone to loadstone, or of iron to loadstone, or of magnetized iron to iron. The second is its tendency to turn to north and south, and its simultaneous declination.[261] The third is the power of penetration through gold, glass, stone, indeed everything. The fourth is its ability to communicate the magnetic power from the stone to iron, and from iron to iron, without communicating any substance. But here I am speaking only of the first power, that is, of attraction. There is also a remarkable motion of attraction between quicksilver and gold; so much so, that gold draws quicksilver to itself, even when made up into ointments; and men working among the fumes of quicksilver usually keep a piece of gold in their mouths to collect the emissions of quicksilver which would otherwise invade their skulls and other bones; whence also the piece of gold becomes white. So much for the Motion of Lesser Congregation.

9 Let the ninth motion be the *Magnetic Motion,* which, although it is similar in kind to the Motion of Lesser Congregation, yet if it operates at great distances and on large masses, deserves a separate investigation; especially since it is neither initiated by contact, as most motions are, nor leads to contact, as all congregative motions do; but merely raises bodies, or makes them swell and nothing more. For if the moon raises the waters or makes moist things swell; or if the starry heaven draws the planets towards their apogees; or if the sun attracts the heavenly bodies Venus and Mercury, so that they depart no further than a certain distance from his body; these motions do not seem to be rightly placed under either the Greater or the Lesser Congregation, but to be, as it were, an intermediate and

---

[261]A magnetized needle supported so that it can move freely about its centre of gravity generally comes to rest with its north pole either higher or lower than its centre. This phenomenon, which is called the declination or dip of the magnet, was thoroughly investigated by William Gilbert, who correctly attributed it to the earth's magnetism.

incomplete congregation and ought therefore to constitute a species to themselves.

10 Let the tenth motion be the *Motion of Flight;* a motion that is the exact opposite to the Motion of Lesser Congregation, whereby bodies out of antipathy flee from and repel those that are hostile, and separate themselves from them, or refuse to mix with them. For although this motion can in some bodies seem to be merely a motion incidental to or consequent on the Motion of Lesser Congregation, because the homogeneous parts cannot unite unless the heterogeneous are excluded and removed, nevertheless it should be classed as a motion in itself, and constituted as a species, because in many cases, the desire for Flight seems to be more important than the desire for coition.

Now this motion is notably prominent in the excretions of animals, and no less in objects that are loathsome to some of the senses, especially to smell and taste. For a fetid stench is so rejected by the sense of smell that it even induces the mouth of the stomach to heave in sympathy; and a bitter and rough flavour is so rejected by the palate or throat as to lead to a shake of the head and a shudder in sympathy. But this motion is found elsewhere as well; for it is plain to see in some antiperistases,[262] as in the middle region of the air,[263] the coldness of which seems to be the rejection of the cold nature from the confines of the heavenly bodies; in the same way that those great heats and conflagrations that are found in underground places seem to be rejections of the hot nature from the earth's interior. For heat and cold, in a small amount, destroy each other, but if in large masses, in regular armies, as it were, then the result of their conflict is that they expel and eject each other from their place. They also say that cinnamon and other aromatics keep their scent longer if placed near latrines and other foul-smelling places, because they refuse to come out and consort with foul smells. Certainly quicksilver, which would

---

[262]*Antiperistasis* was defined by Bacon in Aphorism II, 27, as "rejection of contrary nature".

[263]At the height of mountain tops, that is, as Bacon indicates in Instance 2 of Table 2, in Aphorism II, 12.

otherwise reunite itself into a whole body, is prevented from
bringing its parts together by human saliva, hog's lard, turpentine, and the like; this is because of the antipathy that they
have to such bodies, from which they shrink when surrounded
by them, so much so, that their Flight from those substances
interspersed among them is stronger than their desire to unite
themselves with parts similar to themselves; an effect which is
called the 'mortification' of quicksilver.[264] The fact also that oil
does not mix with water is not so much due to their different
lightness as to their antipathy, as is seen in spirit of wine,
which, while lighter than oil, nevertheless mixes well with
water. But most remarkable of all is the Motion of Flight in
saltpetre and crude bodies of that kind, which abhor flame; as
in gunpowder, quicksilver and also in gold.[265] But the Flight of
[magnetized] iron from one pole of a loadstone is well observed
by Gilbert to be not a true Flight, but a conformity and coming
together to a more suitable position.[266]

11 Let the eleventh motion be the *Motion of Assimilation,*[267]
or *Self-Multiplication,* or again *Simple Generation.* By this last
I do not mean the generation of whole bodies, as in plants or
animals, but of bodies that are homogeneous. That is to say,
through this motion, homogeneous bodies convert bodies that

---

[264]In early chemistry, mortification denoted the destruction or neutra-
lization of the active qualities of substances. In his *Physiological and
Medical Remains* (*Works,* III, p. 817), Bacon defined mortification as whatever "gives impediment to union or restitution . . . as when quicksilver is
mortified with turpentine, spittle or butter". For Paracelsus, mortification
was effected by chemical reaction; thus, he classified rust as a mortification of iron. His book, *Concerning the Nature of Things,* devotes its fifth
chapter to the "Death of Natural Things" and to recipes for these chemical
murders.

[265]The motions of flight of salts and quicksilver are also discussed by
Bacon in Aphorism II, 36 (9).

[266]William Gilbert (*On the Magnet,* book 2, ch. 4): "There is properly
no such thing as magnetic antipathy. For the flight and declination of the
ends [of a loadstone and "iron when excited by loadstone"], or an entire
turning about, is an action of each towards unity by the conjoint action
and *synentelechia* of both."

[267]By assimilation is here meant conversion into a similar substance,
for instance the conversion by an animal or plant of extraneous material
into fluids and tissues identical with its own.

are related, or at least well-disposed and prepared, into their own substance and nature; as flame, which over vapours and oily substances, multiplies itself and generates new flame; as air, which over water and aqueous substances multiplies itself and generates new air; vegetable and animal spirit, which over the finer parts of both watery and oily substance in its foods multiplies itself and generates new spirit; the solid parts of plants and animals, such as the leaf, flower, flesh, bone and so on, each of which assimilates and generates new substance and supply out of the juices of their food. For let no one choose to be so foolish as to say with Paracelsus who (blinded presumably by his own distillations) would have it that nutrition is only the result of separation; and that in bread and meat are concealed the eye, nose, brain and liver, and in the juices of the earth are hidden the root, leaf and flower. For just as the craftsman produces leaf, flower, eye, nose, hand, foot and the like, out of the raw lump of stone or wood, through separation and rejection of what is superfluous, so too that *arch-craftsman*[268] within, according to Paracelsus, produces all our limbs and other parts from our food, by separation and rejection. But to leave this nonsense, it is very certain that the several parts, the homogeneous as well as the organic, in plants and animals, first extract by some process of selection those juices of their food that are more or less akin to them, or not very different, and then assimilate and convert them into their own nature. Nor does this Assimilation, or Simple Generation, take place only in living bodies, but inanimate ones also take part in this process, as I have just said about flame and air. Moreover, the non-living spirit, which is contained in every tangible animate thing, is perpetually at work to digest the denser parts and turn them into spirit, which then escapes; from which comes the diminution of weight and desiccation, of which I have spoken elsewhere [in Aphorism II, 40]. And when considering Assimilation, we should not ignore that process of accretion, which is commonly distinguished from that of nourishment; as

---

[268]Bacon is explicitly referring to the *Archeus,* the immaterial principle or vital force, which in the Paracelsian system produces and regulates animal and vegetable life.

when clay between small stones solidifies and is turned into a stony material, and scales around the teeth are turned into a substance no less hard than teeth themselves, etc. For I am of opinion that there must be a desire to assimilate in all bodies, no less than the longing to come together to homogeneity;[269] but this power is restrained, just as the other is, though not by the same means. But it is these means, and also how to remove them, that we should make every effort to investigate, because they have a bearing on the re-kindling of vigour in old age. And lastly, it seems worth mentioning that in those nine motions I have just described, bodies seem to be seeking only the conservation of their nature; but in this tenth one they seek its propagation.[270]

12 Let the twelfth motion be the *Motion of Arousal,* which seems to be of the same kind as *Assimilation,* and which I sometimes indiscriminately call by that name. For it is a motion that is diffusive [i.e., spreading], communicative, transitive [i.e., operating beyond itself] and multiplicative, as is that other; and they mostly agree in their effect, although differing in the mode of achieving it, and in their subject. For the Motion of Assimilation proceeds by authority and power; it orders and compels the assimilated body to turn and change into the assimilator. But the Motion of Arousal proceeds stealthily, as if by art and insinuation; it merely invites, and persuades the aroused body to assume the nature of arouser. Moreover the Motion of Assimilation multiplies and transforms bodies and substances, as when it produces more flame, more air, more spirit, more flesh; whereas in the Motion of Arousal, it is the powers alone that are multiplied and transferred, more heat being generated, more magnetic power, more putrefying power. And this motion is most conspicuous in hot and cold things. For heat in the act of heating does not diffuse itself by communicating the original heat, but simply by

---

[269]This is an allusion to the Motion of Lesser Congregation, the eighth in Bacon's list of motions.

[270]As Ellis points out, the first motion in Bacon's catalogue relates to matter in general, while all the succeeding ones concern concrete bodies. Thus the Motion of Assimilation is the tenth of those relating to such bodies, though it is the eleventh in the general arrangement.

Arousing the parts of the body to that motion which is the form of heat, about which I spoke in the First Vintage on the nature of heat [in Aphorism II, 20]. And therefore heat is aroused far more slowly and with more difficulty in stone or metal than in air, because of the awkwardness and unreadiness of those bodies for that motion. So that it seems likely that there may be materials down among the bowels of the earth that utterly resist being heated, because, on account of their greater compression, they lack that spirit by which this Motion of Arousal begins. In the same way, a loadstone imparts to iron a new disposition of its parts and a motion conforming to its own, without losing any power itself. And likewise leaven in bread, and yeast, and rennet from milk, and certain poisons, arouse and induce a successive and continuous motion in lumps of dough, in beer, cheese and the human body, respectively; not so much from a power of arousing as from the predisposition and readiness of the aroused body to yield.

13 Let the thirteenth motion be the *Motion of Impression,* which is also of the same kind as the Motion of Assimilation, and is the most subtle of the diffusive motions. I have decided, however, to constitute it a separate species, because of a notable difference between it and the former two. For the simple Motion of Assimilation transforms bodies themselves, so that if you took away the first motive force, there would be no difference in what follows. For the first lighting of a flame, or the first conversion into air, do nothing to the flame or air generated afterwards. Likewise, the Motion of Arousal continues unaltered for a very considerable time if the first motive force is taken away, as in a heated body, when the original heat is removed; in magnetized iron, when the loadstone is removed, and in lumps of dough, when the leaven is removed. But the Motion of Impression, though diffusive and transitive [i.e., spreading and operating beyond itself], nevertheless seems to be always dependent on the first motive force, so much so, that if the latter is removed or ceases, it straightway fails and dies; therefore the effect must take place in a moment, or at least in a very short space of time. And for this reason, I like to call those Motions of Assimilation and Arousal *Motions of the Generation of Jupiter,* because their generation persists; but this motion I call the *Motion of the Generation of Saturn,*[271] because once born it is immediately devoured and absorbed. And this motion is shown in three things: in rays of light, in the percussions of sounds, and in magnetism, as far as communicating its power is concerned. For if light is taken away, its colours and other images at once disappear; take away the first percussion and the resulting vibration of a body, and the sound dies away soon after. For although sounds, even in their mid-flight, are disturbed by winds as if by waves, yet it should be carefully noted that the sound does not last so long as does the resonance of it. For if a bell is struck, the sound appears to continue for quite a long time; from which one could easily make the mistake of thinking that all that time the sound was floating and lingering in the air, which is absolutely wrong. For that resonance is not one and the same sound but a renewal of it. This is shown by the quieting or stopping of the body struck. For if the bell is held tightly, so that it cannot move, the sound dies at once and does not resound further; as when the strings of an instrument are touched after first being struck, either by the finger as in a lyre, or by a quill, as in spinets, the resonance ceases at once. And when the loadstone is removed, the iron falls immediately. But the moon cannot be removed from the sea, nor the earth from a heavy object while it falls, so we cannot conduct any experiment involving them, but the principle is the same.

14 Let the fourteenth motion be the *Motion of Configuration,* or *Position,* whereby bodies appear to desire, not coition, nor any separation, but a position, an arrangement and a configuration with other bodies. Now this is a very abstruse motion, and has not been well investigated. In some cases, it almost

---

[271]Hesiod's *Theology,* 453 ff., tells how Rhea bore numerous children to Cronos (Saturn), whose habit was to swallow each of them, so that 'no other of the proud sons of heaven should hold the kingly office amongst the deathless gods'. However, when Rhea gave birth to Zeus, she presented Cronos, not with the new-born child, but with a stone wrapped in swaddling clothes, which he promptly devoured, unaware of the deception. Jupiter, who corresponds to the god Zeus in Roman mythology, was amongst other things regarded as the preserver and increaser of Roman power.

seems to have no cause, although I think this is in fact not so. For if it be asked why the heavens revolve from east to west rather than from west to east, or why they turn around poles positioned near the Bears rather than around Orion or any other part of the heaven, this question seems beside the point, since those things should rather be accepted from experience, as positive [i.e., uncaused]. Admittedly there are some things in nature that are ultimate and uncaused, yet this does not seem to be one of them. For in my opinion this phenomenon comes about from a certain harmony and agreement of the world, which has not hitherto been looked at. And if we were to accept that it is the earth that moves from west to east, the same questions remain. For it also moves upon certain poles, but why then should those poles be located where they are, rather than somewhere else? Again, the polarity, direction and declination of a loadstone all come back to this motion [of Configuration]. There are also found in both natural and artificial bodies, especially in solids rather than fluids, a certain arrangement and disposition of parts, like hairs and fibres, which should be carefully investigated; since unless these are discovered, those bodies cannot easily be handled and controlled. But those eddies in liquids, by which when pressed before they can get free, they relieve each other, so that they may all bear that pressure equally, are better assigned to the Motion of Liberation.

15 Let the fifteenth motion be the *Motion of Transition,* or the *Motion According to the Passages,* whereby the powers of bodies are to a greater or lesser degree either impeded or promoted by their media, according to the nature of the bodies and of the powers being exercised, and also of the medium. For one medium suits light, another sound, another heat and cold, another magnetic powers, and so on, with respect to several other effects.

16 Let the sixteenth motion be what I call the *Royal* or *Political Motion,* whereby the predominant and ruling parts in any body restrain, tame, subdue, order and compel the other parts to unite, separate, stand still, move and position themselves, not according to their own desires, but in such order as will conduce to the well-being of that governing part; so that there is a kind of Regime and State exercised by the ruling part over the subject parts. This motion is especially apparent in the spirits of animals, where, provided it is in full vigour, it tempers all the motions of the other parts. It is, however, found in other bodies to a somewhat lower degree; just as I have already said [under the Motion of Lesser Congregation] with regard to blood and urine, which are not resolved [by cold] until the spirit which mingles and keeps their parts together, shall have been discharged or smothered. And this motion is not entirely confined to spirits, although in most bodies it is the spirits that dominate, because of their quick motion and penetration. But in more condensed bodies which are not filled with active and vigorous spirit (such as exists in quicksilver and vitriol), it is rather the denser parts that dominate, so much so, that unless this restraint and yoke are by some contrivance shaken off, there can be very little hope of any new transformation of such bodies. But no one should think that I have forgotten the point at issue, because while this series and distribution of motions is concerned only with the better investigation of their Predominance through Wrestling Instances, I now make mention of Predominance among the motions themselves.[272] For in my description of that Royal Motion, I am not talking of the Predominance of motions or powers, but of the Predominance of parts within bodies. For this is the Predominance that constitutes this particular species of motion.

17 Let the seventeenth motion be the *Motion of Spontaneous Rotation,* whereby bodies, delighting in motion and favourably situated, enjoy their own nature, and follow themselves, not any other body, and as it were court their own embraces. For bodies seem either to move endlessly, or to remain entirely at rest, or to be carried to a limit, at which they either rotate or remain at rest, according to their nature. Those that are favourably situated, if they delight in motion, move in a circle; that is, with an eternal and infinite motion. Those that are favourably situated and hate motion simply remain at rest. Those not favourably situated move in a straight line (as by the

---

[272]It may have been forgotten by the reader that this very long aphorism concerns Wrestling Instances, also called Instances of Predominance.

shortest path) towards assemblies of those of like nature. But this Motion of Rotation includes nine differences. The first difference is in their centre, around which the bodies move; the second, in their poles, upon which they move; the third, in the distance from the centre of their circumference or orbit; the fourth, in their speed, according as they turn more quickly or slowly; the fifth, in the direction of their motion, whether from east to west, or from west to east; the sixth, in their deviation from a perfect circle, by spirals more or less distant from the centre; the seventh, in their deviation from a perfect circle by spirals more or less distant from their poles; the eighth, in the nearer or further distance of these spirals from each other; the ninth and last, in the variation of the poles themselves, if they are moveable, which has nothing to do with their rotation, unless it is circular. And it is the common and long-held opinion that this motion is peculiar to the heavenly bodies, though there is serious dispute about this between some, both ancients and moderns, who have ascribed rotation to the earth. But a much more justifiable debate might be (if only the matter were not entirely beyond debate) as to whether that motion (allowing that the earth stands still) is confined to the heavens, or does not rather descend and is imparted to the air and the waters. But the rotatory motion in missiles, such as in darts, arrows and musket-balls, I refer entirely to the Motion of Liberation.

18 Let the eighteenth motion be the *Motion of Trepidation,* to which, as it is understood by astronomers, I do not give much credit.[273] But when I search carefully everywhere for the appetites of natural bodies, this motion presents itself, and it seems that it should be constituted a species. Now this motion is like that of a certain eternal state of captivity; that is to say, when bodies are not situated entirely in accordance with their

---

[273]Astronomers since Greek times recognized a phenomenon known as the precession of the equinoxes—an extremely slow motion of the celestial pole through the stars. Some astronomers believed that the precession was continuous, making a complete revolution over 26,000 years. But others claimed, wrongly, that the direction of precession changed periodically; this supposed effect was called *trepidation.* See Thomas Kuhn, *The Coper-nican Revolution* (Cambridge, Mass.: Harvard University Press, 1957).

nature, and yet not wholly ill at ease either, they are for ever trembling and in restless agitation, neither content with their state nor venturing to proceed further. Such a motion is found in the heart and pulses of animals, and must necessarily occur in all bodies which pass their time in an uncertain state between comfort and discomfort, so that in their distraction they try to free themselves, and are again repulsed, yet always try once more.

19 Let the nineteenth and last motion be that which the name of motion hardly fits, yet it clearly is a motion. I like to call it the *Motion of Repose,* or *of Aversion to Motion.* By this motion the earth stands still in its mass, while its extremities move towards the middle; not to an imaginary centre, but to union. Because of this tendency, all things that are condensed to a considerable degree are also averse to motion, and indeed, their only wish is not to be moved. And though they may in numberless ways be teased and provoked to motion, they nonetheless preserve their nature as best they can. And if forced to move, they nevertheless always seem to do this just so as to recover their state of rest, and to move no further. And while doing this they certainly show themselves agile, and struggle nimbly and quickly enough (as if weary and impatient of all delay). But we can see the picture of this tendency only in part, because in the realm of our experience, every tangible thing is, by the action of the heavenly bodies in preparing and concocting,[274] not only not condensed to the utmost, but also has some spirit mixed with it.

I have now therefore set out the species or simple elements of motions, appetites, and active powers, which are most general in Nature. And it is no small part of natural knowledge that is outlined in them. Not that I deny that yet other species could perhaps be added, and those very divisions may be adjusted to accord with the truer veins of Nature, and could then be reduced to a smaller number. Nor, however, do I mean this in respect of any abstract divisions, as if one were to say that bodies have an appetite either for the conservation or maximization or propagation or fruition of their nature; or

---

[274]To concoct is to prepare by means of heat.

were to say that the motions of things tend to the conservation and good either of the world, as do the Motions of Resistance and Connection; or of greater wholes, as do the Motions of Greater Congregation, of Rotation and of Aversion to Motion; or of special forms, as the others do. For although these are true, unless they are defined in accordance with true lines in the material structure, they are speculative and of little practical use. Meanwhile, they will suffice and will serve well in weighing the Predominances of powers and in investigating Wrestling Instances, which is my present concern.

For of these motions which I have set out, some are absolutely invincible, some are stronger than others and tie down, restrain and arrange them, some extend much further than others, some excel others in time and speed, some assist others and strengthen, enlarge or hasten them.

The Motion of Resistance is altogether adamantine and invincible, but I am still unsure whether the Motion of Connection is also invincible. For I will not affirm for certain whether there is a vacuum, either concentrated in one place or spread throughout a body. But what I am certain of is that the reason why a vacuum was introduced by Leucippus and Democritus (namely that without it the same bodies would not be able to embrace and fill both larger and smaller spaces) is wrong. For there quite plainly is a 'folding of matter', folding and unfolding itself through spaces, within definite limits, and without the introduction of a vacuum. Nor is there in air two thousand times the vacuum that there is in gold (for such would have to be the case).[275] This is clear enough to me from the very great strength of the powers of pneumatic [i.e., spirituous] bodies (which would otherwise be swimming about in a vacuum like fine dust) and by many other demonstrations. But the other motions govern and are governed in turn, in

[275]In Aphorism II, 40, Bacon stated that gold was 21 times denser than spirit of wine, which in turn was 100 times as dense as its vapour. It is evidently from these or similar premises that Bacon deduced that on the vacuum hypothesis, there would have to be 2000 times as much vacuum in a given weight of air than in the same weight of gold. Bacon's own explanation of expansion and contraction through a folding of matter is obscure.

proportion to their vigour, quantity, excitation, or force of discharge, and in proportion also to the assistance or impediments they meet.

For example, some armed loadstones can hold suspended a piece of iron up to sixty times their own weight, so great is the domination of the Motion of Lesser Congregation over that of Greater Congregation; but if the weight were increased, it would be overcome. A lever of a certain strength will raise a given weight, so greatly does the Motion of Liberation dominate over that of Greater Congregation; but if the weight were increased, it would be overcome. Leather stretched to a certain tension does not break, so greatly does the Motion of Continuity dominate over that of Tension; but if the tension is increased, the leather breaks and the Motion of Continuity is overcome. Water runs out through a fissure of a certain size, so far does the Motion of Greater Congregation dominate over that of Continuity; but if the fissure were smaller, it would be overcome and the Motion of Continuity would prevail. If you put just a ball and powdered sulphur into a musket and apply fire, the ball is not discharged, the Motion of Greater Congregation overcoming in this case the Motion of Matter. But if gunpowder is put in, the Motion of Matter in the sulphur prevails, aided by the Motions of Matter and of Flight in the saltpetre. And so also for the rest. For Wrestling Instances (which indicate the Predominance of powers and by what rules and computations they will either predominate or give way) must be collected from every side with keen and constant care.

And the measures and rules of the succumbing of these motions should also be carefully studied, that is to say, whether the motions cease entirely, or on the other hand struggle on, but are restrained. For in bodies as we know them there is no true rest, neither in whole bodies nor in their parts, but only the appearance of it. But that apparent rest is caused either by equilibrium, or by an absolute Predominance of motions; by equilibrium, as in scales, which stand still, if the weights are equal; by Predominance, as in perforated jugs, in which the water does not move and is kept from running out by the Predominance of the Motion of Connection. It should be noted, however (as I have said), to what extent those succumbing motions are struggling. For if anyone in a fight were held

pinned to the ground, and bound hand and foot, or held down
in some way, he may still struggle with all his might to rise;
the struggle is not any less for not succeeding. Now this state of
things (namely whether the yielding motion is, as it were,
annihilated by the Predominance, or whether, on the other
hand, the struggle continues, although unobserved), which is
hidden in such conflicts, will perhaps show itself when they
concur. For example, have an experiment performed with
muskets, to see whether a musket, for such a distance as it will
send a ball in a direct line, or point-blank as they say, will give
a weaker impact when firing upwards, when the Motion of
Striking is by itself, than when downwards, when the Motion
of Gravity concurs with that of Striking.

Also, the rules of Predominances which we find should be
collected. For instance, the rule that the more general the good
that is sought, the stronger the motion; so that the Motion of
Connection, which relates to the communion of all things, is
stronger than the Motion of Gravity, which relates [only] to the
communion of dense things. Also that the appetites that are
for a private good seldom prevail against those for a more
public good, except in small quantities; a rule which one could
wish held true in politics.

49

Among prerogatives of instances, I will put in twenty-fifth
place *Hinting Instances,* which are those that hint at or point
out what is advantageous to man. For Power and Knowledge by
themselves enlarge human nature, they do not bless it. We
should therefore cull from the whole world of things those that
are most useful to our life. But a more suitable place to discuss
these will be when I deal with *Applications to Practice.*[276]
Moreover, in the work of interpretation itself in each separate
subject, I always devote a place to the *Human Chart* or the

---

[276]Application to Practice is one of the parts of *Novum Organum* which
was announced in Aphorism II, 21, but not completed, nor, so far as we
know, started.

Chart of Desiderata.[277] For it is the role of science both to seek and to desire wisely.

50

Among prerogatives of instances, I will put in twenty-sixth place *Instances of General Use*. These are ones that apply to a variety of things and occur fairly often, so that they save no small amount of work and new trials. Now a more suitable place to speak of instruments themselves and ingenious contrivances will be when I come to deal with the Applications to Practice and the Modes of Experimenting. Moreover, those which are already known and have been put to use will be described in particular histories of individual arts.[278] For the present, however, I append some general remarks about them, merely as examples of Instances of General Use.

Now besides simply bringing bodies together and separating them, men act on natural bodies in seven principal ways: *1.* by the exclusion of things that hinder and disturb them; *2.* by compressions, stretchings, shakings and such like; *3.* by heat and cold; *4.* by the elapse of time in a favourable place; *5.* by the curbing and regulation of motion; *6.* by special consents; or *7.* by the timely and appropriate alternation, in a series and succession, of all or at least some of these.

1 With respect to the first, then: common air, which is with us and presses on us from every side, and also the rays of the heavenly bodies, cause much disturbance. Whatever therefore acts to exclude them can fairly be held to be of General Use. So this applies to the material and thickness of vessels holding

---

[277]Bacon drew up such charts, or tables, at the end of his *History of the Winds* and his *History of Dense and Rare*. Examples of desiderata in the former are: "A better method of ordering and disposing the sails of ships, so as to make more way with less wind; a thing very useful in shortening sea voyages"; and "A method . . . of foretelling the diseases and epidemics every year; a thing useful to the reputation of physicians . . .".

[278]See *below*, in Aphorism 5 of the *Description of a Natural and Experimental History*.

bodies ready for operation. Likewise, the efficient means of stopping up the vessels, by consolidation and what chemists call 'lute of wisdom'.[279]

The sealing-in of substances by means of liquids surrounding them is also extremely useful, as when they pour oil onto wine or juices of herbs, which by spreading over the surface like a lid preserves them perfectly unimpaired by the air. And powders too have their uses, for although they contain air mixed with them, they yet keep out the action of the air massed around them, as occurs in the preservation of grapes and other fruits in sand and flour. Also wax, and honey, pitch and sticky substances of that kind smeared on make a more perfect seal to keep out air and celestial influences.[280] I have also sometimes performed an experiment of placing a jar and some other bodies into quicksilver, which is far the densest of all bodies capable of being poured round another. Caves too and underground caverns are of great use in warding off the heat of the sun and the injurious action of the open air; the North Germans use these for granaries. This is also the purpose of putting bodies under water, as I remember hearing of bottles of wine lowered into a deep well to be cooled, which however, through chance and oversight and forgetfulness, stayed there for many years, and were then taken out; whereby the wine was rendered, not insipid or flat, but much finer to the taste, as a result, apparently, of the more delicate mingling of its parts. But if bodies need to be placed under water, either in rivers, say, or the sea, and yet neither be touched by the water nor enclosed in sealed vessels, but surrounded by air alone, there is a good use for that vessel that has sometimes been brought into operation under water over sunken wrecks,

---

[279]Lute of wisdom (*lutum sapientiae*) was a material employed by alchemists for hermetically sealing vessels. "It was compounded of linen strips and flour, or better still of mixtures of common clay, potter's clay, horse manure and chopped straw or glass powder, quicklime, powdered bricks, white lead and white of eggs." See R.J. Forbes, *A Short History of the Art of Distillation.*

[280]Some of these methods for preserving fruit were described and recommended by Porta (*Natural Magic,* book 4).

to enable divers to stay longer under water, and yet breathe from time to time. It was like this. A large hollow, metal bell was made, which was lowered level with the surface of the water, so that in this way, the bell carried all the air contained in it to the bottom of the sea. Now it stood like a tripod, on three legs, which were a little less in length than the height of a man; thus the diver, when out of breath, could put his head into the hollow of the bell and draw breath and then continue with his task. And I have heard that a machine, like a little boat or skiff capable of carrying men for some distance under water, has now been invented. Now any bodies could easily be suspended in such a vessel as I have just described, and it is for that reason that I have mentioned this experiment.

There is also another use for the careful and complete sealing of bodies, namely to prevent not only the admission of air from outside, as just described, but also the emission of the spirit of the body, which is the object of the operation inside. For it is necessary that anyone working with natural bodies should be certain of his quantities, [certain] that is, that nothing will evaporate or leak out. Because profound alterations take place in bodies when, Nature forbidding their annihilation, man's art also forbids the destruction or escape of any part. And on this subject a wrong opinion has gained currency (which, if it were true, would lead one almost to abandon hope of ever preserving a certain quantity without any diminution), viz., that the spirits of bodies, and also air rarefied by a considerable degree of heat, cannot be contained in any enclosed vessels without escaping through their subtler pores. Men have been led to this opinion by those common experiments, in which cups are inverted over water with a candle or piece of paper burning inside, as a result of which the water is drawn up; and likewise with cupping-glasses, which when heated over a flame draw up the flesh. For they assume that in both experiments the rarefied air is emitted, and its *quantity* thereby reduced, so that the water or flesh takes its place by the Motion of Connection.[281] But this is quite wrong, for the air is not diminished in *quantity,* but contracts in volume, and this motion of the water to take the place of the

---

[281]The Motion of Connection is described in Aphorism II, 48 (2).

air does not begin until the flame is extinguished or the air is cooled; so that physicians place sponges soaked in cold water onto cupping-glasses, to make them draw more strongly. There is, therefore, no reason for men to be much afraid of the easy escape of air or spirits. For although it is true that even the most solid bodies have their pores, neither air nor spirit readily allows itself to be broken down so very finely, just as water refuses to leak out through a very small fissure.

2   As regards the second way [that men act on natural bodies] of the seven mentioned above, the chief thing to note is that compressions and similar violent actions certainly do have a most powerful effect on movement in space and other such motions, as in machines and missiles, and they also lead to the destruction of an organic body, and those of its powers that depend entirely on motion. For all life, in fact all flame and intense heat too, is destroyed by compressions, just as every machine is damaged and thrown into disorder by them. It also leads to the destruction of those powers that depend on the arrangements and the somewhat coarser dissimilarity of parts; as in colours (for the colour of an unbroken flower is not the same as that of one crushed, nor that of unbroken amber the same as of amber ground to powder);[282] and also in flavours (for the flavour of an unripe pear is not the same as that of one squeezed and pressed, for it manifestly takes on a greater sweetness). But these acts of violence do not have much effect on the more striking transformations and alterations of homogeneous bodies; because bodies do not acquire by them any new, constant and fixed consistency, but one that is transitory and striving always for the restoration of its former state and freedom. And yet it would be as well to conduct some more careful experiments on this matter; namely, to see whether the compression or rarefaction of a body that is thoroughly homogeneous (such as air, water or oil) performed by the same violent means, could become constant and fixed, and as it were changed in nature. This should first be tried by simple lapse of time, then with helps and consents. And this could easily have

---

[282]The essential nature of colour in a body consisted, in Bacon's view, in the particular arrangements of the body's 'optical parts'. The theory is given in footnote 187, p. 184.

been done, if only I had thought of it, when, as I have said
elsewhere,[283] I was compressing water using hammer-blows
and presses, until it burst out. For I ought to have left the
flattened sphere to itself for some days and only then extracted
the water; so that the experiment would have been made as to
whether the water would have immediately taken up the same
volume that it had before compression; because if it had not
done so, either immediately or at least shortly after, this
compression might appear to have been made permanent. But
if it had, then restoration would appear to have taken place,
and the compression would have been only transitory. And a
similar thing should also have been done over the expansion of
air in glass eggs.[284] For after sucking strongly, I should have
quickly and firmly stoppered the eggs, and left them stopped
up for several days; and then I should have tested whether, on
opening the hole, air would have been drawn in with a hiss; or
also whether, after submersion, as much water would have
been drawn in as would have been [drawn in] at the beginning,
before the lapse of time occurred. For it is probable, or at least
it is worth testing, that this might have happened, and may
happen again; since in bodies that are slightly less homogeneous, a delay produces similar effects. For a stick bent under
pressure for some time does not spring back, which should not
be put down to any loss of quantity in the wood as a result of
the delay; for with a longer delay, the same effect occurs in a
strip of steel, which cannot evaporate. But if the experiment
does not succeed by a simple lapse of time, the business should
not be given up, but other means introduced. For it would be
most advantageous if permanent and fixed natures could be
imparted to bodies by violent means. For in this way air could
be turned into water by condensation, and many other effects
of that kind produced. For man is a master of violent motions
more than of others.

3 And the third of the seven ways relates to that great
instrument (*organum*) for operating both in Nature and in art,
namely heat and cold. And in this respect, human power is

---

[283]In Aphorism II, 45.

[284]Bacon discussed this experiment in Aphorism II, 45.

lame, and limps on one foot. For we have the heat of fire, which is infinitely more powerful and intense than the heat of the sun (so far as it is conveyed to us) and the warmth of animals; but we have no cold, except what we can get during winter weather, or in caverns, or by applications of snow and ice, which can be compared with the heat of the midday sun in some torrid zone, increased by reflection from mountains and walls: for both heat and cold, of this intensity at any rate, can be endured by animals for a short time. But they are practically nothing compared with the heat of a burning furnace, or with any corresponding degree of cold. All things with us therefore tend towards rarefaction and desiccation and wasting; almost nothing to condensing and softening, unless by, as it were, spurious mixtures and methods. Instances of cold, therefore, should be collected with all diligence, such as seem to be found in the exposure of bodies on towers during a sharp frost; in caverns underground; packed round with snow and ice in deep sites dug for that purpose; in lowering bodies into wells; in burying them in quicksilver and other metals; in immersing them in those waters that turn wood into stone; in burying them in the earth (as the Chinese are said to do in the manufacture of porcelain, when masses made for the purpose remain, they say, in the earth for forty or fifty years and are passed on to heirs, as if they were a kind of artificial minerals); and so on. So too all naturally-occurring condensations caused by cold should be similarly investigated, so that when their causes are understood they can be applied in the arts. We see such things in the sweating of marble and other stones; in the mists that form on glass on the insides of windows towards dawn, after a night of frost; in the formation and gathering of vapours into water underground, from which springs often gush forth; and anything of this kind.

Besides those things that are cold to the touch, we find others having the power of cold, which also condense, but which seem to work only on the bodies of animals, and hardly at all otherwise. There are many examples of this to be seen in medicines and plasters, some of which condense the flesh and the tangible parts, like astringent and thickening medicaments; some condense the spirits, which is chiefly seen in soporifics. Moreover, there are two methods of condensing the spirits by soporific or sleep-inducing drugs; one, by sedating their motions, the other by dispelling the spirits themselves. For violets, dried rose petals and lettuce[285] and soothing, benign things like that, by their friendly and gently cooling vapours, coax the spirits to unite, restraining their keen and restless motion. And rose-water also, applied to the nostrils of one in a faint, makes the broken and over-relaxed spirits recover themselves and as it were cherishes them. But opiates and kindred drugs utterly scatter the spirits by their malign and hostile quality. Therefore, if they are applied to an outer part, the spirits fly away from it at once, and do not readily flow back; and if taken internally, their fumes, ascending to the head, scatter in all directions the spirits contained in the ventricles of the brain; and when these spirits withdraw, and cannot escape to any other part, they perforce come together and are condensed, and are sometimes completely extinguished and suffocated. If, on the other hand, these same opiates are taken in moderation, they comfort and strengthen the spirits, by a secondary contingency (namely the condensation which succeeds the coming together), and curb their useless and inflammatory motions, as a result of which they are most beneficial in the cure of diseases and the prolongation of life.

And we should not omit the ways of preparing bodies to receive cold, such as the fact that slightly tepid water freezes faster than water that is quite cold, and things of that kind.

Moreover, since Nature is so sparing of cold, we must copy

---

[285]According to Gerarde, "The juice of Lettuce cooleth and quencheth the natural seed if it be too much used, but procureth sleepe". In fact, the concentrated juice of various kinds of lettuce was known as Lettuce-opium. Gerarde also says that the "leaves of Violets are used in cooling plaisters, oiles and comfortable . . . pultices'; and they are said by him to be "of great efficacy in burning fevers, and pestilent diseases, greatly cooling inward parts." And "The leaves of the floures of Roses . . . have a predominant or over-ruling cold temperature" (*The Herball or Generall History of Plantes,* by John Gerarde, enlarged by Thomas Johnson, 1636). According to Porta (*Natural Magic,* book 8, ch. 1), "Sleep is caused by cold, and therefore Dormitives have a cooling quality", a view which was also reported by the Greek writer Plutarch (ca. AD 46–120) in his *Symposiaques,* book 3, 3 (5).

the apothecaries, who when a particular simple[286] is not to be had, take a substitute or *quid pro quo* as they call it, such as lign-aloes for xylobalsamum, cassia for cinnamon.[287] In the same manner, we should look around carefully for any substitutes for cold, that is to say, ways in which condensation could be produced in bodies other than by cold, this being the natural operation of cold. Such condensations, as far as we can yet see, appear to be limited to four in number. The first of these seems to be that which comes from a simple thrusting together, which is not very effective in producing any lasting density (as bodies spring back), but nevertheless could perhaps be of some assistance. The second occurs with the contraction of the coarser parts in a body, after the escape or departure of the rarer parts, as happens in the tempering of metals by fire and repeated quenchings, and similar processes. The third occurs with the coming together of those homogeneous parts in any body that are the most solid, and were formerly scattered and mingled with the less solid, as in the restoring of sublimate of mercury [to its original state], which in powder form occupies much more space than plain mercury,[288] and similarly in all purification of metals from their dross. The fourth occurs by sympathies, when bodies are applied which condense things by their occult power. These sympathies so far rarely show themselves, which is hardly surprising, seeing that until we succeed in discovering forms and schematisms we have little hope of investigating sympathies. Certainly, as far as animals' bodies are concerned, there are, no doubt, very many medicines, both for internal and external use, that

---

[286]*Simple* is an archaic term denoting a plant used for medical purposes.

[287]Lign-aloes is the aromatic wood obtained from a Mexican tree of the genus *Bursera*. Xylobalsamum is the fragrant wood of the tree *Balsamodendron Gileadense,* which yields Balm of Gilead, a golden, resinous substance once highly regarded as an antiseptic and healing agent for wounds. According to Gerarde's *Herball,* cinnamon "is dry and an astringent, it provoketh the urine, cleereth the eies and maketh sweet breath"; while of cassia it is said that "used in a larger quantity [it] serveth well for the same pourposes which Cinnamon doth".

[288]Sublimate of mercury is mercuric chloride.

condense as if by sympathy, as I said a little earlier. But this kind of operation is rare in inanimate bodies. To be sure, a story has spread abroad, both in books and by word of mouth, about a tree in Terceira [one of the Azores] or the Canary Islands (I forget which) which drips a continual dew, so as to provide the inhabitants with a fair supply of water.[289] And Paracelsus says that a plant called 'Sundew' is full of dew in the burning sun of midday, when other plants around it are dry.[290] However, in my opinion both stories are fables. But of course if they were true, these instances would be outstandingly useful and very much worth investigating. Also, I do not believe that those honey-dews, like manna, that are found on oak leaves in the month of May are formed and condensed from any consent, or from a property specific to the oak leaf, but that while they fall equally on other kinds of leaves, they are held and remain on oak leaves, because they are well unified and not spongy like most other leaves.

As regards heat, man has certainly a wealth and abundance at his command, but there is no observation or investigation in some cases, and those the most necessary, whatever the alchemists keep saying. For the effects of intense heat are explored and brought to light, but those of milder heat, which belong mostly to Nature's ways, are not explored, and so lie hidden. Thus we see that, with those heats generally favoured, the spirits of bodies are greatly exalted, as in strong solvents and other chemical oils; the tangible parts are hardened and, with the emission of the volatile parts, sometimes fixed; the homogeneous parts are separated, and the heterogeneous parts are more or less blended and mixed together; most of all, the complex structures of composite bodies and their subtle schematisms are thrown into confusion and destroyed. On the other hand, the operations of milder heat ought to be tested

---

[289]Richard Hakluyt reported having heard that in the island of Ferro, in the Canaries, there was "a certaine tree that raineth continually, by the dropping whereof the inhabitants and cattell are satisfied with water, for other water they have none in all the island" (*The Principal Navigations, Voyages, Traffiques and Discoveries of the English Nation,* 1589, vol. 10).

[290]Sundew is a herb of the genus *Drosera,* whose leaves secrete drops that glitter in the sun like dew and, being sticky, trap insects.

and explored, by which more subtle mixtures and orderly
schematisms might be generated and elicited, after Nature's
example and in imitation of the sun's works; some of which I
sketched out in the aphorism on Instances of Alliance.[291] For
the operations of Nature are performed in far smaller portions,
and by arrangements much more delicate and varied, than the
operations of fire, as we use it now. But the power of mankind
will only be truly increased when, by the use of man-made
heats and agencies, the works of Nature can be represented in
appearance, perfected in power, and varied in quantity; to
which should be added acceleration in time. For iron rust
develops slowly, but the conversion into Mars yellow is immediate; and it is the same with verdigris and white lead;[292]
crystal is formed over a long time, but glass is quickly blown;
stones grow over a long time, bricks are quickly baked and so
on. Meanwhile, to come to business, all the different kinds of
heat and their respective effects must be carefully and indus-
triously collected from every side and investigated: the heat
of the heavenly bodies, through their rays, direct, reflected, refracted and concentrated in burning-glasses; the
heat of thunderbolts, of flame and of coal fire; of fire from
diverse materials; of fires open and enclosed, confined in a
narrow space and spreading, modified in short, by the various
structures of furnaces; of fire aroused by blowing, fire quiet
and unaroused; of fire removed to a greater or lesser distance;
of fire passing through various media; damp heats, such as
that of bain-maries,[293] of excrement, of the external and
internal warmth of animals, of enclosed hay; of dry heats, of

---

[291]Aphorism II, 35.

[292]Mars is the old chemical name for iron, and Mars yellow a powder of
iron oxide obtained by burning iron or iron sulphide in air. Verdigris is the
green oxide of copper which forms slowly when copper is exposed to the air
and more quickly by reaction with acetic acid. White lead is a compound of
lead carbonate and hydrated lead oxide; it was used as a pigment, and as
a cosmetic to whiten the skin.

[293]The bain-marie (*balneum Mariae*) was a double-walled heating vessel filled with water, which was described in connection with the very
earliest distillation apparatus by an alchemist known as Mary the Jewess,
after whom it is said to have been named. The term is still used for a kind
of large cooking pot.

ashes, lime and warm sand; of heat in short of every kind, together with their degrees [should be collected and investi-
gated].

But above all, we must try to investigate and discover the
effects and operations of heat when it approaches and recedes
gradually, and in an orderly way, and intermittently, and over
appropriate spaces and periods of time. For such systematic
variability is in truth the daughter of the heavens and the
mother of generation, and nothing much is to be looked for
from heat that is either violent or sudden or comes by fits and
starts. This is very clearly to be seen in vegetation; and there
is also a great variability of heat in the wombs of animals,
resulting from their movement, or sleep, or nourishment and
from the sufferings of females in gestation. Finally, in the very
wombs of the earth, namely those in which metals and
minerals are formed, this same variability exists and flourishes; which makes all the more remarkable the stupidity of
some of the reformed alchemists, who think they will achieve
results by using the even warmth of lamps and equipment
of that kind, burning continually at a uniform level. This then
is all I have to say about the operations and effects of heat.
For the right time to examine them closely will be when the
forms of things and the schematisms of bodies have been
further investigated and brought to light. For only when
we have established the exemplars [i.e., the models to be imi-
tated] will it be time to seek and apply and adapt our
instruments.

4   The fourth way of operating is through lapse of time, which
is the steward and almoner, as it were, of Nature. I call it lapse
of time when any body is left to itself for a considerable length
of time, protected and defended meanwhile from any external
force. For only when the extraneous and adventitious motions
[that is, motions originating from outside] cease do the inward
motions display and perfect themselves. Now the effects of
time are far more subtle than those of fire. For instance, it is
not possible to produce such clarification of wine by fire as by
time, nor are the ashes after incinerations by fire so fine as the
dust of dissolution and decay over long ages. Also, blendings
and mixtures suddenly precipitated by fire are much inferior
to those resulting from time. And the diverse and various
schematisms (such as putrescences) which bodies experience

through lapse of time are destroyed by fire or too violent heat. It is as well in the meantime to note that there is some violence in the motions of bodies that are completely enclosed. For this imprisonment hinders the spontaneous motions of a body. For this reason, some time in an open vessel is best for separations; [some time] in a completely closed vessel [is best] for mixtures; [some time] in a vessel partly closed, allowing air to enter, [is best] for putrefactions; indeed instances of the operations and effects of time should be carefully collected from all quarters.

5　The regulation of motion, which is the fifth mode of operation, is of no small value. I call it regulation of motion when one body, meeting another, hinders, repels, admits or directs the spontaneous motion of that second body. It mostly depends upon the shapes and position of vessels. For an upright cone helps the condensation of vapours in alembics,[294] while an inverted cone helps the removal of the dregs from sugar in upturned vessels. Sometimes a curving vessel is needed, and ones that alternately narrow and widen, and such like. And all percolation depends on this, namely, that the incoming body, as it opens the way to one part of the other body, closes it to another. Nor does percolation or other regulation of motion always take place from outside, but also occurs by a body within a body; as when small stones are put into water to collect its muddiness; and as when syrups are clarified with the whites of eggs, so that the coarser parts stick thereto and can then be separated. And it is also to this regulation of motion that Telesio rather frivolously and foolishly attributed the shapes of animals, which he maintained are due, if you please, to the small canals and nooks of the womb. But he ought then to have seen a similar formation in the shells of eggs, which have no wrinkles or irregularities. It is true, however, that the regulation of motion brings about the shaping of things in moulds and casts.

6　Operations by consents or aversions, which comprise the sixth way, are often hidden deep down. For those so-

---

[294]An alembic was part of the distillation apparatus, in which the distilled vapour condenses and from which it is carried in liquid form to the receiver through its spout.

called occult properties, and specifics, and sympathies and antipathies are for the most part corruptions of philosophy. Nor can we have much hope of discovering the consents of things until we discover Forms and simple schematisms. For consent is nothing but the mutual symmetry of forms and schematisms.

The greater and more general consents of things, however, are not entirely obscure, so I should therefore begin with them. Their first and chief diversity lies in the fact that some bodies, while differing to some extent in the quantity and rarity of their matter, yet agree in their schematism, and others, on the contrary, agree in the quantity or rarity of their matter, but differ in their schematism. For it has been well observed by the chemists, in their triad of first principles, that sulphur and mercury pervade as it were the whole universe. (For the case for salt is absurd, and is added only so that their triad can embrace bodies earthy, dry and fixed.[295]) But certainly there does seem to be, in those two, one of the most general consents to be seen in Nature. For there is consent between sulphur, oil, with its fatty fumes, flame, and perhaps the body of a star. Mercury, on the other hand, consents with water and aqueous vapours, with air, and perhaps, the pure interstellar ether. Yet these two quartets or great tribes of things (each within their groups) differ widely in quantity and density of their matter, but agree quite well in their schematism, as is shown in many examples. But, by contrast, metals agree very well in quantity [of matter] and density (especially compared with vegetation, and so forth), but differ in many ways in their schematism. And in the same way, diverse vegetation and animals vary almost infinitely in their schema-

---

[295]Alchemists identified three main elements of matter, which they called sulphur, mercury and salt. These were not to be identified with the ordinary substances of those names, but with the sources of general properties. Thus ('philosophical') sulphur was the principle of combustibility; mercury that of metallic behaviour; and salt that of solubility. Bacon accepted the first two of these principles as "the most primeval natures", though he was just as happy to call them sulphur and mercury as oily and watery; or fat and crude; or inflammable and non-inflammable. But he rejected any independent third 'salt' principle (*The History of Sulphur, Mercury, and Salt, Works,* V, pp. 205–206).

tism, but in quantity or density of matter vary only by a few degrees.

There follows the consent most general of all, except the first, namely that between principal bodies [i.e., those that act as a source or origin] and their supplies; that is to say, between the seeds of things and what nourishes them. We should therefore investigate in which climates, in what earth and at what depth particular metals are generated; and similarly for gems, whether born out of rocks or in mines; and in which soil particular trees, bushes and plants grow best and, so to speak, rejoice; and at the same time which fertilizers are most beneficial, whether dung of any kind, or chalk or sea-sand, ashes, etc.; and also which of these are most suited and helpful for different soils. Also the grafting and inoculation of trees and plants, and the principle governing it, that is, which plants are most successfully grafted on which, depends very much on consent. In this connection, it would be a pleasing experiment, which I have heard has been recently tried, of grafting forest trees (for this hitherto has usually been done with garden trees), whereby their leaves and fruit have been wondrously enlarged and the trees become more shady. In the same way, the respective foods of animals need to be studied, under general heads together also with negatives [i.e., what is harmful]. For carnivores cannot survive on a diet of plants; and it was for this reason also (although the human will has more power over its body than has that of other animals) that the Feuillant Order,[296] having made the experiment, they say, practically disappeared, as if this was more than human nature could stand. Also, the various substances involved in putrefaction, whereby tiny animals are generated, should be studied.

The consents of principal bodies with their subordinate bodies (for the ones I have noted may be held to be such) are reasonably obvious. To these I might add the consents of the senses towards their objects. And since these consents are very

---

[296]The Feuillant order was a short-lived French monastic order which in the late sixteenth century took self-denial well beyond vegetarianism; so much so, that fourteen monks died in a single week, causing the Pope to intervene, in order to curb these excesses.

clear to see if they are well observed and keenly examined, they can also throw much light on other consents that lie hidden.

But the internal consents and aversions of bodies, or their friendships and enmities (for I am somewhat weary of the words *sympathy* and *antipathy,* on account of the superstitious and meaningless ideas associated with them) are either falsely ascribed, or mixed up with fables, or through lack of observation, very rare. For if anyone should assert that there is disagreement between the vine and the cabbage, because if planted near together they never thrive, the real reason is clearly that both plants are succulent and voracious, so that one robs the other.[297] And if any one should assert that there is consent and friendship between corn and the corn-cockle, or the wild poppy, because those plants as a rule only grow in tilled fields, he should rather say that they disagree because the corn-cockle and poppy are born and created from a juice of the earth that the corn has spurned and left, so that the sowing of the corn prepares the ground for them to flourish in. And there are a great number of false ascriptions of this kind, and they should be utterly extirpated as fables. There does remain, it is true, a small number of these consents, which have been proved by reliable experiment, such as those of a loadstone and iron, also gold and quicksilver, and the like. And in chemical experiments with metals, some others are found that are worth noticing. But they are most frequent (though still only few) in some medicines which through their so-called occult and specific properties affect either the limbs, or the humours or the diseases, or sometimes individual natures. Nor must we overlook the consents between the motions and states of the moon and the behaviour of lower bodies, as far as these can be gathered and accepted, after strict and impartial

---

[297]The information concerning the cabbage and the vine appears in Pliny's *Natural History,* xxiv, i: "The oak and the olive are parted by such inveterate hatred that if the one be planted in the hole from which the other has been dug out, they die, the oak indeed also dying if planted near the walnut. Deadly too is the hatred between the cabbage and the vine." This antipathy is also reported in Porta's *Natural Magic,* book 1, ch. 1, together with numerous other supposed operations of sympathy and antipathy.

selection, from experiments in agriculture, navigation and medicine, and so on. And the fewer instances there are of the more secret consents, so much the more carefully should they be looked for, by traditions and reliable and faithful reports; provided that this is done without any levity or credulity, but in a diffident and almost sceptical spirit. There remains the consent of bodies that is, as it were, natural in its mode of operating, yet of General Use, which should by no means be overlooked, but thoroughly observed and explored. This is the union or coming together of bodies, whether eager or reluctant, through combination or juxtaposition. For some bodies are mixed and thoroughly blended together easily and freely, others with difficulty and obstinacy, just as powders mix better with water; lime and ashes with oils; and so with similar substances. Nor should we only gather instances of the *propensity* or *aversion* of bodies to form mixtures, but also of the disposition of their parts, and of their distribution and digestion, once they have become mixed, and finally of their predominance after the mixture has taken place.

7   There remains, last of all, the seventh and final mode of operation, namely, that through the alternation of the other six, concerning which it would be premature to give examples, before we look a little more deeply into each of them. Now a series or chain of such alternations, so far as it can be suited to particular effects, is a matter both extremely difficult to find out, and very important for the production of works. But men are full of impatience with both this sort of inquiry and with practice, though it is like the thread of the labyrinth as regards works of any importance.[298] But let these suffice for examples of General Use.

51

Among prerogatives of instances, I will put in twenty-seventh and last place *Magic Instances.* I call by this name

---

[298]In Greek mythology Theseus was led to the Cretan Minotaur's secret lair, at the centre of the Labyrinth, by following a thread laid down for him by Ariadne.

those instances in which the material or efficient [cause] is slight or small in relation to the magnitude of the ensuing work and effect, so that even when they are common, they seem to be miraculous, some at first glance, others even after more attentive thought. To be sure, Nature furnished these from herself only sparingly, but what she may do when the folds in her robe have been shaken, and after the discovery of forms and processes and schematisms, time will show. Now these Magical effects, as I now suppose, occur in three ways; either through self-multiplication, as in fire, and in poisons, which are called specific; also in motions that are increased in power by passing from wheel to wheel; or by stimulating or drawing in another body, as with a loadstone, which activates numberless needles yet loses none of its power; or in yeast and the like; or by preventing motion, which has already been mentioned [in Aphorism II, 36 (9)] in regard to gunpowder and mortars and mines. Of these ways, the first two call for the investigation of consents, the third for investigation of the measurement of motions. But whether there is any way of changing bodies, as they say, *per minima* [i.e., through the smallest particles] and rearranging the more subtle schematisms of matter, which applies to all manner of transformations of bodies, so that art may be able to do in a short time what Nature toils to achieve after many tortuous labours—as to this, I say, I have so far no sure indications. And just as in matters solid and true I aspire to the very height of perfection, so I always hate what is swollen and empty and do what in me lies to strike them down.

52

Now this is all I have to say about the dignities or *prerogatives of instances.* I must tell you, however, that in this my *Organon* I am dealing with logic, not philosophy. But my logic teaches and instructs the understanding to this end, not that it may with the slender tendrils of the mind snatch and seize abstract notions of things (as ordinary logic does), but that it may actually dissect Nature and discover the powers and actions of bodies, and their laws as they are determined in matter; so that this knowledge proceeds not only from the nature of the mind, but also from the nature of things; it is not surprising, therefore, that it is sprinkled and illustrated throughout with conjectures and experiments in Nature, as examples of my art.

Now, as will be clear from what I have said, there are twenty-seven prerogatives of instances, namely, 1. Solitary Instances; 2. Migratory Instances; 3. Revealing Instances; 4. Clandestine Instances; 5. Constitutive Instances; 6. Conforming Instances; 7. Singular Instances; 8. Deviating Instances; 9. Boundary Instances; 10. Instances of Power; 11. Instances of Companionship and of Hostility; 12. Subjoined Instances; 13. Instances of Alliance; 14. Crucial Instances; 15. Instances of Divorce; 16. Instances of the Door; 17. Summoning Instances; 18. Instances of the Road; 19. Supplementary Instances; 20. Dissecting Instances; 21. Instances of the Measuring Rod; 22. Instances of the Running-Track; 23. Doses of Nature; 24. Wrestling Instances; 25. Hinting Instances; 26. Instances of General Use; 27. Magic Instances.

Now the use of these instances, in which they excel common instances, is found in general either in the informative or the operative part, or in both. As regards the informative, they assist either the senses or the understanding. The senses, as the five Instances of the Lamp [16 to 20, in the above list]; the understanding, either by hastening the exclusion of the form, as Solitary Instances; or by narrowing and pointing more closely to the affirmative of the form, as do Migratory and Revealing Instances, Instances of Companionship and Subjoined Instances; or by encouraging the understanding and leading it to general kinds and common natures; either immediately, as Clandestine and Singular Instances, and those of Alliance; or in the next degree, as the Constitutive; or in the lowest degree, as Conforming Instances; or by correcting the understanding in regard to ordinary things, as Deviating Instances; or by leading it to the great form, or structure of the universe, as Boundary Instances; or by guarding it from false forms and causes, as Crucial Instances and those of Divorce. And as regards the operative part, they either point out practice, or measure or support it. They point it out, either by showing with what to begin, so that we do not repeat work already done, as Instances of Power; or what to aspire to, given the means, as Hinting Instances; the four Mathematical Instances [instances 21 to 24, in the above list] measure practice; the Instances of Magic and those of General Use support it.

Again, of those twenty-seven instances there are some which should be collected at once, as I said above, without waiting for the particular investigation of natures. In this group are Conforming, Singular, Deviating, Boundary, Hinting and Magic Instances, and those of Power, of the Door, and of General Use. For these either help or cure the understanding and the sense, or equip practice for its work. The rest we should only inquire into when we come to compile Tables of Presentation for the work of the interpreter of some particular nature. For instances marked and endowed with these prerogatives are like a soul among the common instances of presentation, and, as I said when first speaking of them [in Aphorism II, 22], a few count for many. For this reason, when we prepare the tables, they must be zealously investigated and set down in them. I had to deal with them first, because it will be necessary to mention them in what follows. But now I must pass on to the Supports and Rectifications of Induction, and then to the concrete, to both Latent Processes and Latent Schematisms and the rest of the topics that I listed in Aphorism 21 [Book II]; so that at the last (like a good and faithful guardian) I may hand over to men their fortunes, their understanding now liberated and come of age. And from this an improvement of the estate of man is sure to follow, and an enlargement of his power over Nature. For man by the Fall fell both from his state of innocence and his dominion over creation. Both of these, however, can even in this life be to some extent made good; the former by religion and faith, the latter by arts and sciences. For the curse did not make creation entirely and for ever rebellious; but in virtue of that ordinance "in the sweat of thy face shalt thou eat thy bread",[299] by every kind of effort (certainly not by disputations

---

[299]Genesis iii, 19.

and empty magic ceremonies), it will at length in
some measure be subdued so as to provide
man with his bread, that is, with
the necessities of
human life.

THE END OF THE SECOND BOOK OF THE
NEW ORGANON

Preparation towards a Natural and Experimental History

Description of a Natural and Experimental History,

such as may serve for the basis and foundations of a true philosophy

My object in publishing my *Instauration* in parts is to put some of it beyond danger. Much the same reason prompts me to add here another small part of the work, and publish it together with those I have just completed. This is a Description and Delineation of a Natural and Experimental History, such as may serve as a foundation for philosophy, and may include good, plentiful and appropriately arranged material for the work of the interpreter which follows. The more suitable place for it would be when I come in due course to the *Preparations for Investigation*.[1] I have thought it wiser, however, to introduce it now, without waiting for its proper place, because a history of the kind I contemplate and shall in a moment describe is a matter of very great magnitude, and cannot be accomplished without great labour and expense; calling as it does on the work of many men, and being (as I have said elsewhere[2]) a kind of royal work. It therefore occurs to me that it would be advisable to find out whether some others might perhaps be able to take on these matters, so that while I bring to completion my part of the work in the intended order, this part, which is so multifarious and onerous, may even during my life (if so it please the divine majesty) be set up and put in hand by others applying themselves diligently to it at the same time as I; especially since my strength (if I should be working

[1]'Preparations for Investigation' is the title of a part of *Novum Organum* announced in Aphorism II, 21, *above*.

[2]In *Novum Organum*, Aphorism I, 111.

on this alone) hardly seems equal to such a great task. For as far as concerns the actual intellectual work, I can perhaps master that by my own exertions. But the materials for that work are so widely spread that they need to be sought and imported from every quarter (as it were, through agents and merchants). Moreover, I consider it a little beneath the dignity of my undertaking that I should spend my own time on such a matter which is open to almost all men's industry. However, I will myself now provide the chief part of the matter, by carefully and exactly setting out the method and description of a history, such as may satisfy my intention, lest men without this guidance may go about things the wrong way, and take as their guide the example of the natural histories now in use, and wander far away from my design. Meanwhile, what I have said often before must be said again here most particularly: that if all the clever minds of all the ages, past and future, were to come together; if the whole human race had devoted or were to devote itself to philosophy, and if the whole earth had been or were to be nothing but academies and colleges and schools of learned men, even then, without such a natural and experimental history as I am going to recommend, there neither would nor could be any advance in philosophy and the sciences worthy of the human race. On the other hand, though, once such a history is prepared and well drawn up, with the addition of such auxiliary and light-bearing experiments as will present themselves or will have to be found in the course of interpretation itself, the investigation of Nature and all the sciences will be the work of only a few years. This therefore must be done, or the whole business abandoned. For this is the one and only way by which the foundations of a true and active philosophy can be laid; and at the same time, men will see, as if roused from a deep slumber, what a difference there is between ingenious dogmas and fictions and true and active philosophy, and, in short, what it is to consult Nature herself about Nature.

In the first place then, I will give general precepts for the making of this history,[3] next, I will set out before men's eyes its

---

[3]Aphorism 10, *below,* makes clear that in this work Bacon gets little further than the general precepts; he merely supplies a catalogue of titles of particular histories instead of its "particular shape".

particular shape, inserting from time to time the purpose to which the investigation is to be adapted and referred, as well as the particular question to be asked, in order that men, having a clear understanding beforehand of the target, may hit on things I perhaps may have overlooked. Now this history I call the *Primary* or *Mother History*.

Aphorisms on the Composition of the Primary History

Nature is divided into three states and is subject, as it were, to three kinds of regime. For she is either free and unfolds herself as she goes on her ordinary way; or she is forced out of her normal state by irregular and unusual material things and the violence of obstacles in her path; or she is constrained and shaped by human art and agency. Now the first state applies to the *species* of things, the second to *monsters* [i.e., marvels or prodigies] and the third to *artifacts*. For in artifacts, Nature is subject to man's authority, and none of them would have been made without him. But through man's activity and intervention a totally new appearance of bodies, and, as it were, another universe or theatre of things comes into view. Natural history is therefore threefold, and deals either with the *freedom*, or the *errors*, or the *shackles* of Nature, so that we can conveniently divide it into the *History of Generations, of Pretergenerations* and *of Arts*, the last of which I also call *mechanical* and *experimental*. However, I do not insist that these three should be handled separately. For why should the histories of monsters in individual species not be combined with the history of those species themselves? And artifacts also are sometimes correctly dealt with alongside species, and sometimes better separated. It is best therefore to consider these questions as they arise; for too much method produces repetition and prolixity as much as none at all.

2

Natural history being, as I have said, threefold in subject matter, is twofold in use. For it is used either for the sake of the knowledge of those things that it contains, or as the primary source of philosophy, and the furniture or stock of true induction. And it is this latter that is now in hand—I say now, for it never has been up to this time. For neither Aristotle nor Theophrastus nor Dioscorides[4] nor Caius Pliny, much less the moderns, ever set before themselves this goal of natural history of which I speak. And it is of great importance in this context that those who in the future take on the writing of a natural history should always remember that they should not consider the pleasure of the reader, nor even the immediate utility that may be derived from their factual accounts, but should seek out and assemble such a diverse abundance of things as will suffice for the construction of true axioms. So long as they bear this in mind, they themselves will determine the method of this history, for the purpose dictates the method.

3

Now the more difficult and laborious this work, the less it should be burdened by unnecessary things. There are three matters therefore on which men need to be clearly advised to be sparing in their efforts, as being efforts that would immensely increase the amount of toil, but yield little or nothing of value.

First then, away with antiquities[5] and citations or the

---

[4]Theophrastus (ca. 370–ca. 287 BC) was a Greek naturalist and writer on natural history who succeeded Aristotle as head of the Peripatetic School of Athens. Dioscorides (active in the first century AD) was a Greek botanist and pharmacologist, who wrote an important work on the uses and properties of medicinal substances.

[5]Antiquities were a branch of what Bacon called civil history, or the history of men, as opposed to natural history; it consisted of scraps of historical anecdote filled out with conjecture: *"Antiquities,* or remnants of

supporting testimonies of authors, likewise with disputes and controversies and conflicting opinions: everything philological,[6] in short. An author should only be quoted in a case of doubtful reliability, and a controversy should be introduced only in a matter of great importance. Things that only serve to adorn a speech and provide similes and a treasury of eloquence and inanities of that kind should be utterly avoided. And each and every thing that is included should be set forth briefly and concisely, so that they may be nothing less than words. For no one collecting and storing materials for building a ship or other such structures thinks of arranging and displaying them prettily to please the eye (as in shops), but is careful only to see that they are sound and of good quality and take up the least room in his stores. And this is exactly what should be done.

Secondly, those copious natural histories that offer a wealth of graphic descriptions of species and their curious variety are hardly what is needed. For such trifling variations are only the sports and wanton freaks of Nature, and come near to being the nature of individuals; they provide a kind of pleasant ramble among the things they describe, but only slight and often superfluous information to the sciences.

Thirdly, all superstitious accounts are to be utterly rejected (I do not mean strange events, when the recollection of them is trustworthy and open to confirmation, but superstitious stories), and also experiments of ceremonial magic. For I do not want the infancy of philosophy, which natural history supplies with its first mother's milk, to become accustomed to old wives' tales. It will be time, perhaps (after we have gone a little deeper into the investigation of Nature), to run lightly through things of this kind, in case we can extract and keep for use any element of natural virtue clinging to these dregs;

---

histories, are . . . like the spars of a shipwreck; when, though the memory of things be decayed and almost lost, yet acute and industrious persons . . . contrive out of genealogies, annals, titles, monuments, coins, proper names and styles, etymologies of words, . . . to recover somewhat from the deluge of time . . ." (*De Augmentis*, II, vi, *Works*, IV, p. 303).

[6]A *philologus*, it may be recalled from the Letter of Dedication, was a man of letters and, in particular, an interpreter of the writings of others.

meanwhile they should be put aside. Experiments of natural magic should also be very carefully winnowed before they are accepted, especially those which as a rule are derived from common sympathies and antipathies, such as lazy minds are all too ready to invent and believe.

And it is no small achievement to relieve natural history of these three unnecessary burdens I have mentioned, which would otherwise fill volumes. Nor is this all; for in a great work, it is no less essential to have all that is included described succinctly than to have the superfluous eliminated, although no doubt such unadorned brevity would give much less pleasure to reader and writer alike. But it should always be remembered that what is being prepared is only a granary and store house of facts, not for pleasurably lingering or residing in but for dipping into as the need arises, when anything there is required for use in the Work of the Interpreter which follows.

4

The history which I require and have in mind must above all be wide-ranging and made to the scale of the universe. For the world is not to be circumscribed within the narrow confines of the understanding (as is now the case), the understanding is rather to be expanded and widened to receive the image of the universe as it is found to be. Thus the maxim 'study few things and pronounce on few things' has been the ruin of everything.

To take up again the divisions of natural history that I made a little earlier (that is, the History of Generations, of Pretergenerations and of Arts), I divide the *History of Generations* into five parts. Let the first be of the ether and of the heavenly bodies. The second, that of meteors and of the so-called regions of the air; that is, of the tracts from the moon down to the surface of the earth; to which part I also assign (for order's sake, however the truth of the matter may be) comets of every kind, both higher and lower. The third, of the land and sea. The fourth, of the elements (so-called) of flame or fire, air, water and earth. Now what I understand by elements is not the beginnings of things, but the greater masses of natural bodies. For the nature of things is distributed in such a way that the quantity or mass of certain bodies in the universe is vast, because their schematism requires a plain and simple material structure, such as those four aforesaid bodies [i.e., fire, air, water and earth] have; whereas the quantity of some other bodies in the universe must be small and sparingly supplied, because their material structure is quite heterogeneous and subtle, and in most cases determinate and organic; as are for example the species of natural things, metals, plants and animals. I therefore call the former kind of bodies the *Greater Colleges* and the latter the *Lesser Colleges*. Now the fourth part of the history is of those Greater Colleges, under the name of elements, as I have said. But this fourth part must not be confused with the second or third part, in that I have mentioned air, water and earth in each of them. For the history of these does come into the second and third, as [the history] of integral parts of the world, and insofar as they relate to the structure and configuration of the universe; but the fourth part contains the history of their own substance and nature, as it exists in their separate homogeneous parts, and without reference to the whole. Finally, the fifth part of the history contains the Lesser Colleges or Species, which up to now have been the main concern of natural history.

As regards the *History of Pretergenerations,* I have already said that it can most conveniently be combined with the history of generations; that is, a history of things that are merely natural prodigies. For I relegate the superstitious history of marvels (of whatever kind) altogether to a treatise of its own; and this treatise should not be undertaken right at the start but a little later, when the investigation into Nature shall have penetrated deeper.

As for the *History of Arts,* and of Nature as changed and altered by man, or Experimental History, I divide this into three. For it is drawn either from the mechanical arts; or from the operative part of the liberal sciences; or from the many crafts and experiments which have not developed into an art proper, but which occur sometimes in the course of the most ordinary experience, without at all needing any art.

Once therefore a history has been compiled of all these

things that I have mentioned—Generations, Pretergenerations, Arts and Experiments—everything by which the sense may be supplied in order to inform the understanding will I think be included. We shall then no longer be capering around in small circles like men bewitched, but shall equal the wide world in our range.

5

Of the parts of history that I have mentioned, the *History of Arts* is the most useful, because it shows things in motion, and leads more directly to practice. Moreover it lifts the mask and veil from natural things, which are often obscured or hidden under a variety of shapes and outward appearances. In short, the vexations of art much resemble the bonds and manacles of Proteus,[7] which betray the ultimate struggles and efforts of matter. For bodies refuse to be destroyed or annihilated, but instead change themselves into different forms. Very great care, therefore, must be taken over this history and all pride and disdain avoided, however mechanical and far from liberal it may seem.

Furthermore, those among the arts are to be preferred that produce, alter and prepare natural bodies and the materials of things; as for example, agriculture; cookery; chemistry; dyeing; and the manufacture of glass, enamel, sugar, gunpowder, artificial fires,[8] paper and the like. Less useful are those arts that depend chiefly on the intricate movement of the hands and of instruments, such as weaving; carpentry; architecture; and the construction of mills and clocks and such things. Not that these should by any means be neglected, both because they involve many things that have a

---

[7]In Greek mythology, Proteus was a subject of the sea god Poseidon. He had the gift of prophecy and, if captured as he slept on the sea shore, would answer questions about the future, but would try to escape by assuming every possible shape in his captors' hands.

[8]The most famous artificial fire was Greek fire, or wildfire, which Bacon mentions a number of times in *Novum Organum,* for example, in Aphorism II, 13, under Instance 21. Porta's *Natural Magic* devotes a whole chapter to a variety of artificial inflammable mixtures.

bearing on the alterations of natural bodies, and because they give precise information about local motion, which is of very great importance in numerous ways.

But in the whole collection of this History of Arts, I have one piece of advice that should never be forgotten; that it should include not only those experiments of arts that lead to the goal of the art, but also those that occur in any way during the process. For example, that lobsters or crabs when cooked become red, though they are only mud-coloured before, means nothing to the dinner table; but this instance is itself not a bad one for inquiring into the nature of redness, since the same effect also occurs in baked bricks. In the same way, the fact that meat is more quickly salted in winter than in summer is not only important for the cook, so that he knows how much salt to use when preserving food, but is also a good instance for indicating the nature and effect of cold. For this reason it would be a world away from the truth to imagine that it would answer my purpose to make a collection of experiments of arts with the sole end of thereby bringing those arts to greater perfection. For though in many cases I would not criticize such action, nonetheless, it is very much my intention that all the streams of mechanical experiments should flow from every side into the ocean of philosophy. But for the selection of the more outstanding instances in each and every kind (which should be most carefully sought and ferreted out) we must look to the prerogatives of instances.

6

At this point I must also take up again what I dealt with at greater length in Aphorisms 99, 119 and 120 of book I [of *Novum Organum*], but which here it may be enough to lay down briefly in the form of a rule; this is, that this history should include, in the first place, the most ordinary things— things which may seem unnecessary to set down in writing, because they are so well known and familiar; then also mean, low and filthy things (for 'to the pure all things are pure',[9] and

---

[9]The Epistle of Paul to Titus i, 15.

if money from urine smelt well,[10] then much more does the light and information from anything); thirdly, things that are trifling and childish (and no wonder, since we are to become entirely like little children again); and finally, things that seem excessively subtle, because in themselves they have no use. For, as I have said, the contents of this history are not gathered for their own sake; and their importance is therefore not to be measured by their worth in themselves, but by their possible bearing on other things, and their influence upon philosophy.

7

I would also lay down that everything, in the case of both natural bodies and natural powers, should (so far as possible) be set forth counted, weighed, measured and marked out;[11] for it is works we are considering, not speculations. Indeed, practical results are produced when physics and mathematics are well blended. And for this reason, in the history of the heavenly bodies, we should ascertain and write down the exact restitutions[12] and distances of the planets; the extent of the land, and its surface area in comparison with the waters, in the history of the land and sea; how much compression air will stand without strong resistance, in the history of air; how much among metals one outweighs another, in the history of metals; and numberless facts of this kind. But when exact proportions cannot be obtained, then resort should be had at least to estimates or rough comparisons; as for example that the moon lies within the shadow of the earth (if we happen to distrust the calculations of the astronomers regarding dis-

---

[10]The allusion here is to the tax levied by the Emperor Vespasian on the product which the fullers had previously collected free of charge from the public urinals to full their cloth. When the propriety of the tax was questioned in the Senate, the Emperor is reputed to have responded by saying *pecunia non olet* (money has no smell).

[11]This aphorism summarizes the Mathematical Instances of Aphorisms II, 45–48, of *Novum Organum*.

[12]The "restitution" of a planet here means the time it takes to return to a previous position; cf. Aphorism II, 46.

tances); or that Mercury lies beyond the moon; and so on. And when mean proportions cannot be obtained, let extremes be given: as for example that a weak loadstone will raise so many times its own weight of iron, while the strongest will raise sixty times its weight, as I have seen done in the case of a very small armed loadstone.[13] And I am well aware that these definite instances do not occur readily or often, but must be sought as auxiliaries in the course of the interpretation itself (when the need for them is greatest). But all the same, if they should occur by chance, provided they do not delay too much the progress of the natural history, they should also be brought into it.

8

Now as regards the trustworthiness of the things to be included in the history, they are of necessity either certainly reliable or of doubtful reliability or of demonstrated unreliability. Things of the first kind should be simply set down; those of the second kind set down with a note, such as the words "it is reported" or "they say" or "I have heard from a trustworthy source", and the like. For to add the arguments on either side would be too laborious, and would certainly delay the writer too much. Nor is it of much importance to the business in hand, since, as I have said in Aphorism 118 of Book 1, errors in experiments, unless they are everywhere in abundance, will soon be refuted by the truth of axioms. Nevertheless, if an instance should be more than usually important, either from its own use or because many other things can hang from it, then certainly its author should be named, not merely with his bare name, but with some mention of whether he had been told it or had read it (as with most of C. Pliny's writings) or was asserting it from his own knowledge; and also whether it was something that happened in his own day or before his time; and whether it was such an event which must, if true, have had many witnesses; and, finally, whether the author was one given to light and empty pronouncements, or sober and

---

[13]Armed loadstones are discussed in *Novum Organum*, II, 25.

serious; and similar things that contribute to the weight of reliability. Lastly, some things that, though of demonstrated unreliability, have yet been talked about and are well-known, and that, partly from carelessness and partly because of the use of similes, have prevailed for many ages now (as that a diamond binds a loadstone, garlic weakens it, or that amber attracts everything except basil, and many other things of that kind[14]), these should be rejected not in silence, but in explicit terms, lest they cause any more harm to the sciences.

Besides this, it would not be out of place to mention the origin of any instance of foolishness or credulity, if it happened to become known; as for example that the plant Satyrion is supposed to have the power of stimulating sexual desire,[15] because, if you please, its root is formed in the shape of testicles, when in fact this is so because each year it grows a new bulbous root, to which the previous year's root stays attached; whence those twin bulbs. This is obvious, because the new root is always found to be firm and juicy, while the old one is withered and spongy, so that it is not surprising that the one sinks in water while the other floats; which nevertheless is considered extraordinary and adds credence to the plant's other [supposed] powers.

9

There are besides a few more things to note that are useful for a natural history, and which can more conveniently adapt and accommodate it for the Work of the Interpreter which follows. They are five in number.

Firstly, questions should be introduced (I am not talking of causes but of fact), which stimulate and encourage further

---

[14]These fallacies were exposed by William Gilbert in his *On the Magnet.*

[15]Paracelsus described a method of extracting from Satyrion "a medicine which leaves far behind all others for every purpose which relates to conception". Satyrion was also called *Orchis,* a Greek word whose normal meaning is 'testicle' (*The Alchemical and Hermetic Writings of Paracelsus,* II, p. 338).

investigation; for example, in the history of land and sea, whether there is a flow and ebb in the Caspian Sea, and at how many hours' interval; whether there is some southern continent, or only islands; and questions like these.

Secondly, in any new and delicate experiment, the procedure for performing it should be added, so that men may be free to judge whether the information yielded by that experiment is reliable or not, and also so that they may be stimulated to exert themselves to discover, if possible, more accurate procedures.

Thirdly, if in any factual account there lurks any element of doubt or reservation, I would never have it suppressed or kept secret, but openly and clearly mentioned by way of a note or warning. For I want this primary history to be compiled with a most religious care, as if the truth of every detail in it was affirmed on oath, since it should be the volume of the works of God, and (so far as one may compare the majesty of things divine with the lowliness of those on earth), as it were, another book of holy scripture.

Fourthly, it would not be out of place to intersperse observations now and then (as C. Pliny did); as in the history of the land and sea, for example, that the shape of the lands, so far as it is yet known, compared with the seas is narrow and pointed towards the south and broad and wide towards the north; the opposite being true of the seas; and that the great oceans intersect the lands in channels running from north to south, not from east to west, except possibly in the furthest polar regions. It is also very good to add canons (which are simply general and universal observations); as for example in the history of the heavenly bodies, that Venus is never further than 46 parts [i.e., degrees] from the sun, Mercury never more than 23; and that the planets situated above the sun move slowest when they are furthest from the earth: those below the sun fastest.[16] And in addition, another kind of observation

---

[16]In the geocentric system of the universe, the planets were ranged in the order Earth, Moon, Mercury, Venus, Sun, Mars, Jupiter and Saturn. The last three were said to be above the Sun. According to modern observations, Venus never deviates from the Sun in the sky by more than 48 degrees, Mercury never by more than 28 degrees.

should be included, which up to now never has been, although it is of some importance. This is that there should be added to those things that do occur those things that do not; in the history of the heavenly bodies, for instance, that no star is found to be oblong or triangular, but that every star is spherical; either simply spherical, like the moon, or apparently angular but spherical in the middle, like the rest of the stars, or hairy in appearance but spherical in the middle, like the sun; or that the stars are scattered without any order at all, so that you never see a quincunx or a square or any other regular figure (for all that they are given names like Delta, Crown, Cross, Chariot, etc.); hardly ever a straight line either, except perhaps in the belt and dagger of Orion.

Fifthly, a thing that completely undermines and destroys a believer may perhaps be of some help to an inquirer: namely, to review briefly currently accepted opinions, with all their variations and sects, just in order to provoke the understanding, but no more.

10

So much for my general precepts; and if they are carefully observed, the work of this history will make straight towards its goal, without growing too unwieldy. But if the work, circumscribed and limited as it is, should appear vast to any faint-hearted person, let him turn his eyes on the libraries, where he will behold, among other things, bodies of civil and canon law on the one side, and the commentaries of doctors and lawyers on the other, and see what a difference there is between the two as regards the size and number of volumes. For we are like faithful secretaries, who only take hold of and write down the laws of Nature themselves and nothing else; it suits us to be brief, and we are almost compelled to it by the nature of the case; whereas there is no end to the number of opinions, teachings and speculations.

Now I have by no means forgotten what I said in the *Plan of the Work* about the *Cardinal Powers* in Nature, and that the history of those powers should also be written before the Work of Interpretation is undertaken, but I have reserved it for myself, since I hesitate to rely very heavily on the industry of others, until men begin to involve themselves more closely with Nature.[17]

Thus I should now come to delineate the *Particular Histories;* however, I am under such pressure of other business that I have time only to append a mere *Catalogue* of their titles. However, as soon as I do have the time for it, I intend, by posing questions on each subject, to explain for every one of the histories what most should be looked into and collected as conducive to my purpose, like a kind of Particular *Topics;* or to put it another way, as if this were a court case, in this *Great Action* or *Law Suit,* granted by divine grace and providence (whereby the human race attempts to recover its rights over Nature), I propose to interrogate Nature herself and the arts point by point.

---

[17]In the *Plan of the Work,* Bacon characterises cardinal powers as the "primary forces of Nature", and the "foremost passions and desires of matter", giving *dense, rare, hot, cold, consistent, fluid, heavy* and *light* as examples. Apart from *consistent,* these qualities also appear in Bacon's list of schematisms which we gave in footnote 113 in *Novum Organum,* II.

Catalogue of Particular Histories,
by Titles

1. History of the heavenly bodies; or astronomical history.
2. History of the configuration of the heaven and of the parts of it towards [i.e., near] the Earth, and also its parts; or cosmographical history.
3. History of comets.
4. History of fiery meteors.
5. History of lightnings, thunderbolts, thunders and coruscations.[18]
6. History of winds and sudden blasts and undulations of the air.
7. History of rainbows.
8. History of clouds, as they are seen above.
9. History of the blue sky, of twilight, of mock-suns, of mock-moons, of haloes, of the various colours of the sun and moon; and of every variety of aspect of the heavenly bodies caused by the medium.[19]

---

[18]In Instance 11 of Aphorism II, 12, of *Novum Organum,* Bacon speaks of a certain "coruscation" arising from sweating horses on a clear cool night. But the reference here is much more probably to the phenomena of the Aurora Borealis, which Bacon is apparently describing in Instance 8 of the same Aphorism.

[19]A mock-sun is a circular patch of light on the solar halo 22 degrees away from the real sun; it is caused by the refraction of ice crystals in the earth's atmosphere. Mock-suns (or parhelia, or multiple suns), and the other phenomena mentioned here, were the subject of speculation in Aristotle's *Meteorology* and in Descartes' work of the same name.

10. History of ordinary, stormy and prodigious rainfalls; also of waterspouts (so called[20]) and the like.
11. History of hail, snow, frost, hoar-frost, fog, dew and the like.
12. History of all other things that fall or descend from the upper region and have been generated there.
13. History of sounds in the upper region (if there are any), apart from thunder.
14. History of the air as a whole, or in the configuration of the world.
15. History of the seasons or climates of the year, both according to the variations of regions, and according to accidents of times and periods of years; of floods, heats, droughts and the like.
16. History of the land and of the sea; of the shape and extent of them, and their configurations compared with each other; and of their broadening or narrowing; of islands in the sea; of gulfs of the sea, and inland salt lakes, isthmuses and promontories.
17. History of the motions (if any there are) of the globe of the land and sea; and of experiments from which such motions may be inferred.
18. History of the major motions and perturbations in the land and sea; namely, earthquakes, tremors and yawnings of the earth, islands newly appearing, floating islands, breakings off of land caused by the entrance of the sea, encroachments and inundations and, contrariwise, recessions of the sea; eruptions of fire from the earth, sudden eruptions of waters from the earth, and the like.
19. Natural geographical history, of mountains, valleys, woods, plains, sands, marshes, lakes, rivers, torrents, springs, and all different ways they bubble forth, and the like; leaving aside nations, prov-

---

[20]Waterspouts are described by Bacon in Aphorism II, 35, of *Novum Organum*.

inces, cities, and things of that kind that relate to civic life.

20. History of flows and ebbs of the sea, violent currents, undulations and other motions of the sea.
21. History of the other accidents[21] of the sea; its saltness, its various colours, its depth; also of rocks, mountains and valleys under the sea, and the like.

Next come Histories of the Greater Masses.[22]

22. History of flame and burning hot things.
23. History of air, in substance, not in configuration.
24. History of water, in substance, not in configuration.
25. History of earth and its diversity, in substance, not in configuration.

Next come Histories of Species.

26. History of the perfect metals, gold, silver; and of their mines, veins and marcasites;[23] and also of their mine workings.
27. History of quicksilver.
28. History of minerals; such as vitriol, and sulphur, etc.
29. History of gems; such as diamonds, rubies, etc.
30. History of stones; such as marble, touchstone,[24] flint, etc.
31. History of the loadstone.
32. History of miscellaneous bodies, which are neither

---

[21]An accident is an attribute that is not part of the subject's essence.

[22]Bacon called these the Greater Colleges in Aphorism 4 of the *Description of a Natural and Experimental History, above.*

[23]"Many species [of marcasite] were known to the old chemists, for all stones which contained any proportion of metal were so called, and even sulphureous stones, vitriolic stones, etc., were included under the same term" ('A Short Lexicon of Alchemy', compiled by Arthur Edward Waite and included in *The Hermetic and Alchemical Writings of Paracelsus,* II, p. 373). Marcasites of gold and silver were apparently specimens of copper and iron pyrites with the lustre of gold and silver.

[24]Touchstone is a dark variety of quartz or jasper used for testing the quality of gold and silver by the colour of the streaks they leave when rubbed against the stone.

entirely mineral nor vegetable; such as salts, amber, ambergris,[25] etc.

33. Chemical history of metals and minerals [i.e., ores].

34. History of plants, trees, shrubs, herbs; and of their parts: roots, stalks, wood, leaves, flowers, fruits, seeds, gums, etc.

35. Chemical history of vegetables.

36. History of fishes, and of their parts and generation.

37. History of birds, and of their parts and generation.

38. History of quadrupeds, and of their parts and generation.

39. History of snakes, worms, flies, and other insects; and of their parts and generation.

40. Chemical history of the things which are consumed by animals.

Next come Histories of Man.

41. History of the shape and external parts of man, his stature, frame, countenance and features; and of the variety of the same, according to races and climates, or other lesser differences.

42. Physiognomical history of the same.

43. Anatomical history, or the history of the internal parts of man; and of their variety, as it is found in the natural frame and structure, and not merely as regards disorders and conditions out of the ordinary course of nature.

44. History of the parts of uniform structure in man; such as flesh, bones, membranes, etc.

45. History of humours in man; blood, bile, sperm, etc.

46. History of excretions; spittle, urine, sweat, stools, hair of the head, bodily hair, whitlows, nails, and the like.

47. History of faculties; attraction [i.e., the ingestion

---

[25]Ambergris is a waxy substance found floating in tropical waters and as a secretion in the intestines of the sperm whale.

of food], digestion, retention, expulsion, the making of blood, assimilation [i.e., conversion] of food into parts of the body, conversion of blood and its flower[26] into spirit, etc.

48. History of natural and involuntary motions; such as the motion of the heart, the motion of the pulses, sneezing, the motion of the lungs, the motion of the erection of the penis, etc.

49. History of motions that are partly natural and partly voluntary; such as those of respiration, coughing, urinating, stool, etc.

50. History of voluntary motions; such as those of the instruments for the articulation of words; motions of the eyes, tongue, jaws, hands, fingers; of swallowing, etc.

51. History of sleep and dreams.

52. History of the different conditions of the body; fat, lean; of the (so-called) complexions,[27] etc.

53. History of the generation of men.

54. History of conception, vivification, gestation in the womb, birth, etc.

55. History of the food of man, and of all things eatable and drinkable; and of all diet; and of their variety according to nations or lesser differences.

56. History of the growth and increase of the body, in the whole and in its parts.

57. History of the onward course of age; of infancy, childhood, youth, old age; of longevity and brevity of life, and the like, according to nations and lesser differences.

58. History of life and death.

59. Medical history of diseases, and their symptoms and signs.

---

[26]Flower of blood can refer to menstrual blood, though this seems unlikely to be the reference here.

[27]Bacon is evidently alluding to the medieval theory that a person's mental and physical qualities are determined by the combination (or 'complexion') in different proportions of the four humours: blood, phlegm, choler and melancholy.

60. Medical history of treatments and remedies and deliverances from diseases.
61. Medical history of those things which preserve the body and health.
62. Medical history of those things which relate to the form and comeliness of the body.
63. Medical history of those things which alter the body, and pertain to an alterative regimen.[28]
64. History of drugs.
65. History of surgery.
66. Chemical history of medicines.
67. History of vision and things visible, or optics.
68. History of painting, sculpture, modelling, etc.
69. History of hearing and sound.
70. History of music.
71. History of smell, and of scents.
72. History of taste, and flavours.
73. History of the sense of touch, and the objects of touch.
74. History of sexual desire, as a species of the sense of touch.
75. History of bodily pains, as a species of the sense of touch.
76. History of pleasure and pain in general.
77. History of the affections; such as anger, love, shame, etc.
78. History of the intellectual faculties; thinking, imagination, discourse, memory, etc.
79. History of natural divinations.
80. History of discernments, or secret natural judgements.
81. History of cookery, and attendant arts, such as those of the butcher, the poulterer, etc.
82. History of baking and breadmaking, and attendant arts, such as that of the miller, etc.
83. History of wine.

---

[28]An alterative regimen is a course of medical treatment which alters the processes of nutrition, with the aim of restoring them to health.

84. History of the cellar, and of different kinds of drink.

85. History of sweetmeats and confectionery.

86. History of honey.

87. History of sugar.

88. History of the dairy.

89. History of baths and unguents.

90. Miscellaneous history concerning the care of the body, such as [the history] of barbers, perfumers, etc.

91. History of the working of gold, and attendant arts.

92. History of goods made out of wool and attendant arts.

93. History of goods made out of silk, and attendant arts.

94. History of goods made out of flax, hemp, cotton, bristles, and other threads, and attendant arts.

95. History of goods made out of feathers.

96. History of weaving, and attendant arts.

97. History of dyeing.

98. History of leather-making, tanning, and attendant arts.

99. History of cushion-making and of the making of things out of down.

100. History of the working of iron.

101. History of stone-cutting.

102. History of the making of bricks and tiles.

103. History of pottery.

104. History of stone-masonry, and decorative working.

105. History of working in wood.

106. History of working in lead.

107. History of glass and all glassware and of glass-making.

108. History of architecture generally.

109. History of wagons, carriages, litters, etc.

110. History of printing, of books, of writing, of sealing; of ink, pen, paper, parchment, etc.

111. History of wax.

112. History of basket-making.

113. History of mat-making, and of goods made out of straw, rushes, and the like.
114. History of washing, sweeping, etc.
115. History of agriculture, pasturage, sylviculture, etc.
116. History of gardening.
117. History of fishing.
118. History of hunting and fowling.
119. History of the business of war, and of attendant arts, such as armoury, bow-making, arrow-making, musketry, ordnance, ballistas [viz., large catapults for hurling stones], engines of war, etc.
120. History of nautical matters, and of attendant crafts and arts.
121. History of athletics, and human exercises of all kinds.
122. History of horsemanship.
123. History of games of all kinds.
124. History of conjurers and circulators.[29]
125. Miscellaneous history of diverse artificial materials, such as enamel, porcelain, various cements, etc.
126. History of salts.
127. Miscellaneous history of various machines, and motions.
128. Miscellaneous history of common experiments, which have not developed into an art.
   Histories must also be written of Pure Mathematics; though they are observations rather than experiments.
129. History of the natures and powers of numbers.
130. History of the natures and powers of figures.

---

[29]Circulators were mountebanks, so called because they gathered a ring or crowd of spectators about them.

It may not be amiss to observe that, whereas many of the experiments necessarily fall under two or more more titles, as for example the History of Plants and the History of the Art of Gardening have many things more or less in common, it may be more convenient to investigate them with reference to Arts, and to arrange them with reference to Bodies. For I care little about the mechanical arts themselves, but only about those things which they contribute towards the equipment of philosophy. But these things will be better regulated as the case arises.

THE END

BIBLIOGRAPHY

A. WORKS BY BACON

The Letters and Life of Francis Bacon. Edited by James Spedding. 7 volumes. London: Longman, Green, Longman, and Roberts, 1862–1874.

The Literary and Professional Works of Francis Bacon. Edited and translated by James Spedding, Robert L. Ellis, and Douglas D. Heath. 5 volumes. London: Longman and Company, 1857–1858.

Farrington, Benjamin. *The Philosophy of Francis Bacon.* Liverpool: Liverpool University Press, 1964. (Contains translations of Bacon's essays: 'The Masculine Birth of Time', 'Thoughts and Conclusions' and 'The Refutation of Philosophies'.)

The Works of Francis Bacon. Edited and translated by James Spedding, Robert L. Ellis, and Douglas D. Heath. 5 volumes. London: Longman and Company, 1857–1858.

B. IMPORTANT WORKS ON BACON

Cohen, M.R. *Studies in Philosophy and Science.* New York: Henry Holt and Company, 1949.

Ellis, Robert L. General Preface. In *The Works of Francis Bacon,* I, pp. 21–67. London: Longman and Company, 1857–1858.

Fowler, Thomas, ed. *Bacon's Novum Organum.* Oxford: Clarendon Press, 1878.

Hempel, Carl. *Philosophy of Natural Sciences.* Englewood Cliffs, New Jersey: Prentice-Hall, Inc., 1966.

Hesse, Mary. 'Francis Bacon'. In *A Critical Review of Western Philosophy,* J. O'Connor, ed., pp. 142–152. New York: The Free Press of Glencoe, 1964.

Horton, Mary. 'In Defence of Francis Bacon'. In *Studies in History and Philosophy of Science,* vol. 4, pp. 241–278, 1973.

Howson, Colin, and Peter Urbach. *Scientific Reasoning: The Bayesian Approach.* La Salle, Illinois: Open Court Publishing Company, 1993.

Jardine, Lisa. *Francis Bacon, Discovery and the Art of Discourse.* Cambridge: Cambridge University Press, 1974.

Lakatos, Imre. "Falsificationism and the Methodology of Scientific Research Programmes", in *Criticism and the Growth of Knowledge,* I. Lakatos and A. Musgrave, eds., pp. 91–196. Cambridge: Cambridge University Press, 1970.

Macaulay, Thomas Babington. 'Lord Bacon'. *Edinburgh Review,* July 1837.

Popper, Karl R. *The Logic of Scientific Discovery*. London: Hutchinson, 1959.

———. *Conjectures and Refutations*. London: Routledge and Kegan Paul, 1963.

Quinton, Anthony. *Francis Bacon*. Oxford: Clarendon Press, 1980.

Rossi, Paolo. *Francis Bacon: From Magic to Science*. Translated from the Italian text of 1957 by S. Rabinovitch. London: Routledge and Kegan Paul, 1968.

Spedding, James. *An Account of the Life and Times of Francis Bacon*. 2 volumes. London: Trübner and Co, 1878.

———. *Evenings with a Reviewer, or Macaulay and Bacon*. 2 volumes. London: Kegan Paul, Trench & Company, 1881.

Urbach, Peter. *Francis Bacon's Philosophy of Science: An Account and a Reappraisal*. La Salle: Open Court Publishing Company, 1987.

Yates, F.A. *The Rosicrucian Enlightenment*. London: Routledge and Kegan Paul, 1972.

INDEX